The FOUNDERS OF MODERN MEDICINE

PASTEUR • KOCH • LISTER

The FOUNDERS OF MODERN MEDICINE

PASTEUR • KOCH • LISTER

By

ELIE METCHNIKOFF

Including

ETIOLOGY
of
WOUND INFECTIONS
by Robert Koch

THE ANTISEPTIC SYSTEM
by Sir Joseph Lister

and

PREVENTION OF RABIES
by Louis Pasteur

WALDEN PUBLICATIONS
New York 1939

CONTENTS

The FOUNDERS OF MODERN MEDICINE

PASTEUR • KOCH • LISTER

CHAPTER I

The second half of the last century was marked by a profound transformation in medicine. This radical change took place both in the clinical as well as in theoretical fields. Such an event must be set down as among the most important happenings in the evolution of human thought, and is deserving of our particular attention. It was my privilege not only to witness this transformation from its very outset, but also to have been a personal friend to its three principal originators: Pasteur, Lister and Koch. I am undertaking to give an account of the history of that reform in the hope of getting the interest of the reader who is uninitiated into the mysteries of medical science.

In order to help him get his bearings I should begin by sketching an outline of the state of this science at the beginning of the second half of the 19th Century, that is, at the time when the first reformer—Pasteur—appeared on the scene.

Theoretical and clinical medicine at the time were, above all, occupied with the symptoms of disease, with diagnostic methods and with the morbid changes in the organs. At the end of the period in question, these morbid alterations, until then studied with the naked eye, were subjected to the microscope. On the basis of these new facts, different hypotheses were constructed in order to explain the morbid processes; in therapeutics it was especially empirical means which were employed.

Medical art consisted almost exclusively of the application of more or less efficacious remedies and of operative interventions in the case of diseases belonging to the field of surgery and obstetrics. Hygiene and prophylaxis were in a rudimentary state. Only *anti-variolic* (small pox) vaccination, worked out by Jenner at the end of the 18th and the beginning of the 19th Centuries, show like a luminous object in the darkness all around.

In order to give the reader a more precise idea of the state of medical science during the period which preceded the coming of Pasteur, we must pause a while to consider the state of the theoritical and clinical medicine of the period.

It is impossible to get one's bearings in the midst of the complexity and confusion of the various morbid phenomena, except by the aid of a clue furnished by the most complete possible study of these phenomena. At the period in question, it was the German scientist Virchow who who wielded the preponderant influence; his theories of pathology became the guide to a generation of physicians. He was the first to praise the microscopic study of morbid phenomena and to extend these studies as much as possible. He was not satisfied with mere observation with the naked eye. The result of this was his theory of "cellular pathology." His conclusion was that the essence of a disease consists in the abnormal activity of the cells of the organism. According to him it was sufficient for these cells to have developed in an unfavorable place or time to bring about a break in the equilibrium of health. The slightest fault in the cellular function could give rise to a lesser or graver disease. To give his theory as general an expression as possible Virchow summed it up as follows: "All diseases may in the final analysis be reduced to passive or active lesions of a greater or lesser number of vital elements or cells, whose capacity is modified in accordance with their molecular composition; in other words they are dependent on the physical and chemical modification of their contents."(1)

This generalized, almost metaphysical formula of cellular pathology, could not penetrate into the clinic which, as of old, remained empirical. Though attributing the diseases to the abnormal modifications of the cellular activity of the organism, neither Virchow himself, nor his adepts had inquired into the causes of those modifications. Nevertheless, there were already at the time, a few investigators who favored the idea that the cause of many diseases was due to infinitely minute living beings, introduced into the organism, where they produced a break in the normal activity of the cell, that is to say, disease. Virchow, however, rejected this theory. In his numerous researches into human disease he had himself observed

(1) Cellulaer Pathologie - Archiv für Pathologische Anatomie, 1855, Vol. VIII, p. 38.

many times, lower parasitical plants within the diseased organs. Thus he had on several occasions observed mildews in the lungs. (2) However, after giving a detailed description of the morbid lesions, verified by autopsy, and of the moulds that attended them, Virchow concluded that the latter had developed only secondarily in the already diseased lungs. In his report he dwelled much on the to him unjustifiable, excessive enthusiasm, with which physicians had received the microbe theory of certain diseases, an enthusiasm, which, according to him, was in need of being cooled off.

Is it surprising that medical practice should not generally have made much of this imperfect science, and that it should have continued in its old empirical way?

Let us stop here for a particular example in order to give an approximate idea of the state of therapeutics during the period in question. The Crimean War afforded opportunities for a great number of interesting observations on the therapeutics of the time. It is in connection with a very detailed report of Dr. Chenu, (3) on the health condition of the French army in Crimea and in Turkey in the years 1854-56, that we shall attempt to give a general picture of the medical practice of the period, recalling to mind that the first reports of Pasteur, who opened the gates to modern medical science appeared some years after the Crimean War.

---

(2) Archiv für pathologische Anatomie, 1856, Vol. IX, p. 557.

(3) Chenu - Rapport au conseil de santé des armées, Paris, 1865.

Of the army of about 300,000 more than 10,000 were killed, 3% of the total. As to the men lost on account of sickness or as the result of wounds, they numbered eight times as many (85,375, that is 27.6%). In other words, a fourth of the army, composed of strong and healthy men, fell victim to diseases, the result of wounds or independently of them.

Now, what were the diseases from which the French troops especially suffered The number of men who died as a result of wounds almost equaled the number of killed—10,000. Of the wounded, a great many succumbed to hemorrhages during transportation; others fell victim to erysipelas, scab, gangrene, general septicemia, and hospital gangrene. The amputation cases, especially, succumbed to the latter (p. 633). "The mortality of the wounded on whom *resection* of the femur was performed was tremendous. Of 1681 individuals submitted to that operation only 136 recovered from it" (p. 662). The mortality, thus, reached up to 92%. Amputations of the tibia had a better record; nevertheless, close to 1000 patients or 71% (p. 666) died of it. Septicemia was wide-spread in all the field hospitals (p. 115).

The imperfect state of surgery of that time is evidenced by the fact that among those amputated for a fracture of the femur the mortality was considerably higher than among those, who, having the same lesion, were not operated on. Of 1666 operated, 1531 or close to 92% died, while of 487 who were not operated only 333 died, that is to say 68.37%. The author notes that the shortcomings of surgery are deplorable.

However high the mortality due to surgery, it was

nevertheless, surpassed by that due to infections diseases. Towards the beginning of the summer of 1854 Asiatic cholera made its appearance in the French camp. Beginning with the months of June, the number of cholera patients increased to such an extent that it necessitated a retreat (p. 27). Three of the surgeon-majors succumbed at the outset of the cholera plague, which assumed frightful proportions. Just at the time when the French were preparing to undertake a vigorous offensive, and after the order of attack had already been given "500 soldiers were forced to take to their beds. Like a thunderbolt the cholera plague descended upon the expeditionary columns. Within eight hours 150 men succumbed and 350 were in agony. This terrifying vision was enough to shake the courage of the boldest. It was impossible to think of fighting, one could only think of how to escape the disease. The dead and the dying lay in heaps in all tents of General Espinosses' column. In spite of the absence of the enemy the corpses were stretched out everywhere. Graves were dug and the turned-up earth exhaled an infectious odor from far off. Often the hands of the grave-diggers would droop before completing their task and those who wielded the spade would lie down at the edge of the grave not to rise up again." (p. 29)

In an army of 55,000 there were in the month of July more than 8,000 cholera patients (8,239). In 1854, in the month of August, the cholera plague became even worse than in July. In the course of a single month—July 18 to August 18—11 doctors succumbed. In September the plague subsided; nevertheless the general-in-chief of the French armies, Marshall Saint-Arnaud, who had tirelessly counseled those about him, regarding methods of avoiding the infection, was himself seized by the plague and died while being transported to Constantinople. The cholera kept up during the entire fall in spite of the cold weather and broke out with even greater fury in 1855; nine doctors fell victim to it, one of them a chief medical doctor, the other a chief surgeon.

Next to cholera, it was eruptive typhus which tried the French army most. It made its appearance in the winter of 1854-55 and persisted, with intermittent periods, until the end of the War. In the month of January 1856 it caused 1523 victims, of whom 464 or 30% succumbed. Eruptive typhus hit especially the medical corps. Thus of approximately 450 military doctors, 58 fell victim to it, i.e. 12.88%.

Typhus fever was much less widespread, though it made its appearance from time to time. A physician-major succumbed to it. Dysentry was epidemic; but it was especially the scurvy which caused most suffering. The first cases of that disease broke out in 1854 among the army and the navy. During the first ten days of November, 1000 cases of scurvy were noted. The disease took on almost formidable proportions. At that period, there were only very few healthy soldiers: "One found only sick ones among them, and their mortality was very high: diarrhea, dysentery, scurvy." (p. 71). The latter disease increased especially during the winter of 1855. "During the month of February scurvy became so wide-spread that the whole army was endangered, though grave cases were rare." (p. 87). This continued for more than a year. At the end of January 1856, the chief doctor stated in his report: "If the scurvy doesn't cease, not a single healthy soldier will remain in the Second Army Corps. The number of cases is formidable." (p.121). In the diary on the health conditions of the army the following note may be read: "The cases of diarrhea, dysentery, the complications of typhoid fever and of eruptive typhus are mortal in the majority of cases . . . . Always the same impotency of medicine." During the months of December 1854, January and February 1855, the failure of treatments was the dispair of the physicians. The greatest care and the most prudent therapeutical practices remained ineffectual (p. 83).

Though no precise and scientific idea was entertained at that period regarding the true cause of these diseases, nevertheless an infectious character was surmised in regard to some of them. Also, certain precautionary measures were adopted during the war, in the camps and dwelling places, and the freshness of the army food was carefully watched. As a measure against cholera, Marshall Saint-Arnaud warned against the excessive use of alcoholic drinks and the eating of raw fruits. The surgeon-genearl of the army recommended the destruction of infected homes, either by means of fire or by disinfection with ferrous sulphate or hypochlorite of lime, as well as the deep burying of the corpses. According to the first paragraph of the instructions, "the numerous graves filled with corpses which are barely covered with earth, in the region occupied by the troops, may spread morbid vapors. It is therefore noted that all such noxious emanations must be checked." (p. 87).

Hygienic measures were especially directed against the "infectious gases" to which the scientists of the times attributed a too great importance. It is for this reason that ventilation and the suppression of the causes of putrefaction, such as corpses, human and animal remains, were so much stressed. Nevertheless, as we have seen, these precautions did not prevent the grave spreading of surgical and other diseases.

The losses were even more considerable in the Russian army from 1853 to 1856. According to Chenu, who does not lay claim to absolute exactness, the number of those killed in the war is estimated as 30,000, while those who died as a result of wounds or diseases numbered twenty times as many or about 600,000 (p. 617). According to other data, the mortality of the Russian armies during the Crimean campaign though less than the above figures still were extremely high. Dr. Pirogoff, who played a very active role at that period, was horrified at the great number of wounded who succumbed to post-operative complications. He expresses himself in the following terms: "In looking on the cemeteries where repose those who fell victim to hospital infections I do not know what to marvel at more: the stoicism of the surgeons seeking for new operative methods, or at the confidence which the governments and society continue to enjoy. Could one count on real progress as long as the physicians and the governments failed to work in harmony for a new way of destroying the source of the noxious exhalation in the hospitals?"

Pirogoff's idea of the nature of these measures characterizes the scientific thought of the period: "Every more or less noticeable lesion is accompanied by a violent displacement of atoms which cause mechanical modifications in the injured part and these are easily transformed into chemical modifications. This transition is almost imperceptible. No extensive solution of continuity may take place without local necrosis nor without *putrid fermentation,* if the shock has been intense, whether or not in the presence of air." This phenomenon may also be observed in the hospitals of the capital. According to the description of the Second Continental Hospital at St. Petersburg made by Pirogoff, "the large, badly ventilated wards are filled with patients suffering from erysipelas, acute and purulent oedemas and septicemia. The nurses, without any scruples, were in the habit of transferring the linen serving as compresses for the wounds from one patient to another. The mal-administration of hospitals went as far as to preserve, for the purpose of resale, soiled and ill-smelling lint taken from the wounds as well as the dressings, compresses and linen, which were put up in special stockrooms situated close to the sick-wards."(4)

The hospitals of Paris were no better. This deplorable state of affairs was due to the inadequacy of medical science. No amount of cellular pathology, with all its fine points of microscopical analysis could

---

(4) Quotation from the report of Dr. Himmelfarb Rous. Vratch, 1912, No. 17, p. 578.

avail against cholera, against complications from wounds or against various other infectious diseases. In order to achieve this it was necessary to reconstruct, from top to bottom, the entire edifice of medical science.

CHAPTER II.

The state of medical science during the Crimean War reflected the prevailing notions regarding the nature of diseases. The violent spread of purulent wound infections was in harmony with the then popular idea of the role of *fetid gasses.* It was enough to enter a sick ward to be immediately met by the characteristic odor of putrefaction. The more that smell was perceptible, the graver the disease. Due to the greater prevalence of wars in former times, this observation could always be made. From this the conclusion was drawn that wound infections were caused by putrefaction, i.e. a process analogous to the one taking place in the decomposition of corpses, of meat, eggs and albuminoid matter in general. The observation of certain other diseases ought to substantiate this point of view. Thus, in inflammation of the bladder, the urine, as at times in a state of decomposition, has an odor of ammoniac, like that of persons in good health whose urine has undergone decomposition by air. Similarly, inflammation of the mammary gland in the cow is at times accompanied by internal coagulation of the milk, resembling that of normal cows whose milk coagulates in contact with air or due to the action of heat.

From these, as well as other facts, which from the first origins of medicine have attracted attention, it was easy to conclude that the putrefaction of albuminous matter, the fermentation of milk and urine are due to the same causes as the putrefaction of wounds, the inflammation of the bladder and of the mammary gland. Even the similarity of the words "pus" and "putrefaction" shows the antiquity of this idea. It is therefore not surprising that for a long time it was expected that a solution of the problem of the nature of fermentation and of putrefaction (which is nothing else but the fermentation of albuminous matter) ought to lead to the clearing up of the cause of infectious diseases. Already in the 17th Century the eminent English scientist, Robert Boyle, had expressed this opinion. He had stated that he who succeeded in discovering the nature of ferments, would even thereby deepen our knowledge of certain morbid phenomena.

What idea then did the science at the period preceding the appearance of Pasteur, have of fermentation? Whereas the medicine of that period was dominated by the ideas of Virchow, in organic chemistry it was the theories of Liebig, which ruled supreme. Liebig often paused in his labors to consider the question of decomposition—putrefaction and fermentation—of organic matter. He obstinately defended the idea that these processes could be led back to the action of the oxygen in the air, to the oxydation caused by the presence of a ferment, which, during the period of decomposition, always appeared in the form of inert matter. The idea was expressed several times during that period that fermentation was due chiefly to microscopic fungi, to yeasts which, through their vital action caused the decomposition of organic matter. For a long time living cells which multiplied with an extraordinary rapidity had been noticed in liquids placed for purposes of alcoholic fermentation. One saw in them the true cause of the transformation of sugar into alcohol. This theory, nevertheless, for want of proofs, left itself open to objections. Liebig was one of its most ardent opponents. According to him, yeast brought about fermentation not because of their vital processes but because they produced quantity of albuminous matter sufficient to oxidize the sugar and convert it into alcohol. Therefore, for fermentation to take place, there was no need of the living cells of yeasts but rather the dead cells in decomposition. The presence of living fungi and infusoria in putrefied and fermented liquids did not at all prove that decomposition would be impossible without them. "To accept it, it would be necessary, first of all, to establish in what manner these fungi and infusoria can bring about the action attributed to them," states Liebig in his famous "Letters on Chemistry". "This, however," he continues, " has never been done. This hypothesis, therefore, leaves the processes of putrefaction and fermentation as obscure as they were before." (p. 209).

Liebig makes sport of the biological theory of fermentation and putrefaction and likens it to "the opinion of a child who imagined that the rapid current of the

Rhine depended on the movement of the many wheels of the mills on the Main River which sent the waters towards the city of Bingen". (p. 221). If fermentation really depended on living yeasts, why did it not occur either in alcoholic fermentation, or in putrefaction, or during the transformation of lactose into lactic and butyric acid, in the transformation of alcoholic acid into vinegar? "If fermentation was the effect of a vital action, the *organism-ferments* should be found in all cases of fermentation." (p. 24).

In his new "Letters on Chemistry" which appeared a few years after the first "Letters", Liebig returns to the question of the cause of fermentation and repeats his old objections. "The fermentation of wine and beer are not isolated phenomena, but particular cases of a whole order of many and similar processes. Insofar as alcoholic fermentation is accompanied by the growth or decomposition of fungi, it is unlike that of other kinds of fermentations which are not attended by any organism." (p. 53).

From these reflections Liebig draws the conclusion —completely convincing in his own eyes—that the true cause of putrefaction is traceable to the decomposition of complex organic particles (of molecules), i.e. to a process diametrically opposed to life. He holds to the commonly accepted idea of the period cencerning the identity of the phenomena of putrefaction and fermentation with the processes attending many contagious diseases and he touches on this serious problem. He believes "that the solution of the nature of miasmas and infections is very easy." According to him, certain forces of decomposition and putrefaction of matter may be transmitted to constituent parts of the organism. In contact with such putrefied matter, these may assume a state similar even to such matter. (p. 25). The infectious principle thus established would have a destructive rather than a vital character and it may spread by means of solid, liquid or gaseous products without the intervention of a more direct cause". (p. 28).

In opposing the biological theory of fermentation, Liebig naturally denied the hypothesis according to which the infectious diseases were due to lower organisms. He pushed his disdain of that theory to the point even of considering it unworthy of discussion. According to him, the fact that the itch is caused by an acacus, and muscardine of the silkworm by a mold (Bothrytis Bassi) does not at all lead us to the assumption that the infectious diseases in men were due to similar causes. "The most meticulous study has not enabled us to discover either infusoria or other organic beings whose presence could explain the contagious nature of small-pox, plague, syphilis, scarlet fever, measles, typhoid fever, yellow fever, anthrax or hydrophobia."

The medical world, always especially partial to the opinion of chemists, favored Liebig's theory of the inorganic nature of decomposing action of ferments and of the causes of contagion. Of what avail were the isolated voices of doctors who did not share this strongly established general opinion, especially since they had recourse only to mere conjecture?

For a long time there was a conjecture about the existence of a *contagium animation,* that is to say, of a living virus, capable of penetrating the living organism and of developing there, in the manner of various lower organisms. This hypothesis had been developed with a fine scientific acumen by the talented German scientist, Henle, in a small monograph appearing in 1840.(5)

In his opinion, contagion is due not merely to organic matter but to *organized* matter. (p. 20). Minute organisms penetrate our bodies and develop there after a longer or shorter period of incubation. The spreading of infectious diseases by contact of sick persons with healthy ones and the entire course of the development of the disease up to the cure, are best explained if one accepts the living nature of the virus of contagion. That no one has as yet succeeded in discovering these minute organisms is attributed by Henle to the imperfection of the microscope, incapable of rendering them visible within the tissues which have the same index of light refraction as these same organisms. Henle's idea, expressed in this hypothetical form was not likely to assure it many followers. This opinion of an extremely young scientist who only much later became one of the most outstanding of anatomists, was shattered by the authority of such a universally recognized scientist as Liebig was. Is it surprising, that under these circumstances the germ planted by Henle fell on barren soil? It is evident he himself did not attach too much importance to his theory. Steeped in the close study of human anatomy, he gave up the search for the causes of con-

---

(5) **Pathologische Untersuchungen, 1840.**

tagious diseases. When in 1866, as a student, I worked under him at Goettingen, at a time when various, serious investigations on the microscopic agents of infectious diseases had commenced, Henle remained indifferent to them. My scholarly task was to study under his direction and from his viewpoint the kidney of amphibians, and the corpus cavernosum of the sexual organ of man. At no time did the question of the causes of infectious diseases came up in his laboratory.

In France where, as of old, the chemical point of view was given preference over the biological, Liebig's explanation of fermentation, putrefaction and infectious diseases imposed itself with the strength of an irrefutable dogma. However, despite some researches culminating in the study of the role of yeasts as living cells in alcoholic fermentation (Cogniard-Latour), ferments and the principle sources of contagion were regarded as organic matter in decomposition, matter capable of causing a rapid decomposition within the bodies they had entered.

In order to batter down such a conviction, deeply rooted in and having complete sway over the mind of man, there was need of a scientist who would not bend before any authority whatever, and who should know exactly where he was going. Such a role was brilliantly fulfilled by Pasteur.

CHAPTER III.

Pasteur made his debut in science in purely theoretical researches in the field of chemical crystallography (molecular dissymmetry). It was only gradually that he passed over into the study of the phenomena of fermentation of lactic sugar.(6) That work was a death blow to Liebig's theory. Pasteur answered the latter's principal objection regarding the absence of yeasts or of other micro-organism in non-alcoholic fermentation by the discovery of an infinitesimally small living being, the germ of lactic fermentation. Here are several citations from his report which has opened up new paths to science:- "According to Liebig the ferment is an extremely *alterable* substance which decomposes and induces fermentation, as a consequence of the alteration which it manifests itself, and which, by means of communication, disturbs and disarranges the molecular grouping of the fermentescible matter. In this,

---

(6) Mémoire sur la fermentation appelée lactique, Paris, 1858.

according to M. Liebig, lies the primary cause of the various fermentations and of most of the contagious diseases." (p. 5). A little further on, Pasteur adds modestly: "I am persuaded to see the whole thing quite differently. We propose to establish in the first part of the present work, that just as there is an alcoholic ferment, barm, which is found whenever sugar is present and which breaks up into alcohol and carbonic acid, so also there is a special ferment, lactic yeast; that if all plastic nitrogenous materials are able to transform sugar into such acid, it is because this material is a suitable food for the ferment." (p. 6). "In the microscope it has the shape of small globules, or of very short bodies (articles), isolated or in mass, composed of irregular flakes resembling those of amorphous precipitates." (p. 8). "It is sufficient to pour a minute quantity of these flakes into a well boiled liquid containing albuminoid matter and sugar, at a suitable temperature (30 to 35 degrees) for the sugar to undergo an immediate and intensive fermentation, resulting in the production of lactic acid."

At the conclusion of his report Pasteur strays from the facts he had himself observed and builds up a theory of fermentation in which he recognizes the insufficiency of the proofs he is adducing. That part of the work is of special interest to us because it shows the greatness of Pasteur's genius. "In the whole course of this report", he writes, "I have reasoned on the hypothesis that the new yeast is organic (*organisée*), that it is a living being, and that its chemical action on sugar is correlative with its growth and organization . Should I be reproached that I am going beyond the facts in making such conclusions, I would say that this is certainly so in the sense that I am placing myself frankly on the side of a class of ideas which can not be irrefutably demonstrated." (p. 14).

And here is the gist of his theory:-

" . . . Fermentation must be regarded as a correlated characteristic of life and of the organization of globules, and not of death or of the putrefaction of these globules; nor does it appear to be a phenomenon of contact, in which the transformation of sugar is carried out in the presence of the ferment without adding to or taking from it." (p. 15).

These last lines contain an entire program of work which Pasteur was to fulfill in order to establish his theory. The flakes of ferment which he poured into the sugary medium to be fermented, contained not only infinitesimally small globules but also amorphous matter. It was necessary, then, to eliminate the latter to warrant the conclusion that globules alone were the cause of the fermentation. Assuming that the amorphous matter, incapable of producing fermentation, served only as a nutrient for the globules, Pasteur replaced it by solution of mineral matter, completely eliminating the albuminous matter which had entered into the experiments of Liebig and of his school. This experiment enabled Pasteur to obtain media of liquid cultures in which he was able to grow absolutely pure cultures of lactic ferment. This method applied to the fermentation of alcohol afforded a new proof of the sound basis of the biological theory of fermentation. Pasteur obtained a pure culture of barms in an artificially sugared medium (a different one from the one which was used in the culture of lactic ferment). These yeasts brought about a more and more intense fermentation in proportion to their growth without the least intervention of any lifeless particles (dead yeast, etc.).

These facts, set up with unexceptionable precision, opened up a new path in the study of all types of fermentation, including putrefaction. After having proven that the fermentation of alcohol is the result of the vital action of yeasts and that lactic fermentation (of milk) was dependent on immobile and extremely minute globules, Pasteur began to inquire into the nature of organisms which induce other fermentations, particularly butyric and acetic fermentation. With the help of methods he had himself worked out, it was an easy task for him to discover that the first was due to the vital action of little rods, rather bulky and very mobile; and that acetic fermentation, on the other hand, is caused by little rods and articulated filaments. But whereas the butyric sticks are marked by such a fine sensitivity to oxygen of the air that they die out rapidly under its influence, the filaments and sticks of acetic acid are not sensitive to oxygen.

It is rather commonly believed among the public at large that we owe to Pasteur the honor of discovering microbes in general. This is, however, not entirely correct. Microbes, discovered already in the 17th Century, had been studied for a long time by various scientists before Pasteur. Attempts had even been made to classify them into families, orders and species. But Pasteur, by his researches on fermentation, was to be the first to demonstrate the true role of microbes in nature, as destroyers of all kinds of organic matter.

The globules of lactic fermentation, which he discovered, were found to be associated not only with the yeasts, properly so-called, but with the group of bacteria; this was true also of the *sticks* of butyric and acetic acid, likewise discovered by him. These researches of Pasteur not only definitely established that fermentation and putrefaction were due to the vital action of lower, microscopical organisms, but, at the same time, they also gave rise to the idea of the "specificity" of ferments. Though the fermentation of alcohol is brought about by yeasts, that of milk (lactic fermentation) depends on special kinds of globules and sticks, which in turn differ from the organisms connected with butyric fermentation. Just as different types of fermentation do not change over one into the other, so also are the various ferments independent of each other and do not change one into the other.

Pasteur's theory, rigorously worked out, and logically unassailable, nevertheless, met with objections. Liebig, engrossed in his strictly chemical theory, attacked Pasteur with great force. He not only repudiated his theoretical conclusions, but even assailed certain facts established by him. Unable to deny the presence of living micro-organisms in the entire fermented medium Liebig, nevertheless, stubbornly held fast to his main theory, according to which an amorphous, albuminous material was necessary in order to call forth fermentation. But Pasteur, past master in experimental method, proved the sound basis of his assertions, and by means of a series of new experiments, he set down the fundamental and unassailable principle that the yeasts and other ferments may grow and induce fermentation in media devoid of albuminous matter. (In these cases, the ferments draw up the nitrogen in the ammoniac.)

Liebig stopped short in his arguments and Pasteur's theory of fermentation ultimately triumphed. Nevertheless, there were new attempts to overthrow the biological doctrine which affirmed that fermentation depended on the vital action of ferments. After the death of the renowned physiologist, Claude Bernard, one found among his papers a rough draft of a report containing his reflexions on fermentation, as well as a series of preliminary experiments whose purpose it was to prove that the formation of alcohol at the expense of sugar was due to a specific inorganic ferment, found in yeasts. His experiments, however, could not be completed and gave no ground whatever for concluding that such a substance really existed. Pasteur hastened to repeat them but was unable to bring to light this unorganized ferment. Nevertheless, he saw no objection to the belief in the real existence of such a ferment. His report in connection with Claude Bernard's manuscript ends with these words(7) "Let me add, in conclusion, that it has always been a puzzle to me why people imagined that I would be embarrassed by the discovery of soluble ferments in fermentation, properly speaking, or by the fermentation of alcohol with the help of sugar, independent of cells." And as a matter of fact, what is of moment in the biological theory of fermentation is the correlation between the growth of the micro-organism fer-

(7) Comptes Rendus de l'Académie des Sciences, July 29, 1878.

ments and the decomposition of organic matter. This however does not imply for Pasteur and his disciples that physical or physico-chemical phenomena, associated with some form or other of inorganized matter, may not take place in the physiological process which is carried out in the living cell of the ferment. Pasteur's theory would have suffered exceedingly if it had been proven that the fermentations were produced not by the physiological action of ferments but by amorphous materials mentioned by Liebig.

After the death of Pasteur, a German chemist, Eduard Buchner, succeeded in extracting from the barm of beer an unorganized substance, which he named "zymase", a material which was able to ferment sugary solutions without any intervention of the living cells of yeasts. Certain scientists saw in this a refutation of Pasteur's theory as well as a vindication of Liebig's. This, however, was based on a misunderstanding. According to the theory of Liebig the intervention of living cells is not at all necessary for fermentation which is induced by the products of the decomposition of the ferments, or, indeed, by other albuminoid materials (the casein of cheese, gluten, etc.). Buchner's discovery, on the contrary, implies that the breaking up of sugar is brought on by the zymase, worked out inside of the living cells of yeast. The dead bodies of yeast (lifeless yeast) are not able to produce fermentation, as Liebig's theory would demand. On the contrary, the fermentation which takes place in nature is always connected with the growth of ferments whose living cells manufacture an inorganic zymase and products similar to it, just as the living cells of the stomach produce an inorganic ferment, pepsin, which digests the albuminoid matter.

Pasteur's theory has been recognized as unquestionably correct in spite of all objection and in spite of all new discoveries. It is wrong to call it a vitalist theory, as some do at times, for this term implies the explanation of fermentation by a vital, mysterious force of some sort. It must, on the contrary, be placed among the biological theories, because it traces fermentation to intercellular physiological processes.

It is not surprising that this theory of Pasteur, so absolutely consistent with reality, should have opened up ways for new conquests in the domain of theory and practice.

CHAPTER IV.

Though, as has been stated, Pasteur was not the discoverer of microbes, nevertheless he had the honor of discovering a whole series of them, microbes which induce fermentation and putrefaction; and what is even more important, it is to him that humanity owes the final explanation of the rôle of microbes in the destruction of organic matter. Being convinced that the organized ferments represented an entire series of lower beings, with precise characteristics, and easy to differentiate, Pasteur naturally asked himself the question: what was the nature of these ferments and where and under what conditions are they to be found in nature? The extremely rapid, one might even say, spontaneous fermentation of fermentescible liquids, such as the juice of fresh grapes, other sugared liquids, milk, wine, etc., might be explained either in assuming that the germs of the organized ferments are present everywhere in very large numbers, or that they originate spontaneously in organic matter. This question thus posed put Pasteur face to face with the problem which had long held the interest of scientists;

namely, whether there was such a thing as spontaneous generation in nature? Though a great many scientists did not dare enter upon this problem, which had engrossed the finest minds of many centuries—so difficult and complicated did it appear—Pasteur took courage and applied himself to the work.

When he tried to obtain pure cultures of ferment, Pasteur was constantly obliged to boil the organic liquid he prepared. These latter would not ferment unless a minute quantity of ferment taken from a previous culture, had been poured into it. Otherwise these liquids would be preserved for a very long time without undergoing the least modification. This forced the conclusion that ferments did not arise spontaneously in these fermentescible liquids, but, rather, that the ferments penetrated them from without. Pasteur proved that the air contained innumerable microscopic particles in suspension, among them yeasts as well as other germs of various ferments. For fermentation to take place within a short time it was suffiicient to introduce into an organic liquid, previously boiled and kept perfectly intact for a long time, a minute quantity of dust taken from the air.

One might suppose that the logical conclusions established on the basis of Pasteur's experiments—experiments which were very simple to carry out—should have been quickly and without any difficulty accepted by the scientific world. However, the very opposite took place. A storm of objections rose up against Pasteur. Step by step, he was obliged to defend his theory of the non-existence of the spontaneous generation of ferments.

The attacks were launched by Pouchet, a French scientist and an ardent follower of the doctrine of spontaneous generation; his allies were Messrs. Joly and Musset. These men repeated Pasteur's experiment in order to prove that his conclusions were ill-founded; but, instead of reproducing them under the same conditions which their opponent had employed, they allowed themselves certain important modifications. However, while Pasteur had employed *an infusion of yeasts,* which, after boiling, fermented only if sown with a living ferment, Pouchet and his collaborators filled their receptacles with an infusion of hay, a modification which led to a rapid growth of bacteria, without any ferment having been added. Being naturalists, unaccustomed to strict experimental methods, Pouchet, Joly and Musset, fell into errors again and again. This rendered victory even easier for such an ingenious experimenter as Pasteur was.

In order to refute these objections once and for all, Pasteur made a proposal to the Academy of Sciences asking them to appoint a commission to consider the question. The two opposing parties were to reproduce their experiments before that commission. Pasteur, certain of victory, and furnished with an arsenal of test-tubes and glass receivers containing his cultures, presented himself, while his opponents found some pretext for stealing away. Under these circumstances, the commission placed itself flatly on the side of Pasteur. Yet, as a matter of fact, truth was on the side of both parties. Particularly, it is true that a boiled infusion of yeasts will not ferment unless it is sown after boiling, while an infusion of hay has no need of subsequent sowing in order to supply an abundant culture of bacteria. This latter fact, observed by Pouchet, was correct, but the deduction he drew from it regarding spontaneous generation was wrong. Still, a great deal of time and labor was required to clarify this misconception which occurred on the occasion of the researches of the English scienist Bastian, who hurled a caustic criticism at Pasteur. He corroborated the experiments of Pouchet, Joly and Musset, and went even further. He also confirmed Pasteur's experiments on urine, subjected to lengthy boiling: namely that it would in no way ferment—but such sterility was noticeable only under certain conditions. It sufficed to add a little alkali for the urine to become turbid and opaque through the growth of innumerable bacteria, even though no ferment had been poured into it. These observations, according to Bastian, was an irrefutable proof of the reality of spontaneous generation.

Pasteur could not remain indifferent to these objections, based on positive facts. Together with Joubert and Chamberland, his collaborators, he repeated and confirmed Bastian's experiments. But he disputed that scientist's conclusion by proving that the urine and the infusion of hay contained spores of bacteria which showed a strong resistance even to prolonged boiling. In the case of hay infusions the spores germinated abundantly from the time that a sufficient quantity of air was admitted to the culture tube. As to the boiled urine, it lent itself to the development of bacteria only when in a slightly alkaline or neutral state. The normal urine being usually acid, the bacteria, though present, do not develop. But it required only the addition of a small quantity of alkali to enable whatever bacteria were present there to swarm and multiply.

Eventually Pasteur's conclusions were, many times, firmly established. Though Bastian's investigations were incapable of proving the existence of spontaneous generation, they nevertheless threw a new light on the question of the growth of bacteria in organic liquids. They helped to establish the exceedingly important fact of the existence in nature of microbes which could resist prolonged boiling. This new idea required the complete modification of experimental technique. Whereas, in his former experiments, Pasteur had been content to boil the liquids, he was now forced, after Bastian's trials, to heat them to a temperature of from 108 to 120 degrees C. To sterilize solid objects polluted with microbe spores, such as glass receptacles, it was necessary even to heat them to a temperature of 140 degrees C.

This radical change called forth the invention of new apparatus, suitable to bacteriological technique. Chamberland adapted Papin's digester, in which the steam under pressure raises the temperature to 120 degrees C and higher. Chamberland's *autoclave* became an apparatus indispensable to every laboratory, and in every surgical and lying-in hospital.

In spite of protracted opposition and strife, the chief principles of Pasteur's theory remained intact: *Putrefaction and fermentation are due to the vital action of micro-organisms or rather, according to the present nomenclature, to microbes; these ori-*

ginate not from spontaneous generation, but from microbes like themselves.

These conclusions were reached thanks to the persistent and prolonged researches of Pasteur, investigations into which no elements alien to science entered. It had been supposed, and this is still held from time to time, that Pasteur was guided in certain of his researches by ideas coming from a different source. It was thus maintained that his theory of ferments had been suggested to him by the belief in a special vital force. This, as we have noted above, is an erroneous idea, for Pasteur at no time denied the chemical nature of vital phenomena. The attempt was also made to trace Pasteur's conception of the non-existence of spontaneous generation to his religious convictions. Pasteur denied this on several occasions. In his investigations he was guided solely by the desire to bring light on the origin of vital ferments. If, from the very outset, he believed that the ferments were not of spontaneous origin, this was not to be ascribed to his religious beliefs, but to facts he observed through experimentation.

Just as Pasteur's biological theory of fermentation could not be disturbed by the discovery of zymase—an unorganized ferment, produced by yeasts—so also his theory of the origin of ferments, coming from ascendants (ancestors) like them, stands a good chance of persevering even after the possible discovery of a future process for the spontaneous growth of any lower organism whatever in an artificial medium. Such a spontaneous generation however will undoubtedly take place under conditions differing from those which we at present know in respect to the growth of living ferments in organic liquids.

Whether or not the future will furnish us with proofs regarding the existence of spontaneous generation, and whether Arrhenius' hypothesis of the meteoric origin of life on earth is corroborated, at any rate, the theory (doctrine) of Pasteur, in the terms he set it down, will remain true and will retain its practical importance.

CHAPTER V.

Pasteur's researches did not restrict themselves to fermentation, in the narrower sense of the word. After discovering the microbes of lactic, butyric and acetic fermentation, he set himself the task of studying the fermentation of albuminoid matter, that is to say, of putrefaction. This phenomenon seemed to him more complex than the fermentation of sugary and alcoholic substances. The bad smell of meats, of eggs and of other albuminoid materials which become putrefied, is due to the growth of bacteria which dread the oxygen of the air, e.g. the bacteria of butyric putrefaction. Pasteur's researches uncovered two phenomena in natural putrefaction: at first, there is a growth of aerobic bacteria which do not fear free oxygen, which absorb it and thus prepare the ground for the true, putrefying bacteria, the anaerobic bacteria, which subsequently develop freely thanks to the absence of the oxygen of the air, detrimental to them.

Just as alcoholic fermentation may be brought about by several kinds of yeasts and lactic fermentation by various types of lactic bacteria, so also putrefaction does not depend on one species of putrefying bacteria, but rather may be produced by different species. Ad-additional new facts observed by the disciples of Pasteur corroborated this view: it was found, particularly, that the fetid odors of putrefied albuminoid substances are not always emitted exclusively by bacteria fearing free oxygen—the anaerobic bacteria—but also by bacteria insensitive to it. In that case, the process of putrefaction becomes simplified, for the previous elimination of free oxygen in the putrefiable matter is no longer found to be necessary. In both cases, nevertheless, putrefaction, like every other form of fermentation, is the result of microbial action.

The description of the health conditions of the French army during the Crimean War has shown, as we have seen, the disastrous effects of the putrefaction of wounds. Physicians and surgeons had known for a long time that the aggravation of diseases coincided with such putrefaction. No means were spared to get rid of this scourge. It is clear that it was this coincidence, especially, which suggested the idea that putrefaction and disease have a common cause.

No sooner had Pasteur demonstrated that the putrefaction of albuminoid substances depended neither on their contact with decomposing matter, as Liebig supposed, nor on the spontaneous generation of putrefying bacteria, but on their introduction from without, and that it is their vital activity that decomposes albuminoid matter, than the logical conclusion forced itself upon the mind that the putrefaction of wounds must be due to the same cause. What could be simpler than to apply this well-established fact to the putrefaction of wounds? Nevertheless, it was necessary first to get the application and cooperation of the ingenious mind of the English surgeon Lister, who was able to implant this theory only after a great deal of struggle.

Lister was not one of those surgeons who become famous by their skill in difficult and complicated operations; nor was he a fashionable operating surgeon like certain of his colleagues. He was a doctor and a capable and thoughtful surgeon. At the outset of his professional career he dedicated himself to the solution of scientific problems; his first study dealt with the contractile tissue of the ciliary body of the eye. Subsequently he made researches on the structure of the muscular and nervous systems; and undertook extensive studies of blood coagulation and of many other problems of pathological surgery.

As a surgeon he had to perform operations at the Royal Hospital at Glasgow. The conditions there were especially unfavorable. Putrefaction of purulent wounds and erysipelas brought on frightful havoc. Lister's sick-wards were opposite a plot of land where, sometime before, the corpses of cholera patients had been buried, at a very shallow depth. Lister inferred that the serious wound complications were related to the microbes coming from that cemetery, microbes which adhered to the wall and other parts of the hospital. Such germs when transferred to the surface of wounds could bring about putrefaction, whose effects could poison the entire organism.

Lister went through the very same experiments which Pasteur had made on fermentation and on the non-existence of spontaneous generation, in order to convince himself and to convey that conviction to others. We have, from his own lips, an account of the history of his beneficent discovery. In spite of "an unconquerable repugnance against talking about himself," he consented to impart it to the members of the British Association for the Advancement of Science, in the year 1906, when he was its president:

"Nothing was formerly more striking in surgical experience than the difference in the behavior of injuries according to whether the skin was implicated or not. Thus, if the bones of the leg were broken and the skin remained intact, the surgeon applied the necessary apparatus without any other anxiety than that of maintaining a good position of the fragments, although the internal injury to bones and soft parts might be severe. If, on the other hand, a wound of the skin was present communicating with the broken bones, although the damage might be in other respects comparatively slight, the compound fracture, as it was termed, was one of the most dangerous accidents that could happen.

"What was the cause of this astonishing difference? It was clearly in some way due to the exposure of the injured parts to the external world. One obvious effect of such an exposure was indicated by the odor of the discharge, which showed that the blood in the wound had undergone putrefactive change by which the blood nutrient liquid had been converted into highly irritating and poisonous substances.

"These and many other considerations had long impressed me with the greatness of the evil of putrefaction in surgery. I had done my best to mitigate it by scrupulous ordinary cleanliness and the use of various deodorant lotions. But to prevent it altogether appeared hopeless while we believed with Liebig that its primary cause was atmospheric oxygen, which in accordance with the researches of Graham could not fail to be perpetually diffused through the porous dressings which were used to absorb the blood discharged from the wounds. But when Pasteur had shown that putrefaction was a fermentation caused by the growth of microbes, and that these could not arise *de novo* in the decomposable substance, the problem assumed a more hopeful aspect. If the wound could be treated with some substance, which without doing too serious mischief to the human tissues would kill the microbes already contained in it and prevent the future access of others in the living state, putrefaction might be prevented, however freely the air with its oxygen might enter. I had heard of carbolic acid as having a remarkable deodorizing effect upon sewage, and having obtained from my colleague, Dr. Anderson, Professor of Chemistry in the University of Glasgow, a sample which he had of this product, then little more than a chemical curiosity in Scotland, I determined to try it in compound fractures. Applying it undiluted to the wound, with an arrangement for its occasional renewal, I had the joy of seeing these formidable injuries follow the same safe and tranquil course as simple fractures, in which the skin remains unbroken.

"Undiluted carbolic acid is a powerful caustic; and although it might be employed in compound fractures, where some loss of tissue was of little moment in comparison with the tremendous danger to be averted, it was altogether unsuitable for wounds made by the surgeon. It soon appeared, however, that the acid would answer the purpose aimed at, though used in diluted forms devoid of caustic action, and therefore applicable to operative surgery. According to our then existing knowledge, two essential points had to be aimed at: To conduct the operation so that on its completion the wound should contain no living microbes, and to apply a dressing capable of preventing the access of other living organisms till the time should have arrived for changing it.

"Even our earlier and ruder methods of carrying out the antiseptic principle soon produced a wonderful change in my surgical wards in the Glasgow Royal Infirmary, which, from being some of the most unhealthy in the Kingdom, became, as I believe I may say without exaggeration, the healthiest in the world; while other wards separated from mine only by a passage a few feet broad, where former modes of treatment were for a while continued, retained their former insalubrity.

"Equally striking changes were afterwards witnessed in other institutions. Of these I may give one example. In the great Allgemeines Krankenhaus of Munich, hospital gangrene had become more and more rife from year to year, till at length the frightful condition was reached that 80 per cent of all wounds became affected by it. It is only just to the memory of Professor von Nussbaum, then the head of that establishment, to say that he had done his utmost to check this frightful scourge; and that the evil was not caused by anything peculiar to his management was shown by the fact that in a private hospital under his care there was no unusual unhealthiness. The larger institution seemed to have become hopelessly infected, and the city authorities were contemplating its demolition and reconstruction. Under these circumstances Professor von Nussbaum dispatched his chief assistant, Dr. Lindpointner, to Edinburgh, where I at the time occupied the chair of clinical surgery, to learn the details of the antiseptic system, as we then practiced it. He remained until he had entirely mastered them, and after his return all the cases were on a certain day dressed on our plan. From that day forward not a single case of hospital gangrene occurred in the Krankenhaus. The fearful disease pyaemia likewise disappeared, and erysipelas soon followed its example."

One would imagine that Lister's method should soon have taken up the place which was its due. But this was not to be so, on account of the stubborn opposition of various surgeons. After a certain period of deliberate silence, Lister's colleagues launched an attack against him. The famous Simpson, who enjoyed a great reputation, especially in England, opposed the new method very vehemently. Spens, Lister's colleague at Edinburgh, utilizing statistical facts he had gathered, attacked the antiseptic method and attempted to destroy it once for all. In other countries, too, the voice of criticism was raised, though not as vociferously as in Great Britain. The antiseptic method, based on Pasteur's experiments, found a more favorable soil in France, where Alphonse Guérin had introduced the use of cotton dressings, independently of Lister, though somewhat later, in 1871. Thanks to the splendid confirmation of the antiseptic method in Germany, by Nussbaum, it found followers in such authoritative men as Volkman, the eminent surgeon. Nevertheless, many years went by before the great discovery of Lister—the application of the theory of the non-existence of spontaneous generation of ferments—became a common possession.

As the new method of treating wounds began to spread throughout the entire world, it underwent important modifications. It began with the discovery that wound infections were due less to the bacteria of the air than to manual contact, to instruments and tissues insufficiently cleaned, contaminated with pathogenic ferments. Later at operations the pulverization of carbolic acid, the purpose of which had been the destruction of the microbes in the air, was omitted.

Although the injurious effects of carbolic acid were not very noticeable, nevertheless, it was desirable to dispense with that substance in order not to subject to it the tissues whose quick repair is so necessary for a complete recovery. Little by little the anti-infectious, antiseptic technique of Lister was replaced by asepsis, except in cases of wounds already infected before surgical interference. In aseptic treatment the dressings no longer contain any antiseptic matter. The older method is employed only for washing the hands of the operator and the patients' skin, which are always, to a smaller or larger degree, contaminated by microbes. The instruments and the tissues are disinfected by raising the temperature. After a trial period lasting several years, asepsis has everywhere taken solid root.

Just as the primitive technique of Pasteur, restricted at first to the boiling of the medium, gave place to heating at a higher temperature, so also Lister's method was replaced by a more improved method in which the dressings were no longer moistened with carbolic solution or other disinfectants. Nevertheless, the main ideas both of Lister and of Pasteur will always retain their importance. According to the former, wound complications are due to the intrusion of infectious microbes coming from the outside; according to the latter, fermentations result from the vital activity of ferments coming from the outside, and not at all from spontaneous generation.

CHAPTER VI.

Lister's main desire was to save his patients, as quickly as possible, from the terrible effects of wound complications, resulting from gangrene. This made him direct his ideas, based on the fundamental principles of Pasteur's theory, towards a practical solution of the problem in keeping with that theory. He did not stop to study the putrefaction of wounds for the purpose of proving the presence of living microbes; nor did he make a detailed study of the nature of ferments. Rather, he went straight to the examination of his carbolic dressings, hoping thereby to remove the microbes from the wounds, without bothering about questions of their genus or species. It was not until much later that he noticed that surgical wounds were not invaded only by bacteria diffusing a bad odor. He also ascertained in his ward that the epidemic of erysipelatic inflammation was not attended by a fetid odor. He remarked, furthermore, that in many cases of purulent wounds there was no putrefaction. From all these observations he concluded that "the wound complications may be as various as the different fermentations, and that every one of these complications must be due to a different species of microbe."

This idea was soon proven, in a brilliant manner. A great many scientists set themselves to study the bacteriology of surgical diseases and this made it possible for the existence of a whole flora of wound microbes to be proven. While certain species of the group showed a very marked sensitivity to the action of the oxygen in the air—the anaerobic bacteria; others, and among them the microbe of erysipelas, were very slightly sensitive to that gas—the aerobic bacteria.

But before science had as yet begun to profit from the knowledge of wound ferments and of pus, facts already began to be gathered about the microbes of certain infectious diseases. What is notable here is the fact that these early observations on these microbes were made before the microbiological experiments of Pasteur.

After gaining the conviction that the infectious diseases might be transmitted by a contagious element, physicians and, above all veterinarians, had for a long time tried to transmit the infection from a sick organism to a healthy one. A classic example of this is the vaccination of people with the contagious principle of human small-pox—variolation—or with small-pox from a heifer—vaccination. The theory of Liebig was the base on which were built all the experiments on the nature of the sources of contagion. In other words, it was believed that this contagious principle consisted of an amorphous albuminoid substance in a state of decomposition.

In 1850, two well-known French physicians, Rayer and Davoine, made the following observation in the course of their researches on the contagious nature of the blood of sheep dead of anthrax:(8) "The blood examined through the microscope behaved like that of sheep, seized with anthrax, which had been used in the inoculation. The globules, instead of remaining very distinct like those of healthy blood, became agglutinated as a whole into irregular masses. There were in addition, *thread-like small bodies* in the blood, about twice the length of a blood globule. *These little bodies showed no spontaneous movement whatever.*" Apparently, this discovery did not appear very important for it was not followed by any new researches about these "thread-like corpuscles." Somewhat later it was noticed in blood affected by anthrax, in Germany and in Russia (at Dorpat or Jurieff). In 1855, Pollender in turn observed them and thought he was dealing with microscopical plants, but he did not go to the point of ascribing to them the causes of the disease. Two years after Pasteur's great discovery of lactic ferment, Branell found thread-like corpuscles in human blood affected by anthrax, as well as in that of bovidae and sheep. However, he mistook them for the vibrios of putrefied blood and failed to understand their significance.

All of these observation took place at a time when Liebig's theories regarding ferments and the sources of infection dominated science. We must also pay especial attention to the opinion of the French veterinarian Delafond, who, ten years after the discovery of

---

(8) Comptes rendus de la Société de biologie, p. 45, 1850.

Rayer and Davaine, in his turn observed, in the blood of animals which had died of anthrax, microscopical corpuscles in the form of sticks (batonnets) or short filaments. "I do not at all think," he states, "that these growths might be the cause of the anthrax, or these bodies contain the infectious principle of the disease. It seems to me, nevertheless, that the blood of animals affected with anthrax acquires a morbid predisposition favorable to the pullulation of those corpuscles." In other words, the bacteria of anthrax were not the cause but the consequence of the disease, which, in keeping with Liebig's theory, was due to an amorphous principle of infection, in the form of albuminous matter about to decompose.

This example demonstrates the fact that a leading but erroneous idea may turn research away from truth. This entire picture however was changed completely after Pasteur, in 1861, had discovered the mobile rods which bring about the fermentation of sugar, giving butyric acid. Davaine, who in the succeeding ten years had forgotten all about his thread-like corpuscles he had discovered, immediately had the idea that these corpuscles must play the same role in anthrax as Pasteur's vibrios in butyric fermentation. To put it in Davaine's own words: "The lack of an opportunity and many other cares prevented me from going into a deeper study of the question, when Pasteur, in 1861, published his monumental paper on butyric fermentation; the ferment, consisting of small, cylindrical rods, having all the earmarks of vibrios or bacilli. The thread-like corpuscles which I had seen in the blood of sheep seized with anthrax being remarkably analogous, as regards form, to these vibrios, I was led to examine the question whether these corpuscles resembling or of the same genus as those which were the cause of butyric fermentation, would also behave like a ferment if introduced into the blood of an animal."(9) From that time on, Davaine threw himself with much spirit into the study of anthrax. In that work he was detained neither by the difficulties of obtaining the necessary material, nor by "other cases". For about ten years he investigated very minutely all facts capable of proving that the bodies found by him were not the secondary products of disease, but their real cause. Nevertheless, he failed to isolate the corpuscles from the ambient blood fluid, the liquid which, according to the ruling theory of the period, should contain the principle of infection. Davaine based his opinion on the fact that the contagion could not be transmitted from the blood of the ewe seized with anthrax to that of the foetus though the blood of the former caused the disease. This agrees with the fact that the corpuscles are absent in the blood of the foetus and yet are abundant in that of the mother. Davaine also leaned on an experiment which consisted in filtering the blood affected with anthrax through a porcelain filter. The filter retains the infectious principle which adheres to the porcelain together with the corpuscles, and the matter which remains in the filter transmits the disease. On the other hand, the liquid which has passed through the filter contains no corpuscles and is not contagious. All these proofs, how-

(9) Comptes rendus de l'Académie des Sciences, July 27, 1863.

ever, could not convince his opponents, who struck tenaciously to Liebig's point of view, asserting that the true inorganized principle could not pass through either the placenta or the filter, just as the corpuscles could not get through it. Davaine's theory was especially unacceptable to his opponents because his "corpuscles" failed to explain the natural spreading of anthrax. It had been known for a long time that the disease was connected with the soil, for in certain localities it reappeared from year to year. It was enough for a flock of sheep to be led out into such a pasturage in the spring, for the first cases of anthrax to be observed, and in the course of the summer it would take on an epidemic aspect. However, when these isolated cases are transferred to other localities, they do not spread. These findings pointed to the extraordinary resistance of the infectious principle of anthrax, whereas his corpuscles, or "bacteria", as he called them, were, in his own words, easily destroyed. Even though the anthrax-affected blood containing them remained contagious for a long time after desiccation, nevertheless, it no longer determined the disease. In his attempt to explain the spreading of anthrax, Davaine stressed the importance of flies, which transferred the infectious bacteria from the blood of animals dead from anthrax, to the bodies of healthy animals. But here again he struck upon difficulties, for cases of anthrax were not at all rare in the winter, before flies made their appearance.

To sum up, Davaine's exacting researches, though productive of new facts, remained ineffectual in the tide of opposition, which instead of subsiding increased in the course of time. The strength of that opposition was due not so much to the ability of the opponents of the theory of the organic principle of contagion as to the awkwardness of its followers. After the doctrine of Pasteur had definitely won the upper hand over Liebig's, many naturalists and physicians began to apply it with excessive zeal to all the infectious diseases. For several years, in the sixties, the 19th Century saw an immense literature appear dealing with the lower pathogenic organisms of various diseases. The problems of disease were solved in a very simple manner: after examining the secretion of the diseased person under the microscope, it was poured into some sort of a medium and the fungus cultures which began to grow there were declared the cause of the disease. The German botanist Hallier excelled particularly in that method. One after another, he came upon parasitic plants in various infections; he took common molds for the sources of skin diseases. Other lower forms of fungi he believed to be the ferments of cholera. It was an easy task for him to discover in quick succession the principle of infection of typhoid fever, eruptive typhus, small-pox, etc. The physician Letzerich made use of the same method; having discovered under the microscope lower forms of fungi in the false membranes of diphtheria he declared them to be the cause of diphtheria. He certifies it in the following words: "My two works on diphtheria prove without a doubt that primary, epidemic diphtheria is due to a fungus whose spores may transmit the disease to other individuals."(10)

Such an unscientific spirit did not fail in bringing about a violent reaction. The famous German botanist, de Barry, considered in his time the best authority on lower plants, launched a strong broadside against Hallier and his followers. He proved to them that their "discoveries" could not withstand criticism, that all their germs of infectious diseases were nothing but blots having nothing in common with the elements of infections. Some fanatics lent a deaf ear to the warning of de Barry, but many others who inquired into the organic ferments of contagion were sobered down by his criticism. It did not take long before the atmosphere began to be cleared of these false ideas; a sceptical spirit took its place, which, in its turn, went to extremes. Physicians who in their researches observed microscopical parasites, preferred to keep that fact secret rather than expose themselves to the crushing attack of the schooled botanist. The following example is not without interest here. Towards the end of the Sixties of last century a severe epidemic of recurrent fever had broken out in Berlin. A number of the patients were placed in the ward of the famous Virchow and confided to the care of his assistant Obermeyer. The latter was in the habit of making clinical examinations irreproachable from the point of view of the medicine of the period. The temperature, the pulse, the respiration, the body weight, the urine of the patient were studied with the most exacting detail. Exceedingly detailed facts regarding the pro-

(10) Archiv für pathologische Anatomie, 1869, Vol. XXXXVI, p. 232.

gress of the disease were gathered in that exemplary piece of work.(11) Only one little fact was left out. In his microscopical examinations of the blood of the diseased, Obermeyer had noticed very minute spiral-formed filaments of very rapid motion which repulsed the red corpuscles with great force. Nevertheless he made not the least mention of them in his article. As we have seen in the first chapter of this book, Virchow was convinced that the cause of disease lay in the abnormal functioning of the cells of the organism; he paid no attention to the lower beings found at times in the morbid products. Obermeyer adopted the ideas of his teacher and chief. Moreover, public opinion, disinclined towards the theory of organic ferments of infection, caused him to shy from venturing too far with his discovery. It was not until five years later, in 1873, that he determined to publish it, for in the interval many changes in medical beliefs had taken place. The Franco-Prussian War made it possible for many observations to be made on wound diseases. The German surgeon Günther and the pathologist Klebs, in the army service, became convinced that the putrefaction and purulence of wounds were the result of the intrusion of organized ferments, just as Lister's theory had stated. At the beginning of the Seventies a new current made itself felt in medicine. The great minds made ready to apply Pasteur's ideas on the nature of infectious diseases. Under these circumstances Obermeyer's discovery of the spiral-formed

(11) Archiv für pathologische Anatomie, Vol. XXXXVII, pp. 161 and 428.

filaments took on a special importance. This fact was soon confirmed from all sides. With a renewed zeal all laboratories began to search for the microscopical parasites of other diseases. The results of these investigations, however, were rather meager. They had to their credit only the bacterium of anthrax and the spirilla of intermittent fever. On the debit side they had many charges, for as regards the other infectious diseases, in spite of some microbes isolated, nothing either convincing or permanent was established in respect to the role they played. Moreover, the bacteria of anthrax and the spirilla of Obermeyer always being distributed in the liquid of the affected organism (blood and exudation), it was impossible to receive as proof that it was these beings and not the unorganized substances which accompanied them, that were the cause of anthrax and intermittent fever.

A powerful impulse was necessary to change this inchoate idea of organized ferments into a rigorously proven scientific truth. Such an impetus was started by Robert Koch in his paper on anthrax written in 1876. (12) This young health officer in the little city of Wolstein, a God-forsaken hole in Posen, suddenly came into the limelight of science. His work was indeed a model of true scientific creativeness. Living in a region in which anthrax was endemic, he set about to study it, without the help of laboratory or library, and always thrown back on his own resources. He worked in his own rooms where for lack of gas illumination

(12) Beiträge zur Biologie der Pflanzen, 1876, Vol. II, p. 277.

he was obliged to use a petroleum lamp. By means of plates covered with moist sand he constructed a semblance of an apparatus for growing cultures of bacteria. Nevertheless he achieved results superior to anything as yet accomplished. He was the first to succeed in changing the thread-like microscopical corpuscles of Davaine into long filaments and the latter into beads consisting of minute grains, the spores. This great discovery of the spore of anthrax removed all doubts regarding the role of bacteria in the causation of anthrax, for it illuminated all points hitherto left unexplained. As was to be expected, the spores were found to have much more resistance than the sticks or filaments. Unlike the latter, which, when deprived of spores, lost their virulence a little while after drying, the spores, subjected to desiccation for several years, would provoke fatal cases of anthrax in animals inoculated with them. This vitality of the spores explained in a very simple manner the correlation observed between anthrax and the soil. It was evident that the places where the cadavers of animals affected with anthrax had been buried and where the sticks were able to become transformed into filaments and these into spores, could for a long period become a source of contagion.

In order to bring proof of his results, Koch went to Breslau, to the celebrated botanist Cohn, and there, in the presence of numerous scientists, he demonstrated his preparations and his cultures. The impression produced was crushing. Koch's discovery spread around the world, convincing even the most obstinate sceptics that the interpretation of the role of bacteria in the etiology of anthrax was quite exact. It opened a new era in the study of infectious diseases.

There were many who now expected that the extraordinary technical skill of Koch would permit him soon to discover the ferments of other diseases, of even greater importance to man than anthrax. Two years of anxious waiting rolled by without anything happening. Finally, in the fall of 1878, Koch deilvered a report to the Congress of German Naturalists at Cassel regarding his new discovery—new microbes of infection. However, it was nothing but the germ found in small laboratory animals, a germ causing a widespread infection, septicemia of mice! The disappointment of the assembled scientists was immense; they failed to realize that this new work represented an important step in bacteriological technique. It was on that occasion that Koch first introduced the idea of aniline coloration of microbes. He combined Abbe's condenser of very intense illumination for microscopical examination with a system of downward immersion in cedar oil.

Obtaining soon afterward a position in the "Imperial Bureau of Public Health" newly instituted at Berlin, Koch organized a good laboratory with two assistants attached to it and everything requisite for scientific research. It was there that he succeeded, after years of hard labor, in separating the tubercular bacillus, the formidable enemy of mankind. This bacillus was considerably smaller than the bacterium of anthrax and even much harder to study and cultivate. Koch communicated this discovery to the Physiological Association of Berlin, on March 24, 1882. The news flashed through the world with the speed of light and made an indescribable and unforgettable impression. As in his first work, on anthrax, Koch, in his new report, his masterpiece, forsaw and forestalled all the objections, so much so, that even his severest critics had to bow to it. The new discovery rapidly became common possession. There was an upsurge of intense and tireless activity in all laboratories and hospitals, aiming towards a practical application of that discovery: to track down, cure and prevent all the different forms of tuberculosis, the horrible disease that spares not even one of the human organs.

In the interval, Koch and his assistants had gone to Egypt and India. When he returned in 1884 he brought back the news of the discovery of the germ of Asiatic cholera—a little stick bent back like a comma, or rather, a *vibrio*.

These exceedingly important discoveries succeeded one another rapidly and gave rise to a new branch of science, medical bacteriology. The fruitful work of this German scientist did not remain without effect on scientific progress in other countries. Pasteur, immersed in his studies of alcoholic fermentation and of the deterioration of wine by noxious microbes, could not for a long time decide to undertake the study of pathogenic ferments. He feared becoming entangled in the labyrinth of official medical science in spite of all the preparation he had in connection with his fruitful studies on the disease of silk-worms. It was not until later when he had secured the assistance of a very talented young physician, Emile Roux, that he overcame his doubts and set about the work with a passion and an energy which always characterized him. He began with the study of the bacteria of anthrax and it was not long before he displayed his own marked initiative. He applied to these microbes his method of raising cultures in liquid media, a method which had brought such good results in the isolation and study of ferments. He found that the bacteria grew well in non-acid and diluted urine. He succeeded in growing a whole series of successive generations, each one of which showed the same virulence as the first culture. He thus gained definite proof that it was these bacteria and not the blood liquid containing them, which were the true cause of anthrax.

In citing this fact I must not pass over in silence a side of the question which appears puzzling in matters pertaining to science. Certain authors, apparently with the purpose of enlarging on the importance of the cultures of anthrax grown by Pasteur, placed doubt on the conclusive value of Koch's experiences. They believed that it was not Koch but Pasteur who had finally removed all doubts as to the role of bacteria in anthrax, for Koch had cultivated only a small number of generations of bacteria, in blood serum and aqueous humor, whereas Pasteur had obtained an infinitely larger number of generations in urine medium. Even the last culture of Koch might still have retained a certain quantity of supposedly inorganic ferment, while all trace of it must have disappeared in the immense volumes of urine Pasteur made use of in his cultures.

Dr. Roux, who entered Pasteur's laboratory in 1878, explains why the arguments of Davaine and of Koch had failed to carry conviction:

"We can not understand nowdays how it was possible for anyone to dispute the fact that bacteria were the cause of anthrax. But in 1878 the great minds were as yet unprepared for the notion that the viruses are parasitic microbes. Most physicians considered the bacteria to be merely accessories to disease. The sticks of Davaine, they claimed, do not exist by themselves, in the blood affected by anthrax. Alongside of them there were globules and the plasma, the true amorphous virus. Nor do Koch's cultures suffice to convince us. Within the drop of aqueous humor into which anthrax blood is poured, Koch not only introduces bacteria but also the amorphous virus contained in the plasma; the successive pourings that he carries out on the drops of liquid merely lead to a dilution of that virus. But do we not know nowadays that the property of viruses is to act in infinitely small doses and that they may be considerably diluted without destroying their action?" However, at the time these objections were put forth, they seemed very forceful.

Such was the state of the problem when Pasteur came up with it. He, too, begins to grow cultures of bacteria; but instead of pouring the anthrax blood into a drop of nutritive medium, he placed it, from the very outset, into a glass container which encloses hundreds of centimeters of organic infusion, where the bacteria pullulate within several hours. He pours a trace of that culture into the second, and so on to the twentieth, to the hundredth generation. And a trace of that hundredth culture will as surely cause anthrax as the blood of a sheep affected with the disease. One can no longer appeal to the dilution of the virus. The original droplet had been drowned in oceans of liquids; it remained in the hundredth culture and the minutest dose of it was mortal. The virus, then, had reproduced itself, was a living thing, it could be nothing else but that bacterium which exists by itself in the glass containers of the culture. It is this bacterium which is mortal and not the chemical substances which accompany it. Indeed, if we place the receptacles containing the bacteria into a place of a very low and constant temperature, such as the cellar of the Observatory, as Pasteur did, the bacteria in suspension will sink to the bottom of the container. The clear liquid which remains, when injected into the body of animals in no matter how large quantities, will not bring about the disease, whereas a very minute portion of the bacterial sediment, when introduced into their bodies will cause them to die of anthrax.(13)

The role of the anthrax bacterium as the sole cause of the disease was also proven beyond any doubt, by Koch's experiments in which he inoculated some animals with blood and desiccated organs not containing spores, and others with blood and desiccated organs containing spores. In the first case, the virulence became extinct after five weeks of desiccation; in the second case it was preserved even after four years. If the blood and the organs had contained an inorganic ferment besides the bacteria, how can we understand the fact that the former had sometimes

(13) L'oeuvre médicale de Pasteur, **Agenda du Chimiste,** 1896, p. 521 (Editor's Note).

lost and at other times retained its effect in measure with the absence or presence of the spores? If the hypothetical ferment showed no resistance to desiccation, how shall we explain the fact that contamination took place even four years later? On the other hand, if it does show resistance to desiccation, why does contamination cease after only five weeks? This dilemma could not be solved except by admitting, with Koch, that the infection must be ascribed to the anthrax bacteria and to their spores, rather than to an inorganic ferment.

Another controversy, relating to anthrax but carried over to the domain of patriotism, concerns the discovery of the bacterium of anthrax. While the French authors ascribed this discovery to the Frenchmen Rayer and Davaine, in 1850, the German writers made Pollender its discoverer, in 1849. Pollender is said to have observed the bacteria before the Frenchmen did, but did not publish his observation until after theirs, in 1855. In reality the principal role in that discovery belongs to Pasteur, for Pollender, Rayer and Davaine failed to understand their bacteriological observations, and their works remained on the dusty shelves of professional libraries.

It is to the Frenchman, Pasteur, that we owe an understanding of the true significance of the bacterium of anthrax and to the German, Koch, that we owe the proof of its role as the sole infectious principle (source) of that disease. It would seem exceedingly desirable to avoid all considerations of patriotism in questions of science!

In his researches into pathogenic microbes, Pasteur

did not limit himself to anthrax. He soon discovered new and exceedingly fruitful fields in the youthful science of medical bacteriology. He did not follow the example of Koch, who concentrated all his efforts upon the discovery of new pathogenic bacteria and upon the improvement of the technique of demonstration and of culture media. Though, on the way, he discovered the microbes causing boils and puerperal fever, his main purpose was to devise a general method of fighting infectious diseases. In preparing himself for that task he made a careful study of the works of Jenner and of everything that concerned vaccination against small-pox. In the laboratory he acquainted his collaborators Chamberland and Roux with his projects and put them to work on many experiments to prove the ideas crowding his brain. Thanks to his delicate sense of observation, he did not omit even the least detail capable of leading him to the passionately desired goal. His untiring activity was interrupted only by the briefest possible vacations, after which he returned to Paris with redoubled energy. One day, his assistants informed him, with confusion, that the cultures of minute microbes of chicken cholera, left in the drying-stove during his vacation, had completely lost their virulence for chickens. Pasteur's attention was immediately aroused. Imbued by the thought of preventing the infectious diseases, he believed that these non-virulent microbes might play the same role as the small-pox of cattle,—a very effective vaccine against the true human small-pox. He worked out a full series of experiments and had the joy of establishing results which proved his assumption. The chicken which had been vaccinated with the culture which had lost the virulence actually acquired a lasting immunity against chicken cholera, which they were inevitably subject to without preliminary vaccination. The new means of fighting infectious diseases, a means so ardently hoped for, was at last found! It was necessary, first of all, to obtain a culture of the given microbe, then to find a means of attenuating it, and finally to establish the degree of attenuation necessary for warding off the infection. Activity at the small laboratory at the Normal School was intensified to such a degree that a whole series of discoveries were achieved there during a brief period, between 1880 and 1885. Following this preventive culture against chicken cholera, similar "vaccines" were found against anthrax in domestic animals and against hog cholera. All this, however, failed to satisfy Pasteur, who ardently desired to crown his scientific achievement with the discovery of preventive against a human disease. Certain external considerations fixed his choice on that of hydrophobia. Though he had succeeded neither in finding the microbe of that disease nor in obtaining cultures of its infectious principle, nevertheless, he was able to solve the problem he had set himself, in a very ingenious manner. A whole stock of jars containing the spinal marrow of rabbits had been laid aside in the laboratory; the vain attempt had been made to cultivate in these bottles the virus of hydrophobia, and these marrows had little by little dried up. Pasteur charged his assistant, Eug. Viala, to determine the degree of their virulence, hoping thereby to find an antirabic. After numerous experiments this new attempt by the ingenious and indefatigable scientist was also rewarded with success. After proving, on dogs, the preventive action of a long series of spinal marrow graded in regard to their virulence, Pasteur at last determined to try his method on people bitten by dogs.

It was not without much struggle that Pasteur was able to attain his shining victories over disease. To begin with, he met with the obstinate resistance of such a formidable adversary as Koch. Apparently stung by Pasteur's failure to appreciate the true value of his classic work on anthrax (which may simply have been due to Pasteur's ignorance of the German language), Koch, as well as his assistants, launched a violent attack against Pasteur. In his opinion, Pasteur did not possess the ability either to study the microbes or to obtain pure cultures of them. Consequently, all of his conclusions were full of errors. He had not proven the attenuation of the virulence of the microbes nor had his claim that preventive vaccination was possible been confirmed by the experiments undertaken by his opponents. Pasteur, invited in 1882 to the International Congress of Hygienists at Geneva, availed himself of that occasion to answer with a public statement of his objections to Koch and to invite him to a friendly exchange of ideas. Koch, however, refused this meeting, but instead wrote a paper, in which he assembled what he considered all the facts suitable to destroy Pasteur's prestige and to prove his total unfitness for dealing with the subject. Leaning on some minor technical inadequacies in Pasteur's work, he enlarged upon them out of due proportions and placed himself in decided opposition to the entire medical labors of Pasteur.

Much water has flowed under the bridge since that controversy. At the present time no one doubts that these attacks of Koch were ill-founded, nor questions the far-reaching scope of Pasteur's researches which have opened up a new vista for medicine. Some time after the Geneva discussions, Pasteur published his work on vaccination against hydrophobia. The Berlin school began by opposing it; but a few years lat[illegible] Koch himself organized at the Institute of Hygiene in Berlin a department for vaccinating against hydrophobia, according to the methods of Pasteur.

In his own country Pasteur had to submit to attacks no less stubborn. The Parisian physicians lashed at him without intermission; they accused him of not bringing enough proof in behalf of his treatment, and said that his vaccinations did not save people from hydrophobia, but, rather, that such vaccinations might in turn bring on grave disease. However, if there was anyone who paid dearly for his anti-hydrophobia inoculations, it was Pasteur himself. His health, already put to the proof, was definitely shaken by excitements due to the accusations and attacks leveled at him from all sides.

Koch, Pasteur's junior by 21 years, continued his relentless work at the laboratory of the University of Berlin, for the greatest good of humanity. At this period he especially attacked the problem of fighting tuberculosis. He endeavored to turn to account his great discovery of the tubercular bacillus, for the purpose of working out a preventive and therapeutic method. For several years he labored in silence. It was not until the meeting of the International Congress of Medicine in 1890 that he determined to come out with the following statement:

"In spite of this failure I have not been daunted, and at last have found substances which both in the test-tube and the living body prevent the development of tubercle bacilli. All such investigations, as everyone knows who has tried them, are very exhausting and slow; and my experiments with these substances, though lasting more than a year, are not yet concluded, so that all I can say at present is that guinea-pigs, peculiarly susceptible to the disease, when exposed to the influence of the substances mentioned, cannot be inoculated with tubercle, and that guinea-pigs which already have the disease in high degree have the malady brought to a complete stop, although the body suffers no ill effects from the measure."(14) These words of a scientist like Koch, so careful and precise; by a great mind whose work on the spore of anthrax and on the tubercular bacillus had been verified from beginning to end—these words electrified the large audience of doctors, in an extraordinary manner. Everyone was convinced that Koch had succeeded in solving the problem of the treatment of tuberculosis and his subsequent communications were looked forward to with great eagerness.

The few months which elapsed between this report and the work in which he recorded his observation on the treatment of human tuberculosis, seemed years to

---

(14) Verhandlungen des X. Intern. Med. Kongresses, Berlin, 1890; also, Gesammelte Werke, 1912, Vol. I, p. 659.

patients awaiting cure, as well as to the physicians and bacteriologists. Finally, in the fall of 1890, the work made its appearance. In it, Koch at full length stated that "tuberculosis at its first appearance may be surely cured by my remedy." In order to ascertain the stage "of the onset of the disease" he insisted on the necessity of the preliminary examination of the sputum. The presence of tubercular bacilli proved the existence of the disease, and, consequently, the need to have recourse to the new remedy. In very advanced stages of the disease, however, when the lungs show cavities, one can no longer look to a cure, but only hope for temporary improvements.

The presence of tubercular bacilli in the sputum is a symptom of *open* tuberculosis. If it could be cured at the outset, an important victory in the struggle against the most terrible plague of humanity would be achieved.

The months which passed after the publication of that work constitute one of the most spirited epochs in the annals of medicine. Patients and doctors from two hemispheres flocked to Berlin. Among the first were incipient cases as well as many cases for which there was no longer hope for cure. For a long time it was impossible to get a clear idea of the truth on account of all the commotion and excitement. At last it came to light. The new remedy, an extract of cultures of tubercular bacilli, frequently improved cases of lupus (one of the forms of cutaneous tuberculosis); it was at times effectual in cases of tuberculosis of the bones and of the articulations, but it could never, or only rarely, cure cases of open pulmonary tuberculosis, with tubercular bacilli in the sputum. Besides, Koch's assertion that it was possible to cure and prevent tuberculosis in guinea-pigs, was not corroborated by the bacteriologists.

The extreme enthusiasm based on Koch's reputation as a first rank scientist, was soon followed by a period of bitter and exaggerated disillusionment. Loud cries of protest and indignation were heard; cases were pointed out where "tuberculine" (the new remedy), instead of curing the disease, had accelerated its fatal progress. Very soon, Koch's old admirers cast him down from his high pedestal, forgetting all the benefits humanity had derived from his earlier labors.

After remaining a few years longer in Berlin, Koch for a time transferred his activities to the tropics. He went there for the purpose of studying impaludism, the bubonic plague, sleeping-sickness, rinderpest and several other diseases of domestic animals. For that purpose he undertook several journeys to the Indies, to Central and Southern Africa, and even as far as New Guinea. Nevertheless he did not give up the idea of again taking up the study of methods of fighting tuberculosis. In 1901, he caused a sensation at a Conference in London, by a report on bovine tuberculosis. Contrary of the general belief, that ailment was hardly or not at all contagious for man; consequently the principal source of contamination was not the milk of tubercular cows but the sputum of tubercular people. In several other reports, he told of the discovery of certain processes for modifying tuberculine, of prophylactic measures against tuberculosis, etc. Two days before he fell ill of the sickness which carried him off, he again wrote a report on the epidemic spreading of tuberculosis.

SECOND PART

Now that the reader has become familiar with the chief discoveries which formed the basis of modern medicine, and he is informed regarding the activity of the three heroes who have heaped innumerable benefits on humanity, I presume that he will desire to gain a more intimate glimpse of these three founders of modern medicine—Pasteur, Lister and Koch. The example of these great men is a striking witness of the role the genius plays in human progress. The life history of these three fathers of modern medicine is interesting in itself, but even more for the light it throws on the conditions engendering and favoring the growth of men of genius.

CHAPTER VII.

Let us begin with Pasteur, who was the first to blaze the trail for the revival of medical science. His beginnings were very humble. His ancestors were peasants, serfs, but his great-grandfather regained his freedom with the payment of 96 francs and was able to set up in the business of a tanner in the Jura mountains. His grandfather and his father took up the same trade. Our hero, thus, was born and passed his infancy in the midst of hides and oakbarks. Pasteur's father, conscripted into the army, fought under Napoleon and was retired with the title of non-commissioned officer. Louis Pasteur was born in the small city of Dôle, Department of Jura, December 27, 1822.

In accordance with certain facts which I have been able to gather, it would appear that geniuses are very rarely first-borns. The latter are usually weaker than their juniors. Mortality and criminality are greater among first-borns, whereas the brothers that follow are more often geniuses. The musical geniuses, Mozart and Wagner, were seventh in the family; Chopin, the fourth child. Among writers, Beaumarchais was the seventh, Shakespeare, Voltaire and Victor Hugo, the third, and Tolstoy the fourth child. The only exception which I can cite here is Goethe, the first child of a mother of 17. Among great political geniuses Peter the Great was the third child, and Napoleon I the fourth.

Pasteur was no exception to this rule which seems to be universal. The third child, he had four sisters, two his seniors and two his juniors.

Genius, at times, appears very early. This was not so in the case of Pasteur. He was a persistent student at public school but showed no exceptional gifts. At the age of 13, he took a liking to art and developed quite a skill at pastels. His schoolmates believed he would become a painter, but his parents did not encourage him in it, in the fear that this would prevent him from gaining an assured livelihood. Pasteur's remarkable gifts did not show themselves until much later. The principal of the school at Arbois where Pasteur was a student was especially interested in him and noted his outstanding characteristics: regularity, and a remarkable accuracy in work, together with great enthusiasm. M. Romanet, the principal, tried to develop these precious qualities in him as much as possible and to encourage his desire for higher studies. He made him visualize the prospect of entering the Normal School at Paris. After much hesitation Pasteur's parents at last decided to part with their only son and when he reached 16, they sent him to an institution preparing students for the Normal School.

There he found himself so much out of his element that he decided to go back home and to take up painting again. Pasteur's son-in-law, M. Vallery-Radot, in his biography of Pasteur (15) says, that "very little is known about that period in the life of the young man, when his will fell victim to his feelings." Certain of Pasteur's friends of that period ascribed that crisis to his timid and retiring character which prevented him from admitting the feeble state of his health.

However, Pasteur did not stay long at Arbois. His ambition for the higher studies had increased to a great degree. He entered the royal college of Besançon, a nearby city. There he received his degree of Bachelor of Arts, and his mind again turned towards the Normal School. Before setting out for Paris he had to pass his examination in mathematics at Dijon. That performance was far from brilliant; he only received a passing mark in chemistry. Nevertheless, he entered the Normal School, after passing a qualifying examination with second honors. He was almost 20 when he arrived in Paris, but this time he did not feel homesick and remained in the capital for good. His parents were overjoyed at the news of his admission to the Normal School, for it would enable him to become a high-school teacher or even a professor. What disturbed them was the state of his health. "You know," his father writes, "how much anxiety your health causes us on account of your excessive work . . . It is bad to be always strained."

As a Normal School student, Pasteur gave himself

---

(15) Vie de Pasteur, Paris, 1900.

entirely to science, spending many hours at the library and at the laboratory where he applied himself assiduously and with great enthusiasm to his studies. He was especially engrossed in the lectures of the famous chemist, Dumas. The life histories of great men of science and of the great national heroes stirred up in him an ardent spirit. He immersed himself early in the study of the molecular structure of chemical combinations and set himself the task of explaining the cause of the difference in the physical characters shown by substances having the same chemical composition. It is characteristic of Pasteur's turn of mind that this thought should have engrossed him like an *idée fixe*. He thought about it all the time and endlessly talked about it to fellow-students who took only a very slight interest in the optical qualities of different crystals.

It was clear that Pasteur was on the way to becoming an independent scientist, eager to discover new truths. Nevertheless, in order to enter upon the career of a scientist it was first of all necessary to have done with the examinations. He was 24 when he obtained the diploma of assistant professor in science. Of the fourteen candidates for the fellowship, only four were admitted, Pasteur being third. His fellowship lecture made an excellent impression and his examiner foretold a glorious future for him as a professor. However, the prospect of becoming a teacher did not at all appeal to Pasteur. Thus he refused the position of professor of physics at a provincial preparatory school and preferred the more modest position of assistant in chemistry to Prof. Bolard at the Normal School.

It was there that he prepared his two doctor's dissertations, one in chemistry, on the subject of "the arsenic of potassium, sodium and ammonia"; the other on "the phenomena of rotatory polarization of liquids." He was especially interested in the latter problem; it served him as an introduction to the study of the correlations between the crystalline state of substances and their chemical composition. Pasteur was hardly 25 when he successfully sustained his two theses. After ridding himself of that formality, he now threw himself into laboratory work and after several months of obstinate labor he was able to make his first report to the Academy of Sciences, on "dimorphism." In it he showed the germs of his future ideas.

Suddenly, an event of extreme importance wrested this ardent scholar from the laboratory. In the month of February 1848, the Revolution against Louis-Philippe broke out in Paris, and the Second Republic was proclaimed. Pasteur, drawn into the movement together with several of his associates, joined the National Guard. "I am very happy," he writes home, "for having been in Paris in the days of February and of being there now. I would loathe being away from Paris at the present moment. The lesson which we are learning here is beautiful and sublime. If necessary I shall fight courageously for the good cause of the Republic."

His civic pride appeased, Pasteur went back to his favorite occupation. He began to study the salts of tartaric acid, which, though of the same chemical composition, differ in their crystalline forms. These salts also show a varying effect on polarized light.

Ordinary tartaric salts cause the light to deviate to the right, whereas *para-tartaric* salts do not manifest this quality. Pasteur supposed that this difference was due to the form of the salts' crystals: whereas the crystals of tartaric salts were asymmetrical, those of paratartaric salts were in his opinion symmetrical. Experiments, however, demonstrated that the latter, too, were asymmetrical. Pasteur was at first perplexed by this unforeseeen result but the confusion was soon dispelled. With that fine sense of observation, peculiarly his own, he noted that whereas the asymmetry of the crystals of tartaric salts always showed a deviation towards the same side, the paratartaric salts show sometimes a right asymmetry and sometimes a left one. One by one, Pasteur, with his customary tenacity and patience, isolated all the paratartaric crystals precipitated in the solution and arranged them according to their asymmetry. He then prepared solutions of the crystals thus selected, and examined them with the aid of the polarimeter. He soon came upon a very important fact, namely, that crystals with right asymmetry cause the polarized light to deviate to the right, and that crystals with left asymmetry cause it to deviate to the left; that a mixture of equal parts of the two kinds of crystals has no effect whatsoever on polarized light. The mystery of paratartaric salts, which had bothered the heads of many a notable scientist such as Mitscherlich, was thus simply solved by Pasteur. The salts of that paratartaric acid were found to be a mixture of equal parts of "right" and "left" crystals! When Pasteur achieved this result for the first time his heart beat wildly and his look was anxious. Then he cried out: "I've got it!" The shock was so great that he had to stop work. He left the laboratory hurriedly and meeting another assistant in the corridor of the Normal School he embraced him and dragged him along to the Luxembourg Gardens, where he explained to him his discovery.

The news of this remarkable work by a young scientist quickly spread among the physicists of Paris and it was not long before it reached the ears of the celebrated Biot who for a long time had been interested in the polarization of light. He received the news of the discovery with great scepticism and wanted to verify it personally. He invited Pasteur to his own apartment and asked him to prepare the crystals under his own eyes; then he prepared the solutions himself and placed them in the polarizer. Ascertaining the truth of Pasteur's discovery, he grabbed hold of his hand and said to him: "My dear fellow, I have been so enamored of science all my life that this causes my heart to beat faster". Pasteur very well understood the far-reaching scope of the discovery he had made. He knew that he had opened a new and unexpected pathway for the molecular study of the structure of elements.

This discovery, made by him when he was 26, formed a solid basis for his career in science, and left its imprint on all his future work. Unfortunately this activity was for some time interrupted by extraneous concerns. Obliged to take a teaching position at a lyceum in Dijon, Pasteur was deterred from his researches by his duties which occupied almost all his time. Soon afterwards he was transferred to the position of substitute professor of chemistry in the Faculty of Strasbourg, where he for the first time felt "an unsuppressible need for a family life." Before long he fell in love with Mlle. Laurent, a daughter of the rector of the University, and hardly two weeks after taking up his new position he addressed the following letter to the girl's father:

"Sir, within a short time you will receive a request of great seriousness both for myself and for your family. I regard it as my duty to address to you the following words about myself as they may help to decide for or against me. My father is a tanner at Arbois, a small city in the Jura Mountains. The care of our household and business is in the hands of my sisters, as we had the misfortune of losing our mother last year in May.

"My family is in easy circumstances, though not rich. I estimate our possessions to be worth about 50,000 fr., but, as to myself, I have for some time been determined to leave my sisters the entire part of the share that might be allotted to me. I have thus no fortune of my own. All that I possess is my good health, my good nature and my position at the University.

"I was graduated about two years ago from the Normal School with the degree of *agrégé* in the physical sciences. I received my degree of Ph.D. some 18 months ago and I have submitted several reports to the Academy of Sciences, which have been well received, especially the last one. Enclosed you will find a very favorable review on this last work.

"Here, then, sir, is my whole present position. As

far as the future is concerned, barring the possibility of a complete change in my tasks, I shall always devote myself to chemical research. As soon as my scientific work will have received some recognition I intend to remove to Paris. M. Biot has advised me on several occasions to give serious thought to the Institute. If I continue to work assiduously I may perhaps realize such a dream within ten or fifteen years. We shall let time do justice to that dream. It is not this prospect which makes me love science.

"My father will come to Strasbourg to make this marriage proposal in person."

Having received the permission to address the young lady directly, Pasteur wrote to her:

"All that I ask you, Mademoiselle, is not to judge me too hastily. You might be mistaken. Time will show that beneath an exterior cold and timid, which may displease you, there beats a heart full of affection for you." Then, as if to reproach himself for forsaking his laboratory too long he added: "I, who have been so much in love with my crystals."

Pasteur's proposal was favorably received and marriage soon followed. He was then twenty-six and a half. After a brief stay at Strasbourg, Pasteur was named professor as well as dean of the new Faculty of Sciences at Lille. Though he remained there but a few years, he nevertheless managed, in his small and ill-organized laboratory at Lille, to make a whole series of his finest discoveries. He pondered tirelessly over his precious crystals and set up a schematic plan of the laws governing them. In his investigation he always gave free rein to his imagination. One of his leading ideas was that asymmetrical crystals were to be found only in organic substances, that is to say in living products. He believed that molecular asymmetry was the sole mark of distinction between living and inert bodies. Imbued by that idea he set about searching everywhere in nature for examples of such asymmetry. Noticing that the products of fermentation contain many substances which give rise to asymmetrical crystals, he conceived the profound and deep-rooted idea that fermentation must be intimately linked up with life. At the beginning of his stay in Lille he jotted down on a small sheet of paper: "What is the nature of fermentation? The mysterious factor in the phenomenon. A few words on lactic acid." At that period he had already conceived the idea of throwing light on that problem, but a special circumstance helped to start it off. Lille was an import center for distilleries. The summer of 1856 was a bad year for alcohol distilling, and the distillers turned to Pasteur for aid. Pasteur of course acceded to their request and set about his task very eagerly. Almost daily he would go to the distilling plants to get the material for his researches, later to examine it under a bad microscope and by means of other very primitive apparatus. In his note-book he would jot down the ideas as they occurred to him. On the margin of one of these notes which he had jotted down a few days previously, but had failed of proof, he wrote, "wrong, false, this won't do." One of Pasteur's students, the son of a distiller, tells in a letter: " . . . I've had the good fortune several times of being the confidant of the enthusiasms and the disappointments of a great scientist." These tests and observations led Patseur to the systematic study of the question of fermentation and his first result was the discovery of the agent of lactic fermentation.

Soon afterwards Pasteur returned to Paris as sub-director of the Normal School. He had the task of organizing the studies as well as " the supervision of rules of economy and hygiene, the care of general discipline and the relations with students' families and the scientific and literary societies frequented by the students." However, what was of prime importance to Pasteur was the opportunity of doing purely scientific work which Paris could offer. He had to begin his researches in a little laboratory in an attic, where he was obliged to clean the glass instruments himself and to do other similar manual work. It was only much later that he was provided with new and somewhat larger premises, which, however, were very unlike the laboratories one expects nowadays even in the meanest places. In spite of all these inconveniences, Pasteur got marvelous results with the means at his disposal. It was at the Normal School that he attacked the problem of the origin of ferments, which led him to the study of spontaneous generation. These labors increased his already great fame.

The normal course of his researches was suddenly interrupted. Dumas, chemist as well as senator, asked him to go to Central France to help fight a terrible scourge, the disease of silkworms, which threatened to ruin the entire silk-growing industry. At first Pasteur refused, saying that the problem was entirely strange to him, that he had never in his life seen a silk-worm.

Nevertheless, he finally gave in to Dumas' entreaties and departed with some of his assistants for Languedoc. He had to struggle for a long time with many difficulties. The problem was especially complicated by the fact that the silk-worms were infected with two diseases at the same time. However, he tackled the problem on a practical basis. Pébrine, the main disease, was found to be hereditary. Its infectious principle is transmitted from the mother to the progeny in the form of microscopical corpuscles which penetrate into the egg. Thanks to this observation Pasteur was able to suggest a method for isolating the females and the eggs laid by them: When the eggs are laid, the butterflies should be examined by the microscope. The eggs of those containing microscopical organisms must be destroyed and only those eggs preserved whose mothers were discovered to be healthy. This method of selection brought about the desired result; the disease was eliminated, and the silk-growing industry put back on its feet.

When Pasteur returned to Paris, he was stricken with an attack of apoplexy, though he had not as yet reached his fortieth year. He had hemiplegia of the left side with speech difficulties. Though he lay between life and death for an entire week, this did not deter him from dictating a report on the disease of silk-worms for the Academy of Sciences. Three months after the onset of his illness he took the train back to the Midi, where he was to continue his studies on diseases of silk-worms.

The grave ailment by which he was seized at a comparatively early age has been especially attributed to intellectual overwork as well as to excitement due to the violent opposition hurled against his work on the diseases of the silk-worm as well as against all of his daring theories.

His general condition improved, and he completely regained his intellectual powers. No traces of the sickness remained except an uneasiness in his walk and a weakness in the left arm.

Pasteur got back to work with renewed energy for he was anxious to complete his two-volume monograph on the diseases of the silk-worm, and to put the finishing touches to his researches in the deterioration of wines under the influence of abnormal ferments.

The War of 1870 was to him such a painful experience that he could never completely recover from it. During the general upsurge of patriotism he expressed the desire to enter the National Guard as a volunteer and to remain in Paris during the siege. His friends, however, dissuaded him from it, and advised him to depart for the country, where his father had left him the house. He departed for Arbois the day after the fall of Sedan and the collapse of the Empire. His emotions were at the highest pitch. He sent back to the University of Bonn the honorary degree which that institution had bestowed upon him for his scientific labors. He solemnly declared that from then on every one of his works would bear this epigraph: "Hate Prussia! Revenge! Revenge!"

Hardly a few months had passed since his departure from Paris when Pasteur was again seized with a fit of activity. "My head is filled with the grandest plans for work. The war has caused my mind to lie fallow. I am prepared for new labors. Alas! Perhaps I am deceiving myself! At any rate, I shall make an attempt," he writes to his disciple and collaborator Duclaux, then professor of chemistry at Clermont-Ferrand. Pasteur joined him there and took up his researches in Duclaux' laboratory. Combining a love for science and hatred for Prussia, he conceived the idea of placing his work on fermentation at the service of his country in the perfecting of the brands of beer so that it might compete with the German product which was known everywhere. With that purpose in mind he took up his old experiments on alcoholic fermentation, in the belief that the employment of pure cultures which he made use of in the laboratory would bring good results in the beer plant. He studied the problem very intensively and, by the way, he threw light on other points of very great importance to alcoholic fermentation. To avoid the spoiling of beer, which may take place very easily, the beer-wort should be protected against the penetration of injurious microbes, for the spoiling of beer and of wine was nothing but a disease caused by foreign yeasts. Pasteur collected all his studies on alcoholic fermentation in an important work entitled "Studies on Beer", which appeared in 1876. The same year saw the publication of Koch's work on anthrax, as we have seen in Chapter V. The notion of microbes as the agents of diseases was already known to medical circles. Davaine's studies had already drawn the attention of French thinkers. Pasteur, more than anyone else, was prepared for solving the problem of the microscopical beings and of the infinitely small. All the circumstances we have cited prompted him to plunge into the study of medical bacteriology. The last chapter summed up all that part of Pasteur's work.

While all of his inquiries on fermentation were worked out at Lille, his researches on infectious diseases were carried out in two small laboratories at the Normal School. There Pasteur passed thirty years of his life filled with constant commotion roused by his discoveries and by perpetual collisions with numerous opponents. A spirited and passionate fighter, he rarely made use in these disputes of guarded and parliamentary language. Especially in opposing the Academy he would throw all discretion to the winds, pointing out the total lack of scientific preparation of physicians and their ignorance of experimental methods. The doctors, in turn, sought to revenge themselves upon him. Their satisfaction was complete when the first cases of death broke out among those vaccinated for hydrophobia. For a time Pasteur even expected to have charges of homicide brought against him. However, certain professors of the Faculty of Medicine, chief among them the celebrated Charcot, took up the cudgels for him, and this intercession somewhat abated the opposition and calmed the situation. But all this strife had a very deleterious effect upon Pasteur's health. In order to remove him from the scene of battle his family took him to the Midi, to Bordighera on the Italian Riviera, where he rested for a short time. His stay had to be cut short however due to the severe earthquakes which at the time shook the Northern Coast of the Mediterranean.

When Pasteur returned to Paris he was a completely changed man. He still showed enough energy to found the new Institute which bears his name, an institution built by means of international contributions. However, his scientific work proper was at an end. He occupied the apartment which was reserved for him at the Institute solemly inaugurated in 1888, but was no longer capable of the laboratory work. He had then just completed his 66th year when death prematurely interrupted his fruitful activities. Death was due to the chronical ailment which had undermined his health. Pasteur's mortal remains rest at the Institute founded by himself.

CHAPTER VIII.

During the early years of medical bacteriology, I was engaged in the study of pathogenic bacteria, and was in search of a laboratory. It was therefore with great joy that I accepted the proposal of the municipality of Odessa and of the zemstvo of Cherson to direct the Bacteriological Institute founded by them. There Pasteur's discoveries were to be applied in practice. This took place in 1886, soon after Pasteur published his methods against hydrophobia. Though I was already corresponding with Pasteur, it was not until 1887 that I first made his acquaintance.

When I arrived in the Rue Vauquelin in the Latin Quarter at the small laboratory reserved for vaccinations against hydrophobia, I perceived an old man of medium height, with the traces of left hemiplegia, his eyes gray and piercing, his beard and mustache cut short, his graying hair covered with a black skull-cap. He wore a large cape over his jacket. His pale and sickly color indicated a man who did not have many more years before him, perhaps only months.

Pasteur received me very kindly and immediately began to talk to me about the matter which concerned me most, namely the struggle of the organism against microbes. "Though my youthful collaborators are very sceptical towards your theory," he said, "nevertheless I have placed myself on your side, for I have recently been struck by that struggle, in several organisms which I observed. I believe you are on the right track." Engrossed in the problem of vaccination against rabies, which was then in its first stage of practical application, Pasteur spoke about it to me and asked me to be present during the vaccinations. He paused at each little detail, the least little obstacle upset him. He would comfort the children who cried during the injection, giving them candies and pennies. Pasteur's devotion to his work could readily be seen; age had not diminished his ardor.

He invited us to dinner for the day after at his apartment in the Normal School. His extreme simplicity caused me to believe that the reception would be just as simple and I thought it would be quite correct for me to come in my frock-coat. But my astonishment was great, when, mounting the stair, I saw the other guests in gala dress and gown. I wanted to turn back immediately to put on a gown I had worn on the occasion of the International Congress of Hygiene, which I had attended before coming to Paris. Pasteur stopped me and in order better to put me at my ease he even changed his gown for a frock-coat. The dinner and the evening were passed in animated talk and my embarrassment was definitely dispelled.

It was thus only during his last few years that I

knew Pasteur personally. At the time he was especially interested in the results of inoculations against rabies and in the fate of the Institute which he had founded.

Of independent character, Pasteur was unwilling to yield to the demands of the Paris municipality. Before deciding in favor of a free grant of land necessary for the building of the Institute, the authorities had tried to meddle in the activities of the great scientist, as for instance inspecting the data of inoculations against rabies. The members of the municipality were hostile to Pasteur for political reasons, he being considered a monarchist and pro-clerical while the former were socialists and anti-clerical. For all of these reasons the city refused to grant the land desired and it was necessary to acquire it for cash, which considerably decreased the financial resources of the new Institute. The building was conceived on a large scale and when it was completed only a small part of the subscription amount remained for its maintenance. This caused Pasteur much concern and his anxieties regarding new resources somewhat poisoned the last years of his life.

The last labor which Pasteur brought to completion was his elaboration of the method of vaccinating against rabies. Though he possessed in Dr. Roux a very capable collaborator, yet his own genius was still undoubtedly evident in that last discovery. Dr. Roux has often repeated to me that without the constant influence of Pasteur who directed and inspired his pupils, the results achieved would never have taken place.

His anxieties regarding preventive vaccinations, his concern over the future of the Institute and, above all, the precarious state of his health caused Pasteur to renounce all scientific labors. He could no longer make use of the laboratory installed for him near his apartment. One day he was shown some turkey hens which had succumbed to some infection. He was eager to study it in collaboration with me, but these researches came to nothing, as also happened to his attempts to treat epilepsy by means of an emulsion of marrow. A doctor who had brought several epileptics to be treated for rabies, remarked that vaccinations were very favorable in epileptical fits. Pasteur, with his customary energy, ardor and devotion endeavored to find a method of treatment. He tried to procure epileptics in all the hospitals, followed closely the incidence of their fits and observed the influence produced on them by injection of marrow. In spite of all this he failed to cure the sick, but instead weakened his own health. This restlessness and perpetual anxiety brought on fits of insomnia and his family and close relations had to insist that he leave off all work he had undertaken.

A great sadness hung upon Pasteur when he saw the impossibility of continuing the scientific labors so dear to him. He believed that he had not completed the work he should have achieved and this regret made him very unhappy. We tried in vain to persuade him that having done so much for science, he had the right to rest on his laurels; but our reassuring words failed to appease his insatiable need for work.

Unable to continue with his work personally, Pasteur would always come to the laboratories. He always questioned me about my experiments and told me about his past. He expressed a desire to transfer his enthusiasm and energy to his students and collaborators and he never discouraged anyone by an air of scepticism so common among scientists who have attained the height of their success. On the contrary, he always kept up their courage and their hope for success. After Dr. Roux had succeeded in discovering the toxin of diphtheria, Pasteur continuously goaded him on to tackle, as vigorously and as quickly as possible, the problem of the preventive treatment of diphtheria in animals. Solicitous of the Institute's success, he encouraged many workers in the hope that their labors would assure the future of the institution so dear to him.

Every morning Pasteur would go down to the hydrophobia ward to witness the inoculations. Then he walked up to the laboratories to keep himself informed of the researches being made there. After breakfast, on days when it was in session, he would go to the meetings of the Academy of Sciences and of the French Academy, of which he was a member. Once a week he would go to the Mortgage-Loan Society, having been named its director. It has been imputed in this connection that a scientist should never participate in any business which does not belong to the domain of science, and, particularly, to shy away from financial matters. But one forgets that Pasteur had a family to support and that his position called for large expenses. I can still remember the time when Pasteur's health was already undermined and he could not go out of doors except in a carriage. The problem arose of renting a one-horse carriage by the year. It was quite a problem and gave rise to many calculations and long considerations before it could be carried out. In the future, when the role of science will become sufficiently appreciated it will seem unbelievable that a man of Pasteur's stature, in spite of the many benefits he rendered to mankind, should, at the height of his glory and during his declining years, have had to face such cares about the means of transportation.

Soon after the founding of the Institute, it became impossible for Pasteur personally to take a hand in its activities and direction. In many respects he was replaced by Duclaux who was the assistant director, but the latter in turn yielded his place to Dr. Roux who from the time of its inauguration up to the present has been the real director of the Institute. The meetings of the council were reduced to almost a formality. Whenever a question was put to Pasteur he always referred it to Dr. Roux. During the period I am speaking of, the beginning of the Nineties, there was a feverish activity everywhere in bacteriological research, to such a degree that Pasteur was unable to follow the whole trend of science, and so he would frequently refer to one of us. This was true especially when visitors came to the Institute. I remember being called in by him on the occasion of the visit of a Mexican doctor, completely unknown, who filled a very important post in his native country. He sat there in an armchair in Pasteur's studio, wearing an enormous gold watch-chain and a look of great importance. He was expounding a new method of treating an infectious disease which was wide-spread, and seemed very much surprised that Pasteur had not heard of his method.

"It is strange," he said, "that, while in Mexico we are closely informed about every one of your discoveries, my own researches should be so completely unknown to you, Monsieur Pasteur!" Of course, the plan of this Mexican Aesculapius was entirely fruitless and it would be impossible at the present time to even have an inkling as to what his method actually was.

Pasteur was always molested by all kinds of visitors who would ask him the most unlikely questions. He was also swamped with floods of letters which he was in the habit of answering with an almost angelic patience. His evenings he passed alone with Mme. Pasteur who was extremely devoted to him. She would read to him in a loud tone, preferably from historical memoirs, and, at times, Pasteur would doze off during the reading. During the evenings I would amuse him by telling him of new discoveries and of new scientific trends in general, which seemed to interest him very much.

Little by little Pasteur's powers began to wane. The minor cerebral hemorrhage which attacked him from time to time gradually destroyed the health and the intellectual force of this giant of brain and work. One autumn day I found him bed-ridden; he was very weak and depressed. His spirit picked up when I told of the plan of a grand celebration in honor of his 70th anniversary, announced in the press. His relatives exerted themselves to buoy up his health and spirits to face that great day, and the care of his friends increased even more. The festival took place December 22, 1892, but, alas, Pasteur's condition was very precarious, when he presented himself before the large audience which came to felicitate him. Pale, suffering, grown old, he had not the strength to repress the tears when he heard all the congratulations accorded to him by an entire world. He was unable to read the address of thanks which he had prepared and his son Jean-Baptiste Pasteur delivered it in his stead.

In my opinion, Pasteur's old age was not at all a happy one. In spite of the fact that his family worshipped him, in spite of the respectful devotion of all those who surrounded him, he considered his work unfinished, and always tormented himself, often without any adequate reasons. Soon after his Jubilee, his powers slowly dwindled until death itself appeared, on September 28, 1895.

The extremely cool days of the first part of summer were followed by very hot ones. Pasteur passed his vacations with his family in Villeneuve-l'Etang, in lodgings which had formerly served as an out-house to the Palace of Saint-Cloud of Napoleon III. This dwelling was situated in a beautiful park, near the station de Garches, on the Marly-le-Roi line. After the war the palace was destroyed but the out-houses remained intact. The government had granted this residence to Pasteur when he expressed a need for a large and secluded place to house the numerous dogs he used in his researches in hydrophobia. Kennels were built in that old place as well as boxes for the smaller laboratory animals. The upper story, of a lighter construction, contained many rooms and these were used as living quarters by Pasteur and his family as well as by the veterinarian in charge of the animals. The horses which were used in the preparation of serums against diphtheria and tetanus occupied the stables underneath Pasteur's apartment. The noise of the animals and the smell of the stables were annoying, but in spite of it Pasteur loved his summer-home for it brought back to his mind his hard-working past; the surroundings of the laboratory pleased his taste. The preparation of curative serums, the raising of laboratory animals, his talks with the veterinarian and the other employees, were a real distraction to him.

Every summer he went to Villeneuve-l'Etang and did not return to Paris until the fall with renewed energy to face life in Paris. Paris was unsuitable to his health. The ailment which carried him off was traceable to an hemorrhage he had suffered many years before, from which he had recovered, but traces of which remained the rest of his life. His left hemiplegia troubled him during his laboratory work and he needed the assistance of those about him.

When in the spring of 1895 Pasteur left for his stay at Villeneuve-l'Etang no one thought that he would never return. However, instead of recovering his strength during the vacation he got even worse. That year I passed my vacation in Dauphiné. At the beginning of September I received a letter from Roux informing me that Pasteur's health was causing him much anxiety. I immediately returned to Paris and went to see Pasteur at Villeneuve. I was surprised to find him in relatively good health, seated under the shade of a splendid red beech-tree. He was cheerful, laughed, joked and though there was a slight catch in his voice nothing seemed to confirm Roux's fears. But this state did not last for a long time. A new cerebral hemorrhage aggravated the paralysis and nailed him down to his bed, which he was never again to leave. The chronic inflammation of the kidneys from which he had been suffering for some time (his urine always showed small quantities of albumen) brought on a crisis of uremia from which he finally succumbed, surrounded by his family and relations. The evening before his death, he was asked to drink some milk but he replied that he felt too weak to take it. His coma lasted close to twenty-four hours.

In connection with Pasteur's last moments there has been much talk regarding his religious feelings. However, he avoided talking about the subject of religion and always showed an extreme tolerance. Whenever, on occasions, I heard him talk of religion, it was always in the most general terms about the Infinite, or on the real impossibility of solving scientifically many problems of great importance.

Pasteur has been unjustly reproached of desiring to fight the materialistic outlook with the aid of his researches, for these proved that fermentations were due to the vital action of microbes, and this, again, destroyed the belief in spontaneous generation. Pasteur always insisted on the exclusion of religious motives from questions of science; he himself always observed this rule strictly. His preconceived idea of the non-existence of spontaneous generation under natural conditions came to him only after he had observed that it was impossible to obtain a fermentation in a sterile medium unless a certain amount of living ferment was poured into it: without such a pouring the medium never underwent spontaneous change. The correlation between fermentation and living microbes caused him to assume that fermentation was due to a vital process. However, he never maintained that there were no ferments devoid of life, i.e. that the ferments elaborated by living microbes (16) could not exercise an independent chemical action on organic matter. He submitted to critical examination nothing but researches made on that subject. His purely chemical theory of acquired immunity against infectious diseases proves that he did not subscribe to the vitalist point of view. At that period it was still unknown that such immunity was in reality connected with vital processes.

According to M. Vallery-Radot, his son-in-law and closest friend, Pasteur believed in life after death. As I have mentioned above he connected questions of religion with ideas of the Infinite, the ideal, the search for truth. He had much respect for the religious beliefs of others and showed an extreme tolerance.

Certain people have reproached Pasteur because he was greatly favored by a monarchist government. The son of an officer in the Napoleonic army, he worshipped the Great Emperor as many other Frenchmen did. He used to remember with great pleasure the hours spent at the court of Napoleon III. where he was invited for scientific chats. As a whole, Pasteur was for order, for the status quo, and for that reason he easily adapted himself to the Third Republic. He was above all an ardent patriot and, during the War of 1870, he hated the Germans. Whenever he received a German book or a pamphlet, he would take

(16) Dead yeasts and microbes never bring about any fermentation.

hold of it with the tip of his fingers and pass it over to me, or he would put it away altogether with an air of disgust. This, however, did not prevent his from following my suggestion of sending Koch a telegram of congratulations on the occasion of his discovery of a remedy against tuberculosis.

At the time of my arrival at the Pasteur Institute there was already talk of a Franco-Russian alliance which he looked forward to with great sympathy. In that connection I recollect the following incident. Among my students there was at the time a very careless doctor. On leaving Paris for a while he left his laboratory all cluttered up with old preparations and other useless trash. After the vacation, when it was necessary to place the newly-arrived students, the table and the closet of the incorrigible doctor had to be cleared off and his things transferred to another place. A short time afterwards he returned and when he learned of what had happened to his things, he took me to task in an unbecoming manner. Naturally I answered him sharply and told him to leave my laboratory. Two days later Pasteur came to see me, very much upset and holding two large sheets of paper in his hands. "Look what you have done," he said, "you have chased away a doctor, a prince sent on a mission by the Russian Government! Here, read what he is saying and also read my reply, which I am sure you will approve of!" The prince complained about me in sharp terms and threatened with sure reprisals by his government; he even indicated dire consequences to the amicable Russo-French relations. In his tentative reply Pasteur made his excuses and assured the prince of his best wishes. Of course, I protested against the dispatching of that letter and I assured Pasteur that my antagonist had clearly deserved the punishment I had inflicted upon him; that this Caucasian prince who had been sent abroad to do research work was but a bad and ill-mannered student who could not be tolerated in our Institute. I had great difficulty in pacifying Pasteur and in persuading him to rewrite the letter. He was soon able to convince himself that the departure of my excitable antagonist had no effect on the Franco-Russian Alliance!

Like every one of us, Pasteur had his weaknesses. But even without mentioning the innumerable benefits he heaped on humanity, it must be said that he combined with his genius a vibrant soul, a profound goodness of heart and an extraordinary loftiness of character.

CHAPTER IX.

It is not without reason that the English are called practical. In France, Pasteur's discoveries in the field of fermentation and the non-existence of spontaneous generation were considered to be merely interesting scientific facts; in Germany, the examination of wounds led to nothing but the minute study of various putrescing microbes, in England, on the other hand, the question was from the very outset placed on a practical basis. As we have seen in Chapter V., this task was brilliantly carried out by Lister.

Pasteur and Lister resembled each other very little. The first, of medium height, ardent, very excitable, used to challenge his opponents and attack them with great violence; the second, tall, of unruffled composure, made no bones about his opponents. But this dissimilarity of character did not prevent them from being great friends and having a great esteem for one another.

Lister was five years younger than Pasteur. He

was born on April 5, 1827, in Upton, County Essex, not far from London. Unlike Pasteur, whose parents had only moderate means, Lister's were well-to-do. His father was a wholesale wine-merchant, but also much interested in science. He was fascinated by the study of optics and undertook the building of microscopes; these were considered the best of his time (the first half of the 19th Century). I have no clear ideas regarding the circumstances of the birth of our hero, Joseph Lister, except for the facts that his parents were married in 1818, that they had seven children, four boys and three girls, and that Joseph was born in 1827. All this leads me to conclude that he was not the first child. This strengthens the hypothesis mentioned in connection with the life of Pasteur.

Lister was born and bred in a very religious environment. His grand-father, his father and he himself were Quakers.

Lister started on his studies at the school of Tottenham and then entered London University College as a student of science and medicine. After completing his five years of medical studies, he was made professor at the Royal School of Surgery in London. At that period he was interested in the study of microscopical anatomy, and in physiology. It was not until much later that he fastened his choice on surgery. For the purpose of perfecting himself in that field he went to Edinburgh in 1853, to study under Prof. Sim, whose assistant he became. A great friendship developed between him and his teacher whose oldest daughter he married in 1856. Four years later, having been named professor of surgery at the University of Glasgow, he was placed in charge of a very important hospital, where his surgical activities could develop to all their fullness. He published a number of works bearing on various branches of surgery and finally tackled the main problem of his life, the antisepsis of wounds, based on principles worked out by Pasteur.

Lister's activity had taken on quite a considerable extent when, in 1869, he was named professor at Edinburgh in place of Sim, who had died a short time before. It was here that he perfected his antiseptic treament, that the method of using carbolic spray in the operating room was introduced, and that the technique of using catgut in sutures and ligatures was worked out.(17)

The conditions he found in Edinburgh were much better than those in Glasgow. Its medical school was considered the finest in Great Britain. Students from all over the world flocked to it and filled its lecture halls. Lister's fame became universal. This, of course, did not hinder some of his envious confreres from attacking him. The eminent surgeon Simpson even dared to bring charges against him, charges which were both inadmissible and unjust. For a short time these charges created a certain sensation, but very soon persons of impartial views leaned to the side of the truth.

In 1877 Lister settled in London where he occupied

(17) This catgut is prepared from the coalls of the small intestines of certain animals.

the chair of clinical medicine at King's College. There he remained five years and then withdrew from his teaching activities having reached the retirement age. From then on he could rest on his laurels. He gave up applied surgery altogether and concentrated on science and literature. He wrote only one treatise on pure surgery (on the fracture of the patella) but he always went back to the history of antisepsis. As president of various societies it was his duty to deliver public reports from time to time. In 1896, he was chosen president of the Royal Society of London, taking the place of Lord Kelvin. The same year he became president of the British Association for the Advancement of Science. On the occasion of his 70th anniversary he was named a lord and a British peer.

In 1893 he suffered the great misfortune of losing his wife while on a trip to Italy. This blow was even harder for him as he was childless and he thus remained all alone at a very advanced age. One of his nieces came to live with him; she would take down his dictations and became altogether an irreplaceable friend to her uncle. Lister soon afterwards suffered an attack of apoplexy from which he never recovered. Sick and aged he quit London for his estate of Wolmer where he spent his last years. He died of pneumonia on April 1912, at the age of 85. His longevity was due partly to hereditary causes, his grandfather having lived to be 98, his father 84. Lister's last rites were very solemn; many surgeons and other scientists from all over the world were present at the funeral. His remains, at first placed in Westminster Abbey, were later transferred to Hampstead Cemetery, to be interred close to his wife's, in accordance with his last wishes.

In 1891, Lister, as organizer of the International Congress of Hygiene, invited me to make a report on immunity. I had not made his acquaintance until a few months before, having seen him for the first time at the auditorium of the Royal Society of London. I was introduced to a man as yet showing no earmarks of old age, very tall, and of a very pronounced English type. His handsome and expressive features, framed by white hair and side-whiskers, was brightened by a broad and gracious smile. He immediately began to tell me of the approaching congress and referred to my report, but it was not easy for him to continue the conversation in the crowded hall of the Royal Society and we soon parted. During the Congress of Hygiene I saw Lister often and for long periods. I expounded to him the role of mobile cells in the defense of the organism against infectious microbes and showed the importance of their influx into the focus of infection. After the sessions Lister accosted me and said: "It seems to me that these movements, predetermined for a fixed purpose, are another manifestation of something higher than mere chemical affinity." These words clearly showed his mystic tendencies and a religious spirit befitting a member of the "Friends". His whole personality was imbued with a lofty idealism. His somewhat cold exterior hid a great benevolence. His statements were very simple; he never made use of hackneyed phrases. His bearing and his manner of living had the imprint of nobility and peaceful contemplation. His home was not extravagantly furnished nor were his repasts those of an epicure; habits and ways so prevalent among his confreres.

On the occasion of our last meeting in 1906, Lister seemed to me much aged but still in good health. He received me in his study which was thronged with books. He no longer pursued any experiments, but read much and showed interest in everything. He expounded to me an entire program of investigation on the blood and advised me to assign to one of my disciples the carrying out of the necessary research. Very soon after that meeting of ours, Lister's health took a sudden turn to the worse and his sojourns at London became rarer and of shorter duration.

From what we know of the character and personality of Darwin, it would seem that Lister resembled him in many respects. Everything base and egotistical was foreign to him. He was a gentleman in the best sense of the word.(18)

---

(18) Biological details about Lister will be found in "The Lancet" of February 17, 1912, and in the "British Medical Journal" of the same date.

CHAPTER X.

Pasteur's theory of ferments and of the non-existence of spontaneous generation was already generally accepted as true; Lister's antiseptic methods were already beginning to become widely known, when Robert Koch appeared on the scene. Before him, we had only vague or insufficient ideas regarding the role played by microbes in infectious diseases. We have already seen in Chapter VI., in how brilliant a manner Koch had definitely proven this role of the microbes. Whereas Pasteur and Lister had first to develop the basic ideas on which their discoveries were built, Koch found the field all prepared. He was able to concentrate his efforts on the working out of a technique which would offer irrefutable results. In his first classic work he was guided by the ideas of the botanist Cohn, who had predicted the existence of spores of anthrax. Koch, undoubtedly, was a man of genius both as technician and as bacteriologist. In the history of medicine his place belongs undeniably on the side of Pasteur and Lister.

Robert Koch was born on December 11, 1843, at Clausthal, in the Harz Mountains, which then were part of the kingdom of Hanover. His father was a mining engineer and had the reputation of being an energetic and capable expert in the mining industry. His means were very limited, for, being the father of eleven children (nine boys and two girls) he had no personal fortune. Our hero was the third child, again confirming our hypothesis regarding the superiority of younger children over first-borns in the family. In such a numerous family, the children could grow up without strict supervision and were able to enjoy a great deal of freedom. Little Robert very early showed signs of great ability which presaged the future scientist. He was not only a very bright student but he used his leisure time to collect all kinds of minerals, plants and insects in his native, mountainous region. At a very early period he also became an ingenious chess-player. He was at first intended for a business career, but later he was given a free choice in that respect. He himself dreamed of becoming a naval physician, for his tastes inclined him especially towards natural history and for journeys. It was with such intentions that he entered the Faculty of Medicine at the University of Goettingen, where he fell under the influence of the well-known physiologist Meissner, who encouraged the scientific spirit in him. Koch finished his medical studies very rapidly and began his practice at the early age of 22. He became a physician at an institution for the feeble-minded at Longenhagen, near Hanover. But he did not remain there long. For some time he was a practicing physician in two small Prussian towns; then, in 1872 he became health officer at Wolstein in Posen. His material condition having somewhat improved, he organized a small laboratory, bought a new microscope and some apparatus, among them a camera. We already know with what extraordinary success Koch tackled the problem of anthrax, soon after he settled down to work. It was here at Wolstein, too, that he studied wound infections in laboratory animals. The work he published on that subject caused a sensation among specialists. These labors brought Koch a world-wide renown, which caused the German Government to appoint him a member of the Department of Health in 1880. There he became famous by his discovery of the tubercular bacillus. Soon afterwards he organized an expedition for the purpose of studying Asiatic cholera. Although his discovery of the vibrio of cholera was not backed up by proofs as irrefutable as that of the tubercular bacillus, still it constitutes one of his best claims to fame.

In 1885 Koch was assigned to the chair of hygiene at the University of Berlin. At first he spent much time in preparing for his lectures, but he soon grew tired of it and he again threw himself into laboratory work. He immersed himself completely in the study of tuberculosis, in the hope of finding a prophylactic and cure against that disease. He closed himself up in his laboratory, pursuing his researches in secret, not even his closest friends knowing about it.

Finally, after five years as a professor he read a report to the Congress at Berlin about his discovery.

Its results, however, were inconclusive, and this brought him many serious reproaches. It is to be regretted that this work of Koch should not have been examined and criticized in advance by his friends, who assuredly would have prevented its premature appearance. This failure, however, does not diminish the extreme importance of his other works. Nevertheless, it should not have been published for the sake of his fame.

Following his report on the discovery of a treatment against tuberculosis, Koch left the University and became the director of the new Institute founded for the purpose of studying infectious diseases. That institution became known as the Koch Institute, similar to the Pasteur Institute at Paris and the Lister Institute at London. For some years Koch tried to improve the treatment of tuberculosis, but soon he was again seized by his passion for long journeys. He undertook the study of tropical diseases, made a tour of almost the entire world, and succeeded in gathering some interesting facts, though of lesser importance compared to his first three discoveries. Towards the close of his scientific activity, he again devoted his time to tuberculosis, in the undying hope of vanquishing that terrible and obstinate plague. It was in the midst of such labors that he was attacked by a heart disease which was not long in bringing him to his end. The history of this last page of Koch's life is of such great interest that I consider it useful to impart to the reader, from the account of Profs. Briege and Krause, who took care of him.(19) During the last months of his life, Koch was troubled with asthma which obliged him to rest when he climbed up the stairs. The pains in the heart region became worse, but this did not prevent him from going to the laboratory daily and fulfilling his duties of medical inspections at the hospital. Towards the end of the Nineties of last century he had a serious attack of pneumonia of the left lung. During the night of April 9, 1910, he suffered a painful attack of the heart. He awoke with a sensation of extreme lassitude, was bathed in perspiration, had fits of asthma and profuse vomiting and at the same time felt a pain in the cardiac region. These pains traveled up to his left shoulder and were attended by violent rattling of the lungs; the pulse was filiform and very irregular. The following day he felt much better. The doctors found his heart to be somewhat hypertrophied, the pulse very rapid and irregular. Koch had pulmonary oedema, a slight hypertrophy of the liver, and water in the abdominal cavity. The urine was infrequent, and contained much albumen, blood corpuscles and renal cylinders. The urine elimination, however, soon improved. The treament consisted of digitalis, morphine and concentrated coffee. He also had warm compresses applied to the region of the heart, to the hands and feet. There was an improvement during the weeks which followed, but the patient suffered much from asthma and from coughing. During that period he underwent a very close examination: electrodiagrams, X-rays and

(19) Deutsche Medicin Wochenschrift, 1910, No. 22, p. 1045.

other delicate devices of modern clinical medicine were applied. The doctors who from the very outset had made a very unfavorable diagnosis said: "Koch stated that at this time he was also tuberculous which set his mind at ease about his asthma, for he was not afraid of tuberculosis. We left him in that error, assuring him that the asthma was really due to his pulmonary disease." When the nice weather returned Koch expressed the desire to go to Baden-Baden. He withstood the hardships of the voyage, but a week later, while seated in an easy chair before a door of the balcony he passed away peacefully. He died in his 67th year. In accordance with his last wishes his body was cremated and the ashes placed in an urn at the Koch Institute of Berlin.

All the biographies of Koch that I know of have clamped down the lid on his family life. This may lead one to believe that it was not worthy of the memory of the great scientist. Therefore, I regard it as my duty to impart to the reader the facts known to me. In the future humanity's munificent geniuses will probably be more appreciated than nowadays and the absurd prejudices which still beset even the most independent spirits shall have vanished.

At the outset of his medical career Koch married a young woman who became an excellent housewife and mother. From that union was born a girl who adored her father and who helped him in his experiments on anthrax, while still very young. Later she married a military surgeon.

The fight against tuberculosis cost Koch a great intellectual effort. Therefore, to be distracted from his labors he was an indefatiguable frequenter of Lessing Theatre, not far from his laboratory. There he became enamored of a young, talented and intelligent actress who played minor roles. A romance followed. Koch divorced his first wife and married this young woman. This event unleashed a moral storm, as was to be expected. During the Congress of German Physicians in 1892, where I was present, Koch's marriage was the topic of all conversation. Koch, whose scientific greatness had not as yet been forgiven him, was exposed to the most serious accusations; his romance certainly interested the professors more than all the reports submitted to the Congress. The facts I have just cited again prove the importance, in the life and the work of a man of genius, of the sentiment which was at the root of Koch's romance.

In time marriage relations will take on a better and simpler form. Future generations will show much more justice and tolerance towards Koch in this matter than his own contemporaries. It is desirable that a great man's private life be not covered up with a veil by his biographers. Koch had no children by his second wife.

CHAPTER XI.

From the time of its appearance, the first work of Koch inspired in me a feeling of respect. That feeling was changed into out-and-out veneration after reading his first report on the tubercular bacillus. This work brusquely tore the veil of mystery, which for many years had covered the most terrible enemy of mankind. The preceding works of Villemin had established without a shadow of a doubt that tuberculosis was an infectious disease, transmitted by a contagious principle. Nevertheless, the difference between the two was enormous. For the actual discovery of the microbe made it possible to cultivate it in an artificial medium, and it could be combatted thanks to our knowledge of its properties. Besides, the technical perfection by means of which Koch was enabled to obtain his extraordinary results brought him the admiration of all professional men.

Koch, who was followed by a whole school of young bacteriologists, was at first an enemy of my theory of immunity against infectious diseases. The subjects of research which he assigned to his disciples were directed against me. In 1887 at the Congress of Hygiene in Vienna, I met his chief assistant who informed me that Koch was anxious to see the preparations connected with my last work on recurrent fever; that he had asked to have them sent to him. Naturally, I welcomed this idea and so I replied that instead of sending them I would bring them myself. Several well-known Munich bacteriologists advised me against it, for they were convinced that Koch would show me out; that he would fail to see in these preparations what I found in them and that he would be able to assert henceforth that he had established the lack of foundation in my conclusions with a full knowledge of the facts. However, I did not heed this warning and betook myself to Berlin. Arriving at the Institute of Hygiene where Koch was teaching, I met his assistants and pupils. After announcing my visit to Koch, the meeting time was set for the day after. In the meantime I had taken out my preparations and shown them to the young assistants. They all stated unanimously that what they observed under the microscope undoubtedly confirmed my conclusions. Much encouraged by that testimony I went to Koch's laboratory the following day accompanied by his chief assistant. There, seated at the microscope, I perceived a rather elderly man. He was rather bald and his thick, bushy beard showed as yet no traces of gray. His handsome face had a serious and almost haughty expression. His assistant with a show of deference made the announcement that I had come to keep the appointment fixed for that day and that I was anxious to show him my preparations. "What preparations!", he exclaimed in a cross tone of voice. "I've told you to prepare everything necessary for today's lecture and I see that many things are still missing!" The assistant excused himself humbly and again pointed me out to Koch. Without shaking hands with me, the latter told me that he was very busy at that moment and that he could devote only very little time to my preparations. Some microscopes were hastily brought together and I managed to show him what to me seemed the most convincing details. "Why, then, have you made use of a violet coloration when a blue one would have been much better?" I explained the reason to him but this failed to soften him. After a while he got up and declared that my preparations were far from convincing and that they failed to substantiate my point of view. Much galled by these words and by Koch's behavior, I replied that a few moments were evidently not sufficient for him to appreciate the fine points of the preparations, and I asked him for another lengthier meeting. At this, the assistants and students who the day before had been on my side, made common front with him.

During the second meeting he showed himself somewhat more conciliatory. After attempting to refute my arguments, he determined to recognize the evidence, but finally concluded with the following words: "You know, I am not a specialist in microscopical anatomy; I am a hygienist. Consequently, it is entirely indifferent to me whether the spirilla are within or without the cells." Upon this I took my leave.

It was not until nineteen years after that meeting

that Koch publicly confirmed in scientific journals what I had a long time before stated regarding my preparations. Much had happened in the interval: Koch had already published his researches on the treatment of tuberculosis; he had been persecuted and had suffered many mortifications. From a director of the Institute of Hygiene he had become the director of the Institute for Infectious Diseases with his own private clinic. During one of my trips to Berlin, in 1894, I went to see Prof. Pfeiffer, one of the heads of his laboratory, having some accounts to settle with him (bacteriological ones, of course). "Do you know that Herr Private Councillor is here?" he said. I remembered too well the cold reception I got from Koch during my first visit to express the desire of again being introduced to His Eminence. Almost immediately Pfeiffer left and soon returned with Koch. He was entirely changed. He very kindly showed me his clinic and his patients. He entered upon minute details of tuberculine treatment and sharply criticized the doctors who failed to avail themselves of it. Finally he invited my wife and myself to dinner and presented us to his wife. The memory of our first meeting was completely forgotten.

During the period that followed Koch made long voyages to the Indies, to Africa and elsewhere. I saw him again ten years later, first in Berlin, then in Paris, which city Koch was anxious to show to his wife. Mme. Koch insisted on visiting the theatres and the famous artists. I feared that these theatre parties and evening entertainments would tire him out as he had already passed his sixties. When on the night before their departure Mme Koch evinced a desire to see the Montmartre cabarets, I suggested as a guide a young doctor who would gladly undertake such a task. Koch, however, insisted on accompanying his wife and the two went to see the absurd shows of Montmartre. Koch enjoyed the Parisian restaurants and mocked at my persistence in following the rules of hygiene, calling it pedantic. I suspect that this absence of "pedanticism" may have done him much harm and even hastened his fatal illness.

Though Koch's stay in Paris was not for scientific purposes, yet he was shown everything that might interest him in his field. The reception accorded him at the Pasteur Institute surpassed that of all the crowned heads. The staff met him at the library and wished him a hearty welcome with a salvo of unanimous applause. Koch visited the laboratories, the stables and everything else, but showed greatest interest for the technical details. He took note of the slightest improvements in procedure—the blood-letting of horses, injections, etc. I introduced him to Curie who showed us his experiments with radium and its emanations.

During his very satisfactory stay at Paris, Koch had the occasion to visit several museums. While visiting the Louvre he evinced a profound knowledge and a fine taste for paintings. As a whole, he was far from being the narrow-minded specialist one might imagine on reading certain of his treatises; on the contrary he was well-versed in many fields of knowledge. In philosophy he was a follower of Mach. Somewhat later he sent me as a souvenir one of the works of that philosopher. We parted good friends.

After their visit to Paris, the Kochs again left for the East-African colonies. Koch would always mention his previous trips to Africa with a certain tenderness in his voice and declared that the African climate suited him wonderfully and that it was inadequately appreciated. He claimed that the African plateaus had the best climate in the whole world. In his letters to his daughter, published after his death, he expresses regret that Europeans should have to live in such bad climatic conditions, without even minding it.

Koch and I met for the last time in the summer of 1909. I found him in his laboratory, immersed in his researches on tuberculosis which he attempted to cure by new preparations of tuberculine. He looked very well, full of life, and nothing indicated his approaching end. He was dead eleven months later.

CHAPTER XII.

Both Pasteur and Koch founded schools. The technique elaborated by Koch had made possible the discovery of a whole universe of living agents of infection. One of Koch's assistants, Loeffler, discovered the true cause of diphtheria, which, as was to be expected, had nothing at all to do with Letzerich's fungus. The microbe of that terrible disease looks like a little rod, like a bacillus which differs clearly from both the tubercular bacillus and the bacterum of anthrax.

Another of Koch's assistants, Goffky, who had accompanied him during the expedition to Egypt and the Indies for the study of cholera, made some five researches on the agent of typhoid fever. Though several other scientists, and especially Eberth, had already before him observed the bacillus of typhoid fever, nevertheless it was Goffky who made the first thorough-going study of it and who cultivated it in artificial culture media. Another group of scientists, though not Koch's actual pupils, worked in the path broken by him and discovered a great many microbes of infection. We might mention the bacillus of leprosy discovered by Hansen; the coccus of purulent inflammation of the urethra, discovered by Neisser; the streptococcus of erysipelas, discovered by Fehleisen; the bacillus of tetanus, discovered by Nicolaier, etc. Later the two Japanese, Kitasoto and Yersin, discovered the microbe of human plague, and the treponema of syphilis was discovered by Schaudinn.

Independently of the infectious microbes a large group of microbes were found belonging to the class of inferior animals. The first among these parasites was found by Loveran, in marsh-fever; the Englishman Bruce discovered the tryponosoma found in animals suffering from the African disease, called nagona; the Italian Castellani found the trypanosoma of sleeping-sickness, etc.

We must not forget to mention also the numerous infectious microbes which are of such minute dimension that they are invisible to the microscope even under the greatest magnification. They are the so-called invisible or ultra-microscopic microbes. They are known also as filterable microbe-viruses, for they are so infinitesimally small as to pass the pores of porcelain filters. These agents of infection include the ferments of yellow-fever, of eruptive typhus and of certain diseases of domestic animals, such as cattle pest, infectious pneumonia of cattle, etc.

This rapid survey indicates clearly the great number of infectious diseases which are traceable to the action of microbes; this, in itself, already constitutes an enormous progress. Furthermore, many scientists began to inquire as to the nature of the process by which microbes brought about diseases. From the very birth of bacteriology Pasteur had surmised that this was due to toxic secretions. With this in view he undertook experiments on chicken cholera. For the purpose of emphasis we must again state that Pasteur was never opposed to the theory which, in the last analysis, reduces the action of living ferments to inorganic substances. Eventually, inorganic toxins were found in several species of microbes. In this connection, the most important results were the discovery of the toxin of diphtheria by Roux and Yersin and of the toxin of tetanus by Knud Faber.

This question may be connected with that of inflammation. This phenomenon has since antiquity been considered a very important one in pathology. What did not the imagination conjure up in order to explain it! For a long time it was thought sufficient to describe the inflammation in order to explain it. The problem was deemed exhausted by the definition of its attributes: "swollen, painful, red and warm." Virchow taking "cellular pathology" as his base, ascribed inflammation to nutrition and to the increased growth of cells in the inflamed region. However, he disregarded the question of the *cause* of such excitation of the cells. Nevertheless, his theory was widely accepted in the medical profession during the period preceding Pasteur. The doctors whose daily task it was to observe inflammations would follow their growth and diminution without having the least idea of their essence. Pasteur's biological theory of fermentation threw a clear light on this problem. Just as putrefaction, according to that theory, results from the growth of living ferments in the putrefying area, so also suppuration must be due to the same cause, i.e. to the prior penetration of living microbes into the suppurating medium. (Even the names of the two phenomena already show their resemblance.) What could be simpler than this phenomenon, so clearly different from the older inorganic theory and semi-gaseous elements of infection! Pasteur proved the correctness of his theory by being the first to discover a small coccus in the pus of furuncle and which was named the staphylococcus.

One after another of these pus-forming microbes were in time discovered, and always accompanied by inflammation. One would then imagine that the question of the nature of the phenomenon was at last solved! Nevertheless, the representatives of the old school would not be convinced, for a long time. They wished to prove, at any price, that suppuration and inflammation were not related to the penetration of microbes, except in certain cases; that in most cases these phenomena could be brought about independently of microbes. The outcome of this difference of outlook was a great number of researches conducted by the rival school. While the adherents of the new school asserted that microbes assuredly had a cause and effect relationship with inflammation, the followers of the old doctrine pursued experiments with the view of provoking inflammations by means of chemical irritants, without the intervention of microbes. Although the adepts of the old school carried off the victory, that victory must actually be regarded as a defeat. It is true that certain substances, such as the essence of turpentine, silver nitrate and croton oil, introduced in animal organism may bring about inflammation, attended by suppuration; this, however, depends on the quantity of such irritant chemical introduced. It was furthermore, easy to show that non-organic microbial products, such as the extract of tubercular bacilli, i.e. the tuberculine of Koch, could at times bring on severe inflammation, together with pus. All these cases of inflammation, however, require conditions which may be attained only artificially. On the other hand, inflammation and suppuration which are due to living microbes are to be met with everywhere, independent of human intervention. When a person shows symptoms of suppuration, one may safely conclude that the pus is brought about by pyogenic microbes. These latter, of course, operate by means of chemical substances which they produce, but in order for these substances to collect in sufficient quantities, it is necessary that the microbes pullulate beforehand, that is to say, that they display their vital activity.

We have dwelled at length on the question of inflammation and suppuration because it will strengthen the conclusions drawn from the biological theory of fermentation, the corner-stone of modern medicine. Just as alcoholic fermentation may be induced by an inorganic ferment, zymase, so also may suppuration be produced artificially by chemical irritants, either worked out by microbes or independent of them. Under natural conditions, however, the inorganic ferments of alcoholic and other forms of fermentation among them also putrefaction, as well as suppuration induced by chemical sources, require the intervention of living microbes, to which fermentation is due.

The example we have just analysed shows clearly the essential difference existing between medical science before Pasteur and that of the period which he inaugurated. In this sketchy outline we have considered microbes only as the cause of inflammation. We have taken the liberty of passing over the question of the role of inflammation as a reaction of the living organism against the intrusion into it and the growth of microbes. Nevertheless, it sufficed to give us the conviction that inflammation and suppuration of wounds result from the penetration of living ferments, incapable of spontaneous generation, and this led to a new therapeutic method of great importance in medical science. We have already mentioned how Lister worked out his method of antiseptic treatment of wounds. After overcoming the strong opposition placed in its path, antisepsis began to spread gradually, both in wartime and in peace. During the Franco-Prussian War scientific methods slowly penetrated the field of sanitary medicine, which resulted in lessening the number of cases of wound complications and infectious diseases. But it was not until much later that real progress took place. The best example of this may be found in the comparative data furnished by two wars in which Russia took part. In the first chapter of this book we gave a resume of the enormous losses Russia suffered in the Crimean War. For every 25,000 men killed, 16,000 died as a result of wounds. The facts of the Russo-Japanese War of 1904-5, were quite different, for the rational treatment of wounds had already made its way into surgical practice. Thus, for an equal number of soldiers killed (25,000) there were now only 6,000 dead from wounds, i.e., only one third the number of those who died in Crimean War. One may conclude then, that in the Russian army alone 10,000 men were saved, thanks to the application of new methods in the treatment of wounds.(20)

We are furnished with results even more conclusively in favor of Pasteurian medicine in the fight against infectious diseases. It was formerly regarded as a general rule that in times of war, the mortality was due more to sickness than to wounds. We have seen this to be true from the example of the French armies during the Crimean Campaign, as well as of the Russian army during the same campaign. The mortality from diseases was more than twice the number of killed and dead from wounds. For 25,000 killed and 16,000 dead from wounds there were 89,000 who succumbed to various diseases. The casualties of the Russian armies during the Russo-Japanese War were quite opposite: for 31,000 dead—25,000 killed and 6,000 dead from wounds—there were only 1,200 who fell victim to mortal diseases. A comparision of the relative figures of the Russian armies during three campaigns,—the Crimean War, the Turkish War, and the Russo-Japanese War—the relative figures of the Japanese armies during the last-mentioned war and of the German armies in 1870, show that "the highest percentage of fatal casualties due to disease and

---

(20) These as well as the following data are taken from the article by Dr. Koslowsky in the **Journal of the Royal Army Medical Corps,** 1912, Vol. XVIII, p. 330.

wounds was found in the Russian armies in the Crimean Campaign, and the lowest percentage in the Russian armies during the Russo-Japanese War." We see, thus, that the highest mortality figures occur during the period preceding Pasteur and Lister, and the lowest during the full bloom of medical science, founded by Pasteur, Lister and Koch. The introduction of antisepsis in surgery made possible a great many new and very difficult operations, which formerly were not even dreamt of.

Cholera, as we have seen, took first place among diseases prevalent during the Crimean Campaign. Although its contagious character was established from its first appearance in Europe in 1828-1830, nevertheless the fight against it was of no avail on account of the erroneous ideas dominating the medicine of that period. Very useless quarantines were set up which interfered with commerce and travel without safeguarding against the spreading of the scourge. One had not the least precise idea of the nature of the infectious principle, but one looked for it everywhere: in the water, in the air, in the earth, in the living human body, in corpses, and in the faeces. Koch's discovery of the vibrio of cholera abruptly changed this state of affairs. The agent of cholera was discovered to be a microscopical bacterium of very motile form which did not bear up under extended dessication and which was very fragile. It was sufficient to heat a culture of the vibrio to a temperature of 55 to 60 degrees to kill it in a very short time. In water it may be preserved for a long time, but has only a short life in putrefying evacuations, in cadavers, or in the soil. It is only rarely to be found in the vomitings of cholera patients but, on the other hand, abounds in the excrements. It perishes in air laden with dust and is preserved only in little humid droplets. As a general rule, cholera is not transmitted through the air; the principle source of infections lies in the faeces of cholera patients or of those who had been cured of cholera, at times even of those who never had it, but who had contact with cholera patients. To avoid infection it is necessary, above all, to take precautionary measures gainst the penetration of the vibrio into the digestive organs by means of beverages, foods or soiled hands, by anything which might harbor the vibrio. Sometimes flies transfer the vibrio of cholera from excrements to food. From all this it becomes evident that all such measures which lead to the disinfection of the faeces of cholera patients are the most efficacious, for they eliminate the principle source of Koch's vibrio. The natural history of this microbe provides us with a means of combatting cholera. Had it been known during the Crimean War, many of its victims would have been saved. If the doctors who furnished such a large percentage of the dead during that campaign, had only refrained from eating raw fruit, if they had used boiled water or tea, if they had washed their hands in boiled water before sitting down to table, they surely would have been saved. If Saint-Arnaud, the general-in-chief of the French army, who gave strict orders against eating of fruits, especially raw fruits, and who probably himself refrained from eating them, had known that it was even more important to forbid the use of unboiled water and of other sources of cholera vibrios, he would not have been forced to give over the command to Canrobert and neither would he have died of cholera. The contagion may have been passed to him by his cook or by other servants, who, though carriers of Koch's vibrios, were healthy themselves.

The example of the latest epidemics proves the efficacy of rational measures against cholera. When an epidemic broke out in the civil population of St. Petersburg in 1908, the military authorities were able to prevent its spread in the army by means of boiling of potable water, the use of tea as a drink and the prohibition of all leaves to soldiers to prevent them from committing imprudent acts. And although cholera raged among the civil population of Cronstadt in the same year, there were only a few unimportant cases of it in the navy.

One may boldly predict that the fight against cholera will soon result in relegating this disease to the archives of history.

Modern medicine has also worked out very efficacious methods against eruptive typhus, a disease from which the French army suffered greatly in the Crimean Campaign. Typhus, which has disappeared from most civilized countries, is still somewhat widespread among semi-civilized peoples. According to Charles Nicolle of Tunis this disease is caused by an invisible or filterable microbe which we have discussed before. This microbe is found in the blood of fever-patients and enters the stomach of lice which suck it. It is then transmitted to healthy persons who are bitten by the infected lice. The fight against eruptive typhus is concentrated on the destruction of these insects. Typhus was very wide-spread among the miners in the phosphate beds of Gafsa in Tunisia. It was an easy task to stem it by destroying the lice. Since the Tunisians shave their heads, the clothes variety of lice prevail among them; the disinfection of clothes was sufficient to stop the epidemic.

It is surprising that Russia has not as yet found a good means of fighting typhus to which a great number of people, including many doctors and nurses, still succumb. Sooner or later, the knowledge of the infectious source of that disease should lead to its disappearance everywhere, Russia included. In time typhus, too, will become a thing of the past.

Typhoid fever, although a lesser plague than typhus during the Crimean Campaign, nevertheless, also played an important role. In general, however, typhoid fever is much more wide-spread than typhus and the number of its victims is much greater.

The natural history of the bacillus of typhoid fever, known to those following the labors of Goffky, gives us a clue to the measures to be employed against the disease. Like cholera, it spreads by means of unboiled water and foods, soiled hands, flies; it may thus be prevented by using same precautionary measures as in cholera. The fight against typhoid fever, however, is more difficult because it is more deeply rooted in Europe than cholera. Whereas, in the case of the latter disease, it is sufficient to take precautions only for a few months and only rarely for a year or more, it is necessary to fight against typhoid fever all the time. Consequently it should be very important to work out some practical method of preventive vaccination similar to the method used against small-pox. Up to the present several methods of prevention have been used, especially in the army, in the United States, England and France. The outcome of such vaccinations are not as yet sufficiently clear, but in all likelihood, it will become more so in the near future.(21) But even outside of these preventive vaccinations the fight against typhoid fever by means of hygienic measures based on the characteristics of the bacillus of typhoid fever, shows signs of making the diseases less and less frequent in civilized countries.

During the Crimean War doctors were not sufficiently familiar with intermittent fever which they perhaps confused with other diseases. Such confusion was even more likely in the case of French doctors, for intermittent fever is not known in France. This disease so wide-spread in Russia, is of especial interest as an index of the progress of modern medicine. We have already commented on the history of the discovery of recurrent fever. Obermayer, the first to observe the spirilla (or spirocheta) of that disease, did not ascribe any importance to them. Following in the footsteps of the times, he immersed himself in the purely clinical study. He caught the disease himself and became the victim of the microbe he discovered. It was not until after his death that the role of the spirocheta as the agent of recurrent fever was established. It has been proven by recent experiments that this disease is spread by means of lice, as in the case

(21) Vaccination against typhoid-fever has in effect proven itself during the World War—**Editor's Note.**

of eruptive typhus. The prevention of this disease may be assured by immediate measures against the insect, by cleanliness of the hair, the clothes; "flop-houses" are veritable breeding-grounds for typhus and intermittent fever. Recently a specific remedy against recurrent fever has been discovered: Ehrlich's arsenobenzol or salvarsan. In many cases a single injection into the blood will suffice to bring about the crisis in a few hours and then the cure. It is to be hoped that recurrent fever will soon disappear from Russia as it has from the other civilized countries of Europe.

Dysentery, one of the infectious diseases, raged in the French armies of Crimean War, as we have seen above in Chapter III. It generally accompanies most wars. Lately the study of this disease has shown very considerable progress. It has been proven that European dysentery is caused by a microbe somewhat resembling the bacillus of typhoid fever. Like the latter, it reaches the human organism by way of water and foods, and for that reason the measures employed in fighting cholera and tyhpoid fever are used also in dysentery. However, contemporary medicine has discovered a curative for it, namey the introduction into the organism of an animal serum prepared by injections of a culture of dysenteric bacilli. Such treatment is often rewarded with success. It is only a specific case of the general method discovered and worked out by the German scientist Behring. Around 1890, about the same time that the entire world was stirred by the announcement of a cure against tuberculosis, Behring and his collaborators issued a first-class work on the treatment of tetanus and diphtheria by means of animal serums injected with the toxins of those diseases. This discovery, at first received with a great deal of scepticism, was soon generally accepted. The anti-tetanus serum, applied immediately after a wound is caused, is very efficient as a preventative, but one cannot always count on its curative effects after the disease has already broken out, for the first symptoms appear when poisoning has already spread.

Though the treatment of tetanus by means of a specific serum does not entirely reward the hope placed upon it, the same cannot be said of the anti-diphtheria, both in children as well as in adults. Employed in medical practice for the last twenty years, it has brought countless benefits to mankind. It is not possible to determine accurately the number of people saved by this serum against diphtheria. According to Rauchfuss, the famous Russian doctor,(22) the mortality figures from diphtheria in the Russian Empire from 1895 to 1897 are as follows: of 6507 children who fell ill of the disease but who were not treated by the serum, 2219 or 34% succumbed; whereas of 44,631 ill who were treated by the serum, only 6522 or 14% fell victim. It follows, then, that for the period mentioned alone more than 8,500 people escaped death. It must be kept in mind, furthermore, that in a great many cases, injection with the serum is not performed at the outset of the disease, but perhaps a day or two later. A more suitable treatment would reduce the mortality about to 9 or 10%.

The specific serum, besides its curative value against

---

(22) Résultats de l'application du serum anti-diphtherique en Russie, St. Petersburg, 1898, 6. 5.

diphtheria which has already set in, is even more useful as a prophylactic. Often the growth of the epidemic may be arrested by administering preventive injections to healthy children, when the first cases of the disease make their appearance in the school or the home.

The anti-diphtheria serum is a triumph of modern medicine. Behring was able to discover it only on the basis of the researches of Roux and Yersin, who were the first to discover the true toxin of diphtheria. They obtained the latter from pure cultures of the diphtheria bacillus, discovered by Loeffler, Koch's collaborator, who used Koch's technique in the study of diphtheria. To get a curative anti-toxin from the diphtheria toxin, Behring was obliged to attenuate it, then vaccinate the animal with it, i.e. apply Pasteur's bacteriological methods. It is thus easy to follow the connections between the chief attainments of modern medicine and the discoveries of its founders, Pasteur and Koch.

It is not our intention to make a complete enumeration of all that humanity owes to the founders of modern medicine. What we have said will suffice to give the reader an idea of the intrinsic difference between it and older medical science, as well as a picture of the extraordinary successes attained by modern medicine. We must not, however, be satisfied with these results for much ignorance harmful to humanity still reigns in medicine.

The example of the Crimean Campaign has shown the extent of the ravages produced by diseases, which are at present successfully combatted. We have already mentioned the scurvy among the plagues which raged in the army. The mortality from this disease was comparatively small, but it nevertheless required the hospitalization of a great number of soldiers. The causes of scurvy are not as yet well known, but it has been observed for a long time to occur under conditions of malnutrition. Sailors who, during long voyages, are forced to eat preserved foods for lack of fresh are usually subject to scurvy. It consists of lesions of the cheek, containing a quantity of microbes, the spirilla predominating. The fact that arsenic and especially preparations of salvarsan (Ehrlich's) are effective against diseases caused by spirilla, such as recurrent fever and syphilis, inspired some physicians to use the same remedies in scurvy. The results obtained, however, are not clear enough to permit us, as yet, to draw conclusions. To prevent scurvy one has recourse especially to dietetic measures, such as the eating of vegetables, fresh fruit, acid foods, and the elimination, as far as possible, of preserved food.

However deplorable the absence of precise medical ideas regarding scurvy, one might yet be content were it not for the great impotence of medicine in its fight against much more serious diseases, such as, in the first place, pulmonary tuberculosis. We have recounted above with what enthusiasm Koch's discovery of the tubercular bacillus and his announcement of a remedy against all forms of the disease were received. We also saw the sad disillusionment which followed when it was found that in most cases *severe* tuberculosis remained as incurable as before. Nothing of all that Koch and a great number of his students and followers had worked out, has proven itself efficacious up to the present. Almost daily we hear of a new remedy against tuberculosis being announced as being infallible. But when verified it is found to be no better than those which preceded it; for example, Friedmann's remedy which has caused so much talk. Under these circumstances, the fight against tuberculosis, except in cases of surgical intervention, is limited to general hygienic measures, most of which have been used for a long time. The question of the prevention and treatment of tuberculosis remains one of the chief problems of the future.(23)

Nor can we see any hopeful signs in regards to the other varieties of pulmonary inflammation. The microbe of "croupal" pneumonia, discovered more than 30 years ago, has been studied in great detail, which however, does not prevent it from remaining a heavy burden on mankind, being chief cause of the death of old men. The other scourge is influenza, which, according to certain scientists is supposed to be caused by a minute bacillus, discovered by Pfeiffer. While all bacteriologists agree as to the role of pneumococcus, the microbe of "croupal" pneumonia, they disagree about that of the microbe of influenza. Medicine is powerless not only against these serious pulmonary ailments, but also against the less serious ones, such as, anginas, grippes and colds. In spite of excellent researches on whooping cough made by Bordet, one has not as yet succeeded in obtaining a remedy against that sickness. How many are the diseases which mic-

---

(23) Metchnikoff died several years before the first vaccinations with B.C.G by Calmette and Guérin—**Editor's Note.**

robiology has not even begun to tackle to any satisfaction! What are the causes of cardiac, vascular and nervous diseases when they are not due to the spirocheta of syphilis?

Doctors are daily confronted with cases of hardening of the arteries (arteriosclerosis) which seems to have no visible cause; as well as with diseases of the heart considered to be the consequence of severe articular rheumatism. Up to the present all efforts of the scientists to illuminate the causes of these diseases have been fruitless. We are afforded a particularly clear proof of the impotence of clinical medicine in connection with cardiac and vascular diseases in the case of Koch himself, referred to in Chapter X. In spite of the most exacting clinical examinations, treatment according to the old methods of treatment brought no improvement to the eminent patient and could not prevent his premature death.

And what about the various inflammations of the kidneys, nephritis? Some of these are due to the effects of scarlatina or to various lesions of the breast angina. Scarlatina and measles are no doubt infectious diseases, caused by certain microbes. But the most persevering efforts have not as yet been successful in discovering them. Medicine knows even less about a great many frightful diseases, which afflict the human race, the mental diseases. Luckily it has been actually proven that at least some of these, especially "progressive paralysis" are due to the effects of the spirocheta of Schaudinn. Science, however, is still groping in the dark when it comes to those mental diseases which are not of a syphilitic origin. All this makes doctors impotent in the face of diseases which they cannot even relieve.

It is not surprising that under these circumstances the older medicine is beginning to raise its head and to drive back the science founded by Pasteur and Koch. This reaction has become so formidable that infectious diseases are coming to be clearly considered unrelated to microbes. For example, diarrhea of young children or in other words cholera infantum, or even gastro-enteric inflammation of young children a disease ascribed by most pedologists to intoxicants in the products of digestion. Their error has been easily proven by the discovery of the microbe which plays the leading role in that disease. But how great is the number of other cases in which it is difficult to discover the truth!

Let us consider in the first place the worst affliction of the human race, the malignant tumors: epithelioma and sarcoma. Why does cancer develop more frequently in the internal organs and on the skin of old men? Its growth there is unlimited and it relapses in spite of operation. Why do different tumors, also frequently mortal, develop in the child and in the adult? Followers of various schools have time and again attempted to solve this problem, one of the most important of all medicine. Common sense would suggest that malignant tumors are caused by the entrance into the organism of microbes suitable for the intensive growth of cells. Many accumulated facts speak in favor of that theory. As in those infectious diseases connected with certain local conditions such as anthrax, malignant tumors, too, are distributed very differently in various localities. There are certain places in North-east Prussia where the mortality due to cancer reaches extraordinary figures. Among European countries, Switzerland, the Tyrol and the Alpine regions generally, are outstanding for their frequency of malignant tumors, while, in the southern regions, in Italy and in Spain, they occur less frequently.

An agent of infection has already been found in the case of certain sarcomas. We have an example of it in a tumor known today under the name "actinomycosis," which formerly was believed to be a sarcoma. After parasitic fungi had been discovered in it, it has without any definite reason, been excluded from the malignant tumors. The American, P. Rous, has discovered in sarcoma of fowl an infectious principle, belonging to the filterable or invisible microbes. The Danish pathologist Fibiger, was able to produce a cancer of the stomach in rats; its infectious principle is transmitted by cockroaches. In this case, the direct carriers of the infection are little round worms, which are found in cancer of rats and which penetrate into the body of the cockroaches. Rats which feed on these infected roaches will contract a true cancer of the stomach. Many other conclusive facts corroborate the theory which ascribes malignant tumors to agents of infection coming from without. Thus, cancer of the skin is very rare among individuals who observe the rules of bodily cleanliness. Cancer of the internal organs occurs most frequently in the digestive duct which connects with the outside. These tumors frequently occur also in the genitals of women, because these organs are situated close to the lower part of the intestine.

All these facts are signs, though not indisputable proofs, which permit us to group the tumors among the infectious diseases. Modern medicine is almost in the same position with regards to these tumors as it was in respect to anthrax and other infectious diseases before the labors of Davaine and Koch. This absence of exact knowlede, of course, favors the adepts of the older medicine who continue to assert that malignant tumors arise spontaneously in the organism and are not tied up with any microbe. These followers of an antiquated school regard Virchow's theory as more probable; according to it cancer is due "to a marked deviation of the epithelial cell from their primitive type." Virchow's theory fails to explain why this "deviation" produces a continuous growth of cells. The theory of infection, on the other hand, argues that such proliferation depended on the toxins secreted by the microbes of the cancer and that these toxins stimulate the growth of cells.

The older medical school, encouraged by the imperfections of the newer school, avoids the difficult question of the cause of diseases and concentrates all its attention on symptoms; they set up a diagnostic, and, at the best, a prognosis! Thus, in the study of chronic inflammation of the kidneys, they seek above all to determine whether these organs rid the organism of more chlorides than of urea. The prognosis is more favorable in the first case than in the second. Certain expert doctors stretch this to the point of determining from the amount of blood in the urea, whether death will take place in 10 months or perhaps in 18 months. Death, however, is inevitable, for there is no remedy for the retention of urea in the blood. It should be much more important to clarify the cause of inflammation of the kidneys. As we mentioned above, this disease develops sometimes as the consequence of scarlatina and of various other inflammations of the throat; but medicine does not know what to attribute it to, nor how to prevent it. The microbiological school has not solved the problem and the older clinical school has not even posed it.

The same thing is true of two other diseases, diabetes and gout. All the fine technical points of chemistry have been tried out in the study of diabetes, volumes upon volumes have been written on the conditions under which the organism eliminates sugar and on the substances at whose expense it takes place. But hardly a line will be found in them regarding the cause of diabetes. As long as medicine limited itself to the details of the clinical picture of recurrent fever, the fight against that disease had no solid basis; but, as we have seen above, no sooner was it found that the spirocheta transported by the louse is the cause of it, such a basis was acquired.

It will be useless to enumerate any other diseases. Our conclusion applies to them all: modern medicine is going through a critical period which should be brought to an end as soon as possible. The seeds sown by Pasteur and Koch have brought a rich harvest of immeasurable benefits to mankind. But the road they laid out has not yet led to a definite goal. A vast field is still open to scientific investigation. As we have seen above pathogenic microbes which enter the organism do not necessarily cause disease. Among human "carriers" of the microbes of typhus, cholera, diphtheria and other diseases, there are many who have not and will not contract the diseases caused by these micrbes. It is unusually striking that in many cases, the carriers of tubercular bacillus, that terrible enemy of mankind, are not themselves affected by the disease. It is clear, then, that besides the presence of the specific microbes we must also consider other conditions, which may either favor the disease or remain neutral. It is extremely important to study these conditions; the knowledge of them will determine the the direction of the fight against tuberculosis. Facts, more and more, corroborate the hypothesis that alongside of the typical bacillus of tuberculosis there exist a great number of bacilli which resemble it in all points but which behave differently in relation to the organism. It is probable that among the great many bacilli of Koch there are some which are incapable of causing the disease but which may be utilized as a vaccine against the virulent bacillus. Just as it was possible, as a result of Pasteur's experiments, to prepare an artificial remedy against anthrax by means of the attenuation of the bacteria, so also a remedy may be found in nature by the spontaneous weakening of certain tubercular bacilli. This assumption would explain the decrease of tuberculosis observed in certain localities in spite of the inefficacy of the fight against that disease. The same phenomenon may be observed in leprosy on an even larger scale. Leprosy, which was wide-spread in Europe during the

Middle Ages has gradually decreased and at the present time there are only small centers of them in Russia, Germany, Norway, France and elsewhere. Such decrease cannot be explained on the basis of any hygienic measures; it has taken place spontaneously, without any human intervention. The cause of such disappearance is probably due to the existence of bacilli resembling those of leprosy, capable of immunizing the body against it. As a matter of fact a bacillus has recently been discovered similar to that of leprosy but which does not bring about the disease. The French doctors, Leboeuf and Janelly, have found bacilli identical with those of leprosy, in the ganglii of two healthy persons living in New Caledonia where leprosy is wide-spread. They were clearly Hansen's bacilli spontaneously attenuated.

All this leads one to believe that microbes which are very favorable in the fight against infectious diseases must be found in the atmosphere as well as in the organism. In the case of tuberculosis and leprosy the beneficent bacilli resemble the virulent ones; but there must be a number of other bacilli differing from the microbes of infection which we are familiar with and which help us in the fight against these diseases. One should investigate the carriers of microbes of cholera, typhus, diphtheria and other diseases, to determine which microbes are not harmful to their carriers, but whose organism they enter. There are numerous microbes on the human skin and on the surface of certain internal organs which still need much study and which play an important role in life. Alongside of beneficent microbes which guard us against pathogenic bacteria, there must exist also noxious microbes, which are capable of producing diseases. It is probably that to the latter group belong the microbes of those diseases whose cause we still fail to grasp.

For example, certain considerations cause us to assume that diabetes develops under the influence of microbes residing in the pancreatic ducts and that certain diseases of the vascular system are caused by the toxins of intestinal microbes.

We have mentioned here only a few examples to show how much mankind has the right to expect from new scientific searchers who will follow the path laid out by the three great founders of modern medicine—Pasteur, Lister and Koch.

THE END

ETIOLOGY
OF
WOUND
INFECTIONS

INTRODUCTION

As at present used, the term "traumatic infective diseases" (Wundinfectionskrankheiten) indicates a group of affections formerly known as traumatic fever, purulent infection, putrid infection, septicemia, pyemia, but which were included at a subsequent period (when the view became generally accepted that these diseases were essentially of the same nature) under the title "pyemic or septicemic processes."

Strictly speaking, we should include in this group all those diseases which are the sequel of wounds, even the smallest, as, for example, the pricks of a vaccinating needle, and which have been proved with certainty, by clinical observation or experiment, to be contagious. For example, vaccine infection, anthrax, glanders, hydrophobia, and even syphilis, must be ranked among the traumatic infective diseases. Nevertheless this term does not commonly have such a wide signification, but is limited to those morbid processes specially interesting to the surgeon, which may complicate injuries and operation wounds; in other words, to septicemia, pyemia, progressive inflammation and suppuration, and erysipelas. Of late the conviction has more and more gained ground that puerperal fever is also to be regarded as an infective disease, starting from the placental surface or from wounds of the genital passages. Further, many authors include diphtheria also among these diseases, because it at times attacks wounds, and because the possibility of transmitting it by inoculation has been abundantly demonstrated.

In the comments introductory to the experimental part of this work, I shall likewise confine myself to the last-mentioned morbid processes; in the second part, however, I shall deviate from the ordinary limitation of the term "traumatic infective diseases" in so far that I shall also take notice of anthrax on account of its manifold relations to the septicemia produced experimentally in animals.

The expressions pyemia and septicemia are often used with different meanings, and it is therefore necessary to indicate precisely what I shall understand by terms so universally employed.

For a long time pyemia was distinguished from septicemia by the occurrence of metastatic deposits in the former and their absence in the latter. But since it has been established that, even in such cases as had been previously described as septicemia, isolated microscopic metastatic deposits are not unfrequently present, and that the two processes cannot be definitely separated in this way, some authors have preferred to designate as septicemia the disease brought about by absorption of dissolved putrid poison, and to call all the other morbid processes connected with the development of microscopic organisms, pyemic processes.

Birch-Hirschfeld, for example, separates pyemia from septicemia in this way. He understands by the term "septicemia" a disease originating in alterations of the blood, which alterations are a consequence of the absorption of the products of putrefaction. On the other hand, he defines pyemia as "a general infection, which proceeds from the surfaces of wounds or from the focus of a primary suppurative inflammation, probably evoked by specific organisms and different from the putrid infection." Cohnheim also identifies septicemia with putrid infection, and attributes it to the entrance of a putrid poison in solution into the fluids of the body. Davaine, whose works I shall have to allude to repeatedly, adheres, on the other hand, to the older distinction between pyemia and septicemia, and includes under the latter term all those cases in which the post-mortem examination shows no metastatic deposits, although in both cases he considers the co-operation of specific organisms as proven.

The terms pyemia and septicemia no longer retain their original signification, for pyemia does not arise, as was at one time believed, from the entrance of pus into the blood-vessels, and septicemia is not putrefaction of the living blood. They now remain only as collective names for a number of symptoms which in all probability belong to different diseases. So long, however, as these diseases are not sufficiently separated from each other, it seems best for the present to retain these terms in their ordinary signification, in order to avoid the necessity of constantly adopting new definitions.

For these reasons I shall in what follows include under the term septicemia all those cases of general traumatic infection in which no metastatic deposits occur, and under pyemia those in the course of which they may be present.

The Present State of Knowledge with regard to THE RELATIONS OF MICRO-ORGANISMS TO TRAUMATIC INFECTIVE DISEASES.

I. The Occurrence of Micro-organisms in the Human Body in Disease.

The first communication regarding the occurrence of bacteria in the organs of those who have died of traumatic infective diseases was made by Rindfleisch in the year 1866. In pyemia, puerperal fever, and like infective diseases, small softened metastatic deposits, of the size of a pin's head, at times occur. These deposits are always found in greater numbers in the substance of the heart, in the muscular tissue of which they have at first the appearance of greyish white spots, these specks becoming, at a later period, cavities filled with a thin fluid pulp. The contents of these cavities consist, as Rindfleisch has shown, not of pus-corpuscles, but solely of "vibriones." These organisms lie at first closely packed between the fasciculi of the muscle; at a later period, however, from disintegration of the muscular fibres, they penetrate into their interior. Rindfleisch was unable to trace the alterations further than to the formation of these small abscess-like softened spots, because the process in question only occurs in those forms of infective diseases which are most severe and rapidly fatal. Rindfleisch has not specially described the organisms termed by him "vibriones", as regards their size or as to whether they were rod-shaped or spherical.

That the development of these miliary purulent deposits, which occur also in other organs in typhus, pyemia, etc., is produced by parasitic organisms, in other words by bacteria, was shown almost simultaneously by Von Recklinghausen and Waldeyer. Von Recklinghausen describes the bodies found in the smallest renal veins, in the glomeruli, urinary tubules, and pulmonary alveoli, under the name of micrococci, and states that they may be distinguished from detritus by the uniform size of their granules and by their resistance to the action of glycerine, acetic acid, caustic soda, etc. He likewise calls attention to the brownish color of the center of the deposit, as well as to the fact that the uriniferous tubules and the vessels in which the micrococci lie are very much distended at intervals.

Waldeyer confirmed Rindfleisch's statement regarding the occurrence of numerous miliary bacteric deposits in the substance of the heart in pyemia, and he also found bacteria in small abscess-like spots in the kidneys.

Attention was directed by these investigations to the bacteria, which are present in metastatic deposits in pyemia, and which up to that time had been overlooked or regarded as unimportant. These statements were confirmed and extended by many similar observations, and it may now be regarded as an established fact that, in most of the metastatic deposits in pyemia, bacteria in the form of the so-called zooglea will, on careful examination, be found. Nothing essentially new, with some exceptions to be noticed directly, has, however, been added by later investigations to the original observations of Rindfleisch, Von Recklinghausen and Waldeyer. It is therefore unnecessary to take special notice of the numerous papers on this subject.

It is worthy of mention that P. Vogt has seen moving "monads", even during life, in the metastatic deposits of a pyemic individual. It now naturally occurred to observers to subject the pus of wounds to examination, in order to ascertain if the bacteria, found in the metastatic deposits, accumulated in the first instance in the pus of the wound, and from thence penetrated into the tissue. Extensive observations of this kind have been made by Birch-Hirschfeld. He came to the conclusion that the unhealthiness of a wound stood in a direct relation to the number of spherical bacteria in the pus of that wound. The more abundantly these appeared the worse became the state of the wound and the general condition of the patient. The most unfavorable cases were those in which the spherical bacteria had become grouped together in colonies (zooglea). As the spherical bacteria increased in number their penetration into the pus-corpuscles could also be observed. Birch-Hirschfeld examined at the same time the blood of pyemic patients, and found that it contained bacteria. He further states that the severity and rapidity of the general infection are in proportion to the number of bacteria which may be detected in the blood.

The channel by which the bacteria gain access to the metastatic deposits would, if these observations were correct, be pretty clearly indicated. The mode by which they pass into the circulation, from the surface of the wound, alone remained unknown. This blank was filled up by the investigations of Klebs. The work of Klebs deserves notice here, not on this ground alone, but also because his researches furnish very numerous and thorough observations on the bacteria of wound diseases, and further because in them the attempt was made for the first time, by the aid of abundant and excellently used materials for observation, to demonstrate a causal connection between bacteria and traumatic infective diseases. Klebs designates the bacteria found in the pus of a wound as microsporon septicum, starting with the view that spherical and rod-shaped bacteria stand in a genetic relation to each other, and also that the micrococci and bacteria commonly found together in wounds are forms of the same organism. The growth of this microsporon septicum in the form of zooglea masses firmly attached to the surface of the wound was observed by Klebs on granulations, joint surfaces, and serous membranes. He was also able to trace the penetration of the zooglea into the interspaces of the cellular tissue. This takes place either with or without the aid of wandering lymph corpuscles. The passage of the microsporon along the lymphatic vessels could not be followed with complete certainty; on the other hand its penetration through the eroded walls of a vein into the circulation was observed in one instance. Further, the elements of the microsporon were found by Klebs in the thrombi which develop behind the valves of veins, and in the metastatic deposits in the lung and liver.

Although the facts which have been hitherto collected with reference to the dependence of pyemia on the development of bacteria in the body are numerous and important, yet the statements relating to the occurrence of organisms in *septicemia* are few and doubtful.

Coze and Feltz as well as Hueter attribute the corrugated form of the red corpuscles frequently seen in septicemic diseases to the adhesion and penetration of bacteria; an observation which has been much and justly doubted.

The only other statement I have been able to find, as to the presence of bacteria in the blood in septicemia, is made by Collmann von Schatteburg. He saw, in one case, rods both in the blood of the body generally and in the vascular loops of the glomeruli.

The observations on erysipelas are much more abundant.

Nepveu found micrococci in the blood of erysipelatous patients, and these were present in greatest number in blood taken from the erysipelatous part.

Wilde obtained the same result and he also states that the pus of wounds, from which erysipelatous inflammation starts, contains numerous micrococci. Orth has also found micrococci in the contents of the bullae in erysipelas.

Of especial importance is the discovery made by Von Recklinghausen and Lukomsky that the lymphatic vessels and canaliculi of the skin at the border of the erysipelatous part are filled with micrococci.

This observation was confirmed by Billroth and Ehrlich, who likewise found micrococci, not only in the lymphatic, but also in the blood-vessels.

Micrococci have also been seen, by Tillmanns, in erysipelatous skin, and by Letzerich in cases of erysipelas attacking vaccination wounds, in the wound itself, in the blood-vessels, muscles, liver, spleen, and kidneys.

With respect to phlegmonous suppurations, the observations have apparently been confined as yet to the contents of the abscesses, while the walls of the latter

—that is to say the adjacent tissue which, as will subsequently be shown, is the true seat of the bacteric development—have up to this time received no attention. In the pus from the abscess, just as in the ordinary pus from wounds, bacteria have often and micrococci have almost always been found. A detailed account of the statements on this point is accordingly unnecessary.

Hospital gangrene differs so little from the diphtheria of mucous membranes that the observations made with reference to the latter also hold good for the former.

According to Cohnheim, after tracheotomy the disease at times spreads from the mucous membrane to the operation wound. But even without any apparent infection wounds often become diphtheritic, and Cohnheim thinks it probable that hospital gangrene is nothing more or less than a diphtheritic inflammation of the surface of a wound.

Hueter found in the greyish diphtheritic deposits on wounds, and, on more accurate examination, in the neighboring tissues, as yet apparently quite healthy, the same small round bodies with dark contours which he afterwards saw in the false membrane in diphtheritis of the larynx and pharynx.

By the researches of Oertel, Nassiloff, Classen, Letzerich, Klebs, and Eberth, it has been placed beyond doubt that in diphtheritic deposits large numbers of micrococci are present. The statements are, however, as yet contradictory with regard to the question whether or not the bacteria penetrate into the tissues.

Oertel found the inflamed mucous membrane crammed with micrococci, and was further able to trace them in the afferent lymphatic vessels of the nearest lymphatic glands, in the glands themselves, as well as in the blood-vessels of the kidney and of other internal organs.

Similar observations have been made by Eberth, Nassiloff, and Letzerich.

The presence of small deposits of bacteria in the cardiac tissue, in the liver, kidneys, and other organs, in cases of diphtheria, has of late been repeatedly demonstrated.

Attention has also been drawn, by different observers, especially by those who have inoculated diphtheria on the cornea of rabbits, to the brownish color of the micrococcus masses.

On comparing the behavior of the bacteria in diphtheria and pyemia, one is at once struck by a remarkable correspondence. In both morbid processes the surface of the wound is covered with masses of micrococci which penetrate into the deeper layers of the tissue and into the lymphatic vessels; in both, peculiar miliary bacteric deposits are present in the cardiac tissue, in the liver, and in the kidney; and in both, these bacteric deposits are of a brownish color. The question is at once forced on the mind: May not the parasitic micro-organisms of pyemia and of diphtheria be identical?

The same appearances may be seen in puerperal fever. In this disease Waldeyer has found spherical bacteria in the affected tissues, in the lymphatic vessels, and in the peritoneal exudation; whilst Birch-Hirschfeld has observed micrococcus masses on vaginal ulcers, in the perivaginal cellular tissue, in the blood, in the spleen, and in the liver. The presence of micrococci in the kidneys, lungs, and cardiac muscular tissue was demonstrated by Heiberg and Orth, and the latter makes mention of the greyish yellow color of those present in the uriniferous tubules which are affected with nodular dilatations.

As standing probably in close relation to puerperal fever, we must here mention the disease affecting new-born infants, first described by Orth and called by him *mycosis septica.* In one such case micrococci were found in the blood, in the pleural cavity, and in the urinary bladder.

The so-called mycosis of the navel in new-born infants (nabelmykose) seems likewise to belong to this group of diseases. Weigert describes a case of this kind, and states that ulcer of the navel was covered with micrococci, and that groups of micrococci were present in the center of small extravasations of blood in the lungs and kidneys.

Hennig has investigated an analogous case and obtained the same result.

The extremely interesting observations with regard to the occurence of bacteria in endocarditis seem less easily explicable.

All investigators who have been engaged in seeking bacteria in morbid tissues agree in regarding the undertaking as one of extraordinary, often even of insuperable, difficulty. To make up for the weakness of the anatomical proofs as to the presence of bacteria, pathological experiment has in most cases been resorted to. In order, therefore, to obtain a complete survey of the facts known respecting the relations of bacteria to traumatic infective diseases, it is now necessary to give a short digest of the results of the experimental investigations on this subject.

II. Relations of Micro-organisms to Traumatic Infective Diseases, as Established by Experiment.

It is known, as the result of experience, that, when traumatic infective diseases set in, the discharge of the wound and fluids in the neighbouring tissues take on a putrid character. These alterations in the wound often, indeed, make their appearance before any perceptible manifestation of the general disease, and it was therefore concluded that the putrefaction of the discharges was the cause of the infective disease. Some, however, disputed the accuracy of this conclusion, and maintained that the infective disease was produced by causes acting from within, and that the deterioration of the wound occurred secondarily. To settle this controversy numerous experiments have been set on foot. Experimenters for a long time contented themselves with ascertaining the noxious influence of putrid substances on animals when injected into the blood or into the subcutaneous tissue, and with isolating the poisonous substance contained in these putrid fluids. The question as to whether the disease produced by the injection of the putrid fluid was only a simple poisoning, or whether it in reality possessed the infective qualities of those diseases observed in man, was left untouched by the older and most of the later experimenters. If in an animal, by injection of a putrid fluid, a disease was produced resembling to some extent the human infective disease in symptoms and post-mortem appearances, this circumstance sufficed for their identification, and from such an experiment extensive conclusions as to infective diseases were drawn. But in order that such experiments should prove the infective character of the disease, it must be definitely ascertained, by further transmission from one animal to another, that the disease produced experimentally is in like manner of undoubtedly infective nature.

As we have here to do only with infective diseases, all the investigations which have reference merely to the toxic properties of putrid materials, as well as those in which the possibility of a confusion between toxic action and infection is not excluded, must be left unnoticed.

The first attempt to produce traumatic infective diseases artificially in the lower animals was made by Coze and Feltz. These investigators injected some grammes of blood, from a patient who had died of putrid poisoning and puerperal fever, into the subcutaneous cellular tissue of rabbits. In consequence of this the animals died with peculiar and characteristic symptoms. A much smaller quantity of the blood of the rabbits thus killed was injected subcutaneously into other rabbits and the same symptoms and fatal termination occurred as took place with the original putrid blood. Coze and Feltz continued this transmission of blood, in gradually diminishing quantities, from the dead animals to others, and they finally succeeded in bringing about infection with an extremely minute amount of blood. This led them to assume that the poison increased in virulence by successive inoculations. In the blood of animals which had died of putrid infection they found bacteria in great numbers, indeed they assert that they have seen at the same time rods, long threads with an oscillating or vermiform motion, and chains of small granules.

The discovery of the increasing virulence of the successively inoculated putrid poison excited the most lively interest.

The experiments of Coze and Feltz were repeated and confirmed by Clementi and Thin, and by Behier and Lionville. These observers likewise convinced themselves that for the first infection a comparatively large quantity of the infective material, be it blood, peritoneal fluid, or the like, is necessary; while for the later infections an extremely minute quantity is sufficient. They also found numerous bacteria in the blood of the animals killed by the inoculation.

Colin, Vulpian, Raynaud, and others obtained similar results.

Davaine, however, has studied these conditions more thoroughly than any other observer. He transmitted the infection through a series of twenty-five animals in succession, and for the last effective transmission of the putrid infecting material he used only a trillionth part of a drop of blood. Davaine saw in the blood of these animals actively moving bacteria, differing in that respect from those of splenic fever, which are quiescent and were for that reason called by him bacteridia.

Although the most diverse fluids were used by him in these experiments for the first infection, e.g., putrefying blood, blood from pyemic cases, from puerperal fever, scarlet fever, small-pox, and typhus, yet the effects produced were always similar, and the post-mortem examination showed in all cases bacteria in the blood, and swelling of the spleen, with absence of metastatic deposits. Davaine accordingly calls this disease septicemia.

Of the other traumatic infective diseases, diphtheria and erysipelas have been artificially produced in animals.

The attempt to transmit erysipelas was first made by Orth. He injected under the skin of a rabbit the contents of an erysipelatous bulla in which were numerous spherical bacteria. There followed an inflammation entirely analogous to erysipelas in man, and, by the application of the oedematous fluid from the subcutaneous tissue of this animal to a second rabbit, the characteristic progressive inflammation was communicated to the latter. In the oedematous fluid in the subcutaneous cellular tissue, and in the affected parts of the skin of the animals suffering from artificial erysipelas, Orth demonstrated the presence of bacteria in large numbers.

Lukomsky has also experimented on rabbits with erysipelatous fluid in order to produce an artificial erysipelas. He, however, obtained in the animals experimented on an extensive phlegmonous inflammation of the subcutaneous cellular tissue with implication of the skin. But in his cases also micrococci were present in the canaliculi of the areolar tissue and in the lymphatic vessels.

That diphtheria may be communicated to rabbits, and that micrococci appear in the artificial diphtheria similar in characters to those found in diphtheria in man, has been demonstrated by Hueter, Tommasi, Oertel, and Letzerich.

The investigations on diphtheria led to the introduction of an experiment of extreme importance in the study of pathogenic bacteria, viz. the use of the transparent cornea of the rabbit as the place for inoculation.

Nassiloff and Eberth were the first to carry out these corneal inoculations. At first diphtheritic substances were alone used, but is was soon found that the most diverse putrid materials, products of inflammation, and the like, could also be inoculated on the cornea with effect.

Similar experiments have likewise been carried out and in various ways modified by Leber, Stromeyer, Dolschenkow, Orth, and more especially by Frisch.

In a successful inoculation of this kind a peculiar stellate patch with conical processes—the so-called "mushroom" appearance—is produced, the centre of which is the point of inoculation. The materials composing this patch are, in diphtheritic inoculations, dense masses of micrococci, which are of a yellow or greenish-brown color like the micrococci of the diphtheritic and pyemic deposits in the muscular tissue of the heart and in the kidneys. The "Pilzfigur" is also obtained by inoculation of putrid fluids, and here it consists of rod-shaped bacteria. Frisch further inoculated materials from splenic fever on the cornea of living rabbits, and observed the development of splendid "Pilzfiguren", which consisted only of Bacillus Anthracis.

In all these experiments the inflammatory appearances in the cornea were exactly in proportion to the development and extent of the bacteria. Eberth found the association of the bacteria with the artificial diphtheria of the cornea so constant that he distinctly says: Without the fungi (i.e., bacteria) no diphtheria.

A special method, and one of much promise for demonstrating the origin of infective diseases from a contagium animatum, was followed by Klebs. He introduced fluids and other substances, taken from patients who were suffering from or who had died of infective diseases, into thoroughly purified flasks containing cultivating fluids. After development of organisms had occurred in these fluids a small quantity was taken and put into a second vessel containing a similar liquid. With the fluid of the second flask a third was inoculated, and so on through a series sufficiently long to enable him to assume that only an excessively small part of the infective substance originally employed, or indeed none at all, could be present in the last cultivating liquid. The fluids, thus freed from the original infective material, were inoculated on animals. Klebs has employed this method, which he terms fractional cultivation, more especially with substances from diphtheritic and septic processes, though also with material from various other diseases. The fluids obtained in this manner by fractional cultivation, when inoculated on animals, produced again septicemia and diphtheria; and Klebs also found, both in the cultivating fluids and in the infected animals, the characteristic micrococci.

In a similar manner Orth has grown in cultivating fluids bacteria from an erysipelatous bulla, and, by the injection of this fluid, has reproduced erysipelas in rabbits.

III. Objections to the conclusiveness of these Facts.

The facts put together in the two foregoing sections are undoubtedly of considerable significance. When taken along with theoretical considerations, and looked at in the light of the brilliant results of the antiseptic method of treatment, they furnish evidence sufficient to enable many to accept as proved the existence of living infective material, especially in traumatic infective diseases. On the other hand, various objections, of more or less weight, have been urged against this assumption; and a short discussion of these is requisite in order to form a judgment as to the significance of bacteria in traumatic infective diseases.

A considerable number of investigators have advanced the statement that the normal blood and tissues of man and of the lower animals always contain microorganisms. From this some infer that these organisms are not the cause of the infective disease, but that an abnormal increase in their numbers followed the morbid process, because the fluids of the animal body, when altered by disease, present conditions very favorable for their development. We need not consider these views, which have as yet never been experimentally proved, but which are advanced on theoretical grounds alone. Were it, however, true that bacteria do occur in normal blood, and that the same bacteria—e.g., micrococci—are found, though in unusual numbers, in organs altered by disease, then the possibility of proving that these micrococci were the cause of the disease would be rendered much more difficult, perhaps indeed quite hopeless. We must therefore enquire how far the assertion in question is correct.

Lostorfer, Nedsvetzki, and Béchamp discovered small moving particles in normal human blood. Lostorfer calls these bodies micrococci, and asserts that he has traced their further development to sarcinae. Nedsvetzki has given to these particles the name of hemococci, and he considers them as identical with the bodies described by Béchamp. Béchamp has in numerous papers expressed his views respecting the bodies called by him microzymes. He found these bodies in almost all animal fluids, and, from experiments which he carried on in conjunction with Estor, he concludes that microzymes can, through their physiological activity, bring about the coagulation of the blood, and the lactic, acetic, and alcoholic fermentations; that they are also active in the transformation of glycogen in the liver, in the development of the embryo in hens' eggs during hatching, and in all possible processes in the animal body. That Béchamp looks on his microzymes as intimately related to bacteria is apparent, because, according to him, the microzymes in the intestine below the iliocecal valve change normally into bacteria; and at diseased spots of the small intestine—as, e.g., where a tapeworm is attached—bacteria develop immediately from microzymes.

J. Lueders, Bettelheim, Richardson, and, later, Kolaczek and Letzerich, also belive that they have seen bacteria in normal human blood.

Tiegel and Billroth have attempted in an indirect manner to demonstrate the existence of bacteria in normal animal tissues. They introduced, with certain precautions, fresh portions of muscle, liver etc., into melted paraffin. The tissues thus enclosed in an air-tight case were, after the lapse of some time, examined to ascertain the presence or absence of bacteria. Numerous bacteria were found, and hence Billroth concludes that in most of the tissues of the body, in greater proportion indeed in the blood, spores of bacteria capable of development are present.

Objections have been urged against the experiments of Billroth and Tiegel, to the effect that the enclosure in paraffin does not protect against the entrance of bacteria, because cracks and fissures form in the paraffin on cooling, and even afterwards, as every one must have observed who has embedded objects in paraffin for microscopical examination.

When normal blood was tested by Pasteur, Burdon Sanderson, and Klebs, as to its power of causing development, by methods excluding all sources of error, negative results were obtained.

Opposed to the alleged direct observations of bacteria in normal blood are the statements of trustworthy microscopists such as Rindfleisch and Riess, who distinctly assert that the normal blood is free from bacteria, but that on the other hand, as Riess more especially pointed out, it contains small round bodies more or less numerous, which are most probably *débris* arising from the disintegration of white blood corpuscles, and which, on account of their resemblance to micrococci, have been confounded with them.

According to my own experience the examination of

blood, with the view of ascertaining the possible presence of bacteria, is excessively difficult, unless one makes use of the aids to be described afterwards, *viz.*, of staining and suitable illumination. Without the assistance derived from these methods it is in most cases impossible to distinguish the bodies so characteristically described by Riess, from true micrococci; and I can therefore easily imagine that, according as one wished to find that bacteria were present or absent, the granular constituents of the blood would be regarded as micrococci, or micrococci when present would be regarded as the remains of disintegrated white corpuscles. I have, however, on many occasions examined normal blood and normal tissues by means which prevent the possibility of overlooking bacteria, or of confounding them with granular masses of equal size; and I have never, in a single instance, found organisms. *I have therefore come to the conclusion that bacteria do not occur in the blood, nor in the tissues of the healthy living body either of man or of the lower animals.*

On the other hand, the following objections which have been raised against the assumption that bacteria are the causes of traumatic infective diseases seem to me to be well founded. In order to establish this assertion (that they are the cause of traumatic infective diseases) it would be absolutely necessary *that the presence of bacteria in these diseases be proved without exception, and further that the conditions as regards their number and distribution be such as to afford a complete explanation of the symptoms.* For, if in some cases of a certain form of infective diseases bacteria be found, while in others of like nature they are absent, and if further the bacteria present be so few in number that is is impossible that a severe disease or a fatal termination could thereby be produced, then of course nothing remains but to regard the irregular appearance of the bacteria as depending on chance, and their small number as insufficient as an only cause of the disease in question; in other words it is necessary, to assume the presence of some other agency. The observations hitherto made with regard to the occurrence of bacteria in traumatic infective diseases do not, however, in reality fulfil the necessary conitions.

On account of the difficulties, before alluded to, attending the demonstration of bacteria in the blood, and more especially in the tissues, many of the above-mentioned statements have been received with considerable suspicion,—whether always with justice must remain uncertain,—for the earlier method of investigation is in most cases a groping in the dark, and its results cannot be otherwise than very doubtful.

But, apart from the uncertain results of much laborious work on the bacteria of traumatic infective diseases, the literature of the subject contains a number of statements as to complete absence of bacteria in undoubted instances of these affections. It would serve no good purpose to enumerate here all these negative statements, as their value is even less than that of the positive. One or two may, however, be mentioned as illustrations.

Birch-Hirschfeld states that negative results with regard to the occurrence of bacteria, especially in cases of spreading (fulminanter) gangrene and putrid infection, are by no means rare.

Orth, after mentioning that micrococci are present in the blood, particularly in septic diseases, puerperal fever, and diphtheria, expressly states that they are by no means constantly found.

Eberth, who has convinced himself of the frequent occurrence of bacteria in septicemia, does not regard that disease as caused by an infection of the blood by bacteria alone, because he has seen the most distinct septicemia without the presence of bacteria in the blood.

Weigert speaks thus of the occurrence of bacteria:- "However certainly one may refer the development of some diseases to the action of bacteria, yet, on the other hand, there exist a far greater number of morbid processes which would theoretically be considered as mycotic, but in which a conscientious observer cannot discover any traces of bacteric agency."

I have intentionally taken these extracts from the writings of those authors who have shown, by having sometimes obtained positive results, that they understood how to overcome the great difficulties connected with the discovery of bacteria, and whose statements, therefore, with regard to their frequent absence in cases of traumatic infective diseases, deserve especial consideration.

The second circumstance, which seems to me of essential importance in considering this question, *viz.*, that in almost all cases in which bacteria were found the number was strikingly small, has as yet received too little attention.

We do not yet know with certainty how many bacteria are necessary to produce in man definite symptoms of disease, or what proportion per kilogram of an animal is required to cause a fatal result. Undoubtedly some definite relations, varying at most only within narrow limits in consequence of differences in the affected individuals, must exist between the number of pathogenic bacteria and their effect, *i.e.*, the symptoms of the disease. The only disease which may with certainty be affirmed to be of bacteric origin, *viz.*, anthrax, gives us sufficient ground for this supposition. Small animals die after inoculation with anthracic blood more quickly than do large ones, and in animals of the same genus and of like size the fatal termination occurs later when the fluid used contains but few spores or bacilli capable of development than when it is rich in them. The explanation of these facts can only be this, that to kill, *e.g.*, a sheep, more bacilli are requisite than to kill a mouse; that bacilli or spores being introduced in about equal quantities into both animals at the time of inoculation, the number of bacilli necessary to cause the death of the mouse, being small, is reached more quickly than the larger quantity requisite to kill the sheep; and further, that in animals of the same species the fatal number of bacilli is longer in being attained when the spores introduced are few in number than when they are injected in large amount.

We learn further from the study of anthrax that the number of bacilli present in the blood must be enormously large before death results. In relapsing fever also, the relations of which to the spirocheta discovered by Obermeier are as yet not sufficiently known, but which nevertheless, on account of the absolutely constant occurrence of these organisms during every attack of fever, must be regarded as in all probability a parasitic disease, the same relation exists between the number of bacteria in the blood and the symptoms of the disease. Of course it must not be assumed that all pathogenic bacteria behave alike in this respect, but it may be concluded from the analogy of anthrax and relapsing fever that a considerable number of bacteria is necessary to produce symptoms. But the observations which have been hitherto made with regard to bacteria in traumatic infective diseases do not in most cases show that this requirement is fulfilled. Mention is generally made of large masses of micrococci on the surface of the wound, which collections, however, can only be regarded as of importance in large wounds; while in internal organs only miliary colonies of bacteria have been found, and these often in small numbers. This result bears no relation whatever to the almost incredible numbers of bacilli in the blood in anthrax. It is therefore only observations which show the presence of a large number of bacteria which can be regarded as affording sufficient explanation of the morbid appearances. Statements no doubt exist with regard to the occurrence of micrococci in the blood and tissues, but unfortunately it is precisely these assertions which for the reasons above-mentioned are the least satisfactory.

A third point remains to be urged against the cogency of the facts known as to the occurrence of bacteria. It is this, that morphologically the bacteria found in the most diverse traumatic infective diseases, and also in other infective processes not in any way connected with wounds, are strikingly similar.

It must at once strike anyone who studies the literature on the subject of bacteria that the two best known bacteric diseases, anthrax and relapsing fever, are notable for the well-marked and easily recognisable form of their parasites; but that in almost all other infective diseases, which apparently stand in close relation with micro-organisms, there exists a remarkable agreement as regards the form, size, arrangement, and color of the bacteria observed. But, for the very reason that in relapsing fever and in anthrax such marked differences in this respect exist, the similarity of the other pathogenc bacteria must awaken distrust as to the accuracy of the observations and of the assumption that diseases which seem to bear so little relation to each other should, nevertheless, be produced by the same organisms.

Such doubts have been often expressed.

Thus, for example, Birch-Hirschfeld says, "the morphological characters of the bacteria found in pyemia, diphtheria, small-pox, and cholera are so similar that the idea naturally arises that identical organisms are being dealt with. But, if this were the case, it would follow that no specific significance could be attributed to these forms. They have to be regarded merely as parasites of the disease and not as its cause."

To the diseases mentioned by Birch-Hirschfeld a number of others may be added in which micrococci, indistinguishable from each other, were found. Such are erysipelas, puerperal fever, mycosis of the navel in newly-born infants, hospital gangrene, intestinal mycosis, endocarditis (with or without acute articular rheumatism), primary infective periostitis, scarlet fever, rinderpest, and pleuro-pneumonia. It is, however, impossible that all these diseases can be produced by one and the same parasite, and we must therefore assume either that the micrococci are in reality always the same, in which case they would be merely associated, as an accidental complication, with the diseases enumerated, or that the micrococci—though, on account of their small size, very similar, and indeed apparently the same—are nevertheless different in nature, and consequently capable of giving rise to these diverse results.

In order to show that this latter assumption does not lie beyond the range of possibility, Cohn has called attention to the apparently similar external and microscopical nature of the sweet and bitter almond, while a great difference exists between them in physiological action. And Virchow, in the same sense, has referred to the fact that one cannot say with regard to the formative cells of the egg and numerous pathological growths what structure will be developed from them, although as compared with bacteria these are truly gigantic in size.

The possibility that the micrococci, in spite of their uniform appearance, may be in reality different, and the true contagium vivum of the disease in which they are found, must assuredly be admitted. But as a practical groundwork, more especially with regard to the prophylaxis and treatment of the traumatic infective diseases, the *possibility* of a contagium vivum does not help us much; we require conclusive evidence that this or that micrococcus, definite in nature and always recognisable under varying conditions by certain characteristics, is the only cause of the disease in question. So long as the existence of a contagium vivum is only a matter of possibility, or even of probability, we can not avoid taking into consideration in all our investigations, the likewise possible presence of other causes of disease, *e.g.*, of the unknown x of a lifeless disease ferment never yet demonstrated, of the y of the genus epidemicus, and of other unknown quantities. It is, however, apparent that the solution of the problem proposed would thus be rendered in the highest degree difficult, and would be endangered through numerous sources of error—in fact might probably be quite impossible.

If we now look at the facts brought together and the remarks on them, we come to this conclusion, that the frequent discovery of micro-organisms in traumatic infective diseases and the experimental investigations made in connection with them render the parasitic nature of these diseases probable; but that a thoroughly satisfactory proof has not yet been furnished, and can only be so when we have succeeded in finding the parasitic micro-organisms in all cases of the disease in question, when we can further demonstrate their presence in such numbers and distribution that all the symptoms of the disease may thus find their explanation, and finally when we have established the existence, for every individual traumatic infective disease, of a micro-organism with well-marked morphological characters.

Is it then possible to fulfill these conditions in any degree? or have we now, as many microscopists assume, reached the limit of the capabilities of our optical appliances?

This question will, indeed, have often enough occurred to every one who has specially devoted himself to the examination of pathogenic bacteria. It has also occupied my attention greatly, and at once forced itself on me when I commenced these general investigations on bacteria, and saw what great advantages might be obtained by a proper use of microscopic aids in recognising and distinguishing the smallest forms of bacteria with their spores and cilia.

Since that time I have unremittingly attempted to improve the means for the discovery of pathogenic bacteria in animal tissues, because I could not get rid of the idea that the doubtful results of investigations with regard to the parasites of infective diseases might have their foundation in the incompleteness of the methods used.

I shall now, before passing on to the experimental part of my work, describe the method which I have finally adopted as most suitable, and which has led me to positive results.

METHOD OF INVESTIGATION.

Von Recklinghausen's method, in which advantage is taken of the property bacteria have of resisting acids and alkalies, a power not possessed by animal tissues, is still used by most microscopists. If a group of extremely minute particles, characterised by the uniform size of its component granules, does not alter either in acetic acid or in caustic potash or soda, and if there are other grounds for suspecting the presence of bacteria, the problem may then generally be regarded as solved, and the micrococcus found. An error cannot easily occur here, because the appearance of a closely-packed heap of micrococci, the so-called zooglea, is so characteristic that he who has once had this picture stamped on his mind will recognise it at any time. Incomparably more difficult are the circumstances when bacteria—and this particularly applies to micrcocci—are scattered through the tissues either singly or in small loose groups. For now the characteristic appearance of zooglea no longer aids the observer, and one has solely to depend on the resisting power of the bacteria to alkalies and acids, because there are a great number of minute particles present in tissues altered by disease which may very easily be confounded with organisms. This method, however, of distinguishing by reagents soon shows itself unreliable. Many bacteria, more especially those which are extremely minute, are as readily destroyed or altered by these reagents as are the animal tissues; and, in the latter, indefinite granules often occur which are not removed by acids or alkalies. This method, therefore, cannot do more than demonstrate zooglea masses.

An attempt has been made to obtain better results

by the use of staining fluids, and the one which has been chiefly recommended, simultaneously indeed by several observers, is hematoxylin. This is a great step in advance of the first method, especially when it is used in the same way as for staining nuclei. But it is very incomplete, inasmuch as the hematoxylin does not stain rod-shaped bacteria at all, and only colors the spherical so slightly as to prevent their certain recognition when isolated. The use of hematoxylin is a great advance on the simple examination of the object with reagents, because when stained the bacteric masses are very much more evident than the rest of the tissue, and one is thus less likely to overlook them or to confound them with other objects. This method, which does not of course exclude examination with reagents, also possesses this great advantage, that the stained preparations can be preserved in Canada balsam, and can thus be used at any time for comparison with others.

Staining with aniline dyes has yielded still better results than staining with hematoxylin. So far as I know, aniline staining, as a means of demonstrating bacteria in animal tissues, was first employed by Weigert. His method, by the communication of which he has laid me under the greatest obligation, is as follows:

The objects for examination are first hardened in alcohol. The sections made from these are allowed to lie for a considerable time in a pretty strong watery solution of methyl-violet. They are then treated with dilute acetic acid, the water removed by alcohol, cleared up in oil of cloves, and mounted in Canada balsam.

Instead of methyl-violet other aniline dyes, *e.g.*, fuchsin, aniline-brown, etc., may be used in the same manner.

This is, of course, only a general outline of the method; for the individual tissues, and more especially the different forms of bacteria show so great a variety of result from such treatment that it would be impossible to lay down rules which would be universal and which would apply to every case. For many objects fuchsin is best adapted; for others the methyl colors are more suitable. Among these latter there exists such a difference in the staining power that the sections must lie in one solution only a few minutes, in another several hours. One must therefore work with a large number of sections at once, and test them as to the most suitable staining material and as to the time required for the staining. The experienced investigator will find out after a few attempts what is the most suitable material. The strength of the acetic acid solution is not of much consequence. The best solution is one containing only a small percentage of the acid, and it is well not to allow it to act too long. The other manipulations, such as the removal of water, clearing up and mounting, are exactly the same as in the preparation of other microscopic specimens. One must avoid leaving the sections too long in alcohol or oil of cloves, otherwise the staining material will be washed out by these fluids.

In preparations which are treated in this way only the nuclei of the cells and the bacteria are seen to be stained. The latter as a rule take up the aniline color, and, in fact, their staining is so marked that the individual bacteria can be much more distincly recognised than after the use of hematoxylin. It is thus very easy to recognise with certainty isolated large bacteria, *e.g.*, bacillus anthracis, in the most diverse tissues, when the preparations have been treated with aniline dyes. As soon, however, as we have to deal with smaller bacteria the method yields uncertain results, and, finally, with the smallest forms becomes quite useless.

In order now to understand how it is that small objects, notwithstanding intense staining, cannot be distinguished at all in the animal tissues, or only with difficulty, one must clearly comprehend the component parts of the microscopic picture. Let us for the sake of simplicity consider only the case of a section of an animal tissue mounted in Canada balsam in the ordinary manner.

If all the constituents of this tissue were colorless, and had the same refractive power as Canada balsam, nothing whatever would be seen. This is, however, not the case. Fibres, nuclei, and many other portions of tissue, differ from Canada balsam in their refractive power, and thus by diffraction of the rays of light passing through them an image consisting of lines and shadows is developed which may be termed shortly the structure picture.

Let us now suppose a second case, namely, that portions of the tissue, *e.g.,* cell nuclei and bacteria, were colored, then the conditions would appear as follows:- With equal refractive power of tissue and Canada balsam, nuclei and bacteria would be alone visible, and that on account of the staining material with which they are impregnated; we should therefore have a pure color picture quite different from the structure picture produced by fibres, membranes, etc., but in part coinciding with that, as for example in the case of the nuclei. For the best possible demonstration of bacteria, which are particularly intensely stained by aniline dyes, such a pure color picture would certainly be the most suitable. The unavoidable structure picture, however, interferes with this.

Large colored objects, as for example bacillus anthracis, are but little affected in this way as regards distinctness. Only when the section as a whole or when portions of the tissue are very thick (*e.g.,* the intestinal mucous membrane in its whole thickness) may the structure picture become so preponderant, the number of the shadows placed above each other so great, that even the large bacillus anthracis can be no longer easily distinguished. When, however, the bacteria are smaller and thinner, and thus take up less pigment, the bad effects of the structure picture are much more apparent; a broad dark line may then so overshadow some bacteria that their color picture becomes too weak to make an impression on the eye. In very thin sections, and in those tissues whose structure consists of but few lines and shadows (*e.g.*, subcutaneous cellular tissue, cornea, etc.), very small bacteria may indeed be distinguished with some accuracy. Ultimately, however, a point is reached where the bacteria are so small that the tiny stained granules and threads are hidden and rendered invisible by even the faintest structure shadows. In some particularly favorable places one may indeed suspect the presence of bacteria, but a sure recognition of them and distinction of their form and size is no longer possible.

This difficulty was experienced by me in these investigations. In materials stained in the manner to be subsequently described I easily found large bacteria, and also smaller ones, particularly when they formed accumulations in the glomeruli of the kidney. But now the thought arose, must not bacteria be present also in the spleen and in the capillaries of the lung? For the spleen was swollen and the blood from the left side of the heart which had just passed through the lungs produced on inoculation on another animal the same fatal disease and the same extremely fine granular accumulations of micrococci in the glomeruli as in the first animal. But in spite of the greatest pains the suspected bacteria could not be found. In the septicemia of mice, which, as I shall afterwards show, is in the highest degree infective, I was quite unable to demonstrate any micro-organisms. I thus obtained the same incomplete results as the investigators who had formerly studied traumatic infective diseases.

At that time, in attempting to photograph bacteria embedded in Canada balsam, my attention was directed to the fact that the microscopic image consists of a structure and of a color picture, and I found that the structure picture can be markedly increased or weakened by the nature of the illumination. In this there is nothing new. Every microscopist knows what is the effect of the diaphragm placed below a preparation. A narrow diaphragm not only darkens the field of vision, but makes the structure of the object more apparent; a wide one, on the other hand, renders the whole picture clearer, but makes portions of the structure more indistinct. The difference between narrow and wide diaphragms becomes still more strikingly apparent, when, as in photography, not merely a concave mirror, but a lens or condenser, is used for the illumination, and for this reason, that—particularly with a condenser of short focal distance—the cone of rays illuminating the object is capable of much greater variation. When a narrow diaphragm is placed before the condenser the base of this cone becomes so small that the whole cone may almost be regarded as a bundle of parallel rays of light. The larger, however, the opening of the diaphragm is, so much the larger does the radius of the base of the cone become, its length still remaining the same, but far surpassing as regards the ratio of breadth of base to length that obtained by an ordinary concave mirror. If now we examine a microscopic preparation with an illumination in which the cone of rays is at first narrow, but is gradually made broader, though always remaining of the same length, we shall at once see that—as indeed cannot be otherwise according to dioptrical laws—the structure picture resulting from diffraction, which picture was most marked when the narrowest diaphragm was used, becomes less and less apparent. In proportion, however, as the structure picture diminishes, does the color picture become more intense and sharply defined. Thus a method is indicated by which the effects of the structure picture may be in so far obviated that even the smallest stained bodies which are within the optical power of the instrument become distinctly discernible. That is to say, an illumination cone must be used of so wide a base that the appearances resulting from diffraction may be completely removed. I tried numerous different lenses and condensers without finding one which removed the structure picture sufficiently till I fell in with the illumination apparatus suggested by Abbe and made by Carl Zeiss in Jena, which I found to answer my purpose in every way.

This apparatus consists of a combination of lenses, the focal point of which is only some millimetres distant from the lowest lens of the objective system. When this compound lens is placed in the opening of the stage of the microscope, a little deeper than the level of the stage, the focal point coincides with the object to be examined, and the latter thus obtains the most favorable illumination. The angle of aperture is so large that on escaping from the condenser into water the outermost rays are inclined at an angle of almost 60 degree with the axis, the whole effective pencil possessing thus an angle of aperture of 120 degrees—a greater angle than is given any other condenser. The rays of light are conveyed to this system of lenses by a mirror which is only moveable round a fixed point in the axis of the microscope. Between mirror and lens, and near the focal point of the former, is a support for diaphragms, which are moveable both laterally and circularly, so that the direction of the illuminating pencil may be altered in any way desired. By the use of diaphragms with larger or smaller apertures the aperture of the pencil may be modified from the largest to the smallest attainable with the apparatus. By lateral displacement of the diaphragm without movement of the mirror, oblique illumination can be obtained, and by shutting off the centre of the opening in the diaphragm the middle of the pencil can be got rid of.

By means of this apparatus the connection before described as existing between structure and color picture can be made evident in the most simple and convincing manner. Let us suppose that a section of a tissue containing very few bacteria stained with aniline is to be examined by the aid of Abbe's illumination apparatus. At first a diaphragm with a narrow opening is used. The illumination of the object is then about the same as in illumination with a concave mirror and medium cylinder diaphragm. The field of vision, therefore, appears pretty dark, the structure of the tissues is distinctly marked, more especially do the nuclei of the cells strike the eye as dark bodies with a but slightly pronounced staining of a dark blue or red color; as regards the smaller granules one cannot ascertain at all with certainty whether they are stained or not, nor can it be made out whether these particles are bacteria or constituents of the tissue. Now let diaphragms with a constantly increasing size of aperture be used one after another. The picture gradually alters in a most striking manner. The dark outlines of the cells and cell nuclei, and the sharp lines of the elastic fibres, walls of vessels and the like become pale and ill-defined; the shadows of the bodies present above and below the visual level disappear more and more; many of the points and granules previously seen, which might possibly have been considered to be bacteria, disappear completely, while, on the other hand, small objects which formerly appeared black are observed to be colored, and the color of the nuclei becomes more distinct. The field of vision at the same time becomes clearer. The more the lines and shadows and all the differences between clear and dark disappear, so much the more sharply and strongly do all colored objects stand out, and so much the more distinctly can one recognise their outlines and minute differences in tone and strength of color. Finally, when the last diaphragm has been removed, all the outlines of mere structure have disappeared, the field of vision is uniformly cleared, and only colored objects can be seen. The clearer the light which one selects for illumination (the best light is that from white clouds illuminated by the sun), so much the brighter and more sharply-defined do these objects appear. It then becomes easy to distinguish among the stained bodies the bacteria of which nothing could previously be seen, or which appeared as dark indefinite granules, rods, etc. And this is the more easy, as there is almost nothing stained but nuclei and bacteria. The outlines and size of the bacteria can thus be recognised, and by their uniform appearance they can be distinguished with certainty from other stained granular masses—*e.g.*, broken down cell nuclei.

A very simple arrangement may serve to demonstrate the action of Abbe's illumination apparatus. This consists of a small glass vessel filled with Canada balsam, in which small colored and colorless glass beads are placed. Here, therefore, conditions are present similar to those in a stained preparation mounted in Canada balsam. The colored beads correspond to the stained nuclei or bacteria, the colorless to the parts of the tissue which are unstained. If one looks through the vessel on to a broad sheet of paper placed immediately below it and brightly illuminated with daylight, the colorless beads cannot be seen, while the colored, on the other hand, are distinct and sharply defined. If now the paper be placed at a greater distance from the glass—that is to say, if the pencil illuminating the pearls becomes longer and its angle of aperture smaller, its base remaining the same—the same appearance occurs as when with Abbe's illumination apparatus diaphragms with smaller openings are used in succession, the colorless beads begin to be gradually visible, acquire more distinct and darker outlines, while the colored ones become darker; and, finally, the two kinds can hardly be distinguished, the colored becoming comletely masked by the colorless. Microscopists who examine for the first time preparations highly magnified and illuminated with Abbe's apparatus without a diaphragm are generally struck with the unusual appearance, the field being too bright and confused, although the outlines of the colored objects are sharply defined. Such observers have been accustomed to the dark field obtained by ordinary illumination with a concave mirror, and they accordingly feel the want of the outline of the tissue structure. For them it is expedient not to dispense entirely with the diaphragm, but to increase the size of the aperture until the stained object under examination appears sufficiently distinct; there will then remain quite enough of the structure picture to enable them to make out the relations of the tissue to the colored objects.

It is well in general to use, in addition to the examination of the bacteria by means of the pure color picture, other methods of investigation, such as the observation of the structure of the tissue at the same time, and the examination of the fresh object, with or without the use of alkalies and acids; and I may here expressly mention that I have often made use of these chemical tests as a check, in addition to my chief method of examination.

Although the aniline staining and the use of Abbe's illumination apparatus so markedly facilitate the investigation of pathogenic bacteria, we must not imagine that all difficulties are thus removed and all sources of error shut out. On the contrary, a considerable amount of practice is necessary before one is in a position rightly to utilise these very efficient means. Some of the difficulties which most frequently occur may be shortly alluded to.

As even isolated bacteria do not escape the observing eye, it not unfrequently happens that one meets with organisms which are derived from the fluids used for staining, washing, etc. For even distilled water is almost never free from bacteria. One, however, very soon learns to distinguish these bacteria from others, and to recognise them immediately as accidental impurities.

Further, incipient putrefaction must be suspected whenever isolated bacteria are found in the superficial layers of organs. But the bacteria appearing in putrefaction, at first generally large bacilli, are so characteristic that they are not easily confounded with the pathogenic bacteria. Nevertheless, it is well to be cautious in drawing conclusions from preparations already containing putrefactive bacteria; indeed it is best not to use such tissues at all. In order to eliminate every risk to confusion with the putrefactive organisms, and to exclude the idea that in arrangement and number the pathogenic bacteria may have undergone alterations after death, I have only used objects for examination which were placed in absolute alcohol immediately after the death of the animal, though in a few cases a delay of some hours has occurred. Consequently I have never found putrefactive bacteria in the preparations obtained in this way. On the other hand, I have seldom failed to find them in preparations obtained from human subjects, although the *post mortem* examination was made ten to twenty hours after death.

I must here draw attention to a remarkable variety of cells which might give rise to confusion with small masses of micrococcus. These are the so-called plasma cells, described and figured by Ehrlich; flat cells, for the most part situated on the external coats of blood-vessels, and consisting of a round heap of granules grouped around a nucleus. Their behavior with respect to aniline staining is exactly the opposite of that of all other cells. In the latter only the nucleus is stained; in the plasma cells, on the other hand, only the finely granular plasma is colored, the nucleus remaining unstained. Now as the granules have exactly the size of many micrococci, the plasma cell presents the appearance of a small micrococcus colony, more especially when the nucleus is indistinct or has disappeared. But the granules are commonly of unequal size. This fact, taken along with the presence of a nucleus and the results of comparision with other similar cells, enables the diagnosis to be easily made. In human tissues these plasma cells are not very abundant, but they occur in great numbers in mice, particularly in the skin of the ear.

If it be wished to exclude entirely all possibility of confusing bacteria with portions of animal tissues, or if it be desired to render the number and distribution of the bacteria in an organ more evident, then the following method may be made use of:- After staining with aniline, the sections are treated with a weak solution of carbonate of potash, instead of with acetic acid. By this means the nuclei and plasma cells—indeed as a rule all animal tissues—lose again the coloring matter, and the bacteria alone remain stained. Large sections, in which bacteria only are stained by the method just described, form splendid objects for affording a general view.

In microscopical *technique* staining methods play an important part, and many of the most valuable discoveries already made have been obtained by their help. But the full benefit which staining affords in microscopic work can only, as my investigations show, be completely obtained by making use also of a suitable apparatus for illumination.

This has not yet, so far as I am aware, been taken advantage of, and I do not therefore consider it superfluous to recommend my method of illumination for other microscopical investigations in which it is desired to differentiate very small stained elements from others.

With regard to the method of using Abbe's apparatus, I must draw attention to the fact that a sharply-defined picture can only be obtained by the use of such objective systems as have all the zones of the objective aperture properly corrected. The objective systems made by Zeiss are tested by means of Abbe's condenser as to the correctness of the individual zones, especially of the marginal ones. These, and more especially the new oil systems constructed after the designs of Abbe, are therefore thoroughly adapted for the observation of color pictures. In other systems which I have tried from this point of view, the marginal zones were almost always insufficiently corrected. The only other lenses with which I have obtained well-defined color pictures were made by Siebert and Kraft.

ARTIFICIAL TRAUMATIC INFECTIVE DISEASES.

I. Septicemia in Mice.

Mice are especially adapted for experiments on infective diseases, as I previously found in my investigations on anthrax. I therefore attempted to produce artificial traumatic infective diseases in these animals by the use of the method which was followed by Coze, Feltz, Davaine, etc.

Accordingly putrid fluids, *e.g.*, putrefying blood, putrid meat infusion, etc., were injected under the skin of the back in mice. The result of such an injection differs much according to the nature of the putrid fluid, and according to the quantity which is introduced. Blood and meat infusion, which have putrefied for a long time, appear to act less injuriously than fluids which have putrefied for a few days only. Of these latter fluids, as, for instance, of blood which has not putrefied too long, five drops is sufficient to kill a mouse within a short time In this case marked symptoms may be observed in the animal immediately after the injection. It becomes restless, running about constantly, but showing great weakness and uncertainty in all its movements; it refuses food, the respiration becomes irregular and slow, and death takes place in four to eight hours.

In such a case the greater part of the fluid injected is found in the subcutaneous cellular tissue of the back in much the same condition as before it was injected. It contains bacteria of the most diverse forms, irregularly mixed together, and as numerous as when examined before injection. No inflammation can be observed in the neighborhood of the place of injection. The internal organs are also unaltered. If blood taken from the right auricle be introduced into another mouse no effect is produced. Bacteria cannot be found in any of the internal organs, nor in the blood of the heart.

An infective disease has therefore not been produced as the result of the injection. On the other hand, there can be no ooubt that the death of the animal was due to the soluble poison, sepsin, which has been shown by the researches of Bergmann, Panum, and various other investigators, to exist in putrid blood. The animal has accordingly died not from an infective disease, but simply from the effects of a chemical poison.

This supposition is confirmed by the fact that when less fluid is introduced into the animal, the symptoms of poisoning which follow are less marked, and are quite absent when one or at most two drops have been injected. After the use of such small quantities of blood, mice often remain permanently without any morbid symptoms. But a third of them, on an average, become ill after the lapse of about twenty-four hours, during which time they have remained apparently healthy. The symptoms which are then present are characteristic and constant, and are in no case preceded by any of the symptoms of poisoning previously described.

Before I describe these symptoms, I must mention that the infection may succeed when even less than one drop of putrid fluid has been used. The less the amount employed in the first instance, the fewer are the animals affected; for example, of twelve animals inoculated in the ordinary manner with one-twentieth to one-tenth of a drop each, only one was successfully infected.

The first symptom in the infected animals is an increased secretion from the conjuctiva. The eye appears dull, and a whitish mucus collects between the lids, and finally completely glues them together. At the same time lassitude sets in, the animal moves little and languidly; as a rule it sits quite still, with its back much bent and its extremities closely drawn up. It then ceases to eat; its respirations become slower, weakness increases more and more, and death comes on almost imperceptibly. Convulsions never precede it (they always do so in anthrax). After death the animal still remains in the sitting posture with its back strongly bent, while, on the other hand, a mouse which has died from anthrax is always found lying on its back or side with its stiffened extremities fully extended. Thus by the position of the body after death, a fatal result produced by the inoculation of putrefying blood is at once distinguished from that occasioned by inoculation with the material of anthrax. The death of mice infected with putrefying blood occurs forty to sixty hours after the inoculation.

On post-mortem examination there is found at the place of injection or inoculation slight oedema of the subcutaneous cellular tissue. This, however, is often absent, and the internal organs, with the exception of considerable swelling of the spleen, appear quite unaltered.

If one now takes a very small quantity (*e.g.*, one-tenth of a drop) of the fluid of the subcutaneous oedema, or of blood from the heart of such an animal, and inoculates another mouse, exactly the same diseased symptoms occur in the latter animal after the same lapse of time and in the same order as in the former, and death takes place in about fifty hours. From this second animal a third may be infected in like manner, and so on through as many successive animals as one pleases. I have performed these experiments on fifty-four mice and have always obtained the same result. Of these, seventeen inoculations were made in succession; of the others the series of successive infections were less extended.

The certainty with which the infective material can be carried from one mouse to another is here even greater than in anthrax. In the latter, in order to obtain constant results the material for inoculation must be taken from the spleen, because the blood of mice affected with anthrax often contains very few bacilli.

In the disease of the mouse produced by putrefying blood it is, on the other hand, a matter of indifference from which organ the material used for inoculation is taken, and even the smallest amount will produce an effect with certainty. It is sufficient, in order to bring about the death of the animal within about fifty hours, to pass the point of a scalpel, which has been in contact with the infected blood, over a small wound of the skin. I have often performed the following experiment:- The subcutaneous tissue of a mouse which had died after inoculation on the tail was touched with a knife on the opposite part of the body to that which had been inoculated, *viz.*, on the head, and with this instrument a small scratch was made on the ear of another mouse. The animals thus infected died, without exception, of the same disease.

This disease is therefore undoubtedly an infective disease, which, from the result of the post-mortem examination, must be called septicemia.

The great virulence which the blood of septicemic mice possesses leads us to suspect that if this disease be a parasitic affection brought about by bacteria, the parasites must be present in the blood, and that in great numbers. But in my first investigations I entirely failed to discover bacteria in the septicemic blood. Not till I used Abbe's condenser did I succeed in demonstrating their presence with complete certainty, in spite of their minute size.

I examined the blood by a method which I have described in another place, and which in this case yielded good results (by drying it on a cover glass and then staining with methyl violet).

The blood of the animals which became ill after *injection* of one to ten drops of putrefying blood was found to contain as a rule different varieties of bacteria in small numbers, micrococci, and large and small bacilli. If, however, the animals died after *inoculation* with putrefying or septicemic blood, small bacilli alone appeared in the blood. This result was invariable, and the bacilli were always in large numbers. These bacilli, which lie singly or in small groups between the red blood corpuscles, have a length of .8 to 1 mikrm. Their thickness, which cannot be measured accurately, but only approximately estimated is about .1 to .2 mikrm.

One can often see the bacilli in septicemic blood attached to each other in pairs, either in straight lines or forming an obtuse angle. Chains of three or four bacilli also occur, but they are rare. They show at first sight a great resemblance to small needle-like crystals, but that they are undoubtedly vegetable bodies is evident, for when septicemic blood is placed on a concave slide and kept in an incubation apparatus the bacilli grow in the same manner as the bacilli of anthrax, not forming, however, long threads like the latter, but dense masses which consist of isolated bacilli. In some cases I have also seen spores appear in the bacilli. I could not, from want of time, study further the conditions of life and of vegetation of these septicemic bacilli. I intend, however, at some future period to investigate these. Without the use of staining materials the bacilli can only with extreme difficulty be recognised in fresh blood, even when one is familiar with their form, and I have not been able to obtain any certain evidence as to whether they move or not. Their relation to the white blood corpuscles is peculiar. They penetrate into these and multiply in their interior. One often finds that there is hardly a single white corpuscle in the interior of which bacilli cannot be seen. Many corpuscles contain isolated bacilli only; others have thick masses in their interior, the nucleus being still recognisable; while in others the nucleus can be no longer distinguished; and finally, the corpuscle may become a cluster of bacilli breaking up at the margin—the origin of which one could not have explained had there been no opportunity of seeing all the intermediate steps between the intact white corpuscle and these masses.

Starting from the point of inoculation, one can easily see the path by which the bacilli have penetrated into the body. In the subcutaneous cellular tissue in the neighborhood of the inoculated spot they are very numerous, and at times accumulated in dense masses, as can be best observed in inoculations on the ear. They are more especially numerous on the surface of the cartilage of the ear, and they are here covered with a layer of lymph corpuscles. The latter are also present along with numerous red blood corpuscles in the loose cellular tissue.

The large number of red blood corpuscles which pass out of the vessels leads to the conclusion that an alteration has taken place in the walls of these vessels, and thus it becomes extremely probable that the bacilli grow into the vessels and enter the circulation through spaces in their walls, which permitted the exit of the much larger red blood corpuscles. I have never found these bacilli in the lymphatic vessels. Even in the greatly enlarged lymphatic glands they can only be found in the capillary blood-vessels which run through these glands, not, however, in the lymph spaces. In the loose cellular tissue they often spread widely, and may reach from the ear to the mediastinum; from the back into the cellular tissue of the pelvis. I have not found them free in the cavities of the body. Their distribution in the blood-vessels can be best observed on the diaphragm, the vessels running on the border of the centrum tendineum being selected for investigation. The larger veins contain considerable numbers of bacilli pretty equally distributed, and also numerous small clusters developed in the white blood corpuscles. The bacilli which are free in the interior of the vessels are almost always arranged with their long axis in the direction of the blood-stream, and it is thus evident that they were placed in this position by the flowing blood, and after its stagnation have neither increased in number nor moved. In the capillaries the bacilli congregate, particularly at the points of division, but I have never yet seen a complete obstruction of the smaller vessels produced in this way. The inner wall of the arteries is often thickly beset with bacteria directed lengthwise.

In exactly the same manner are the bacilli distributed in the rest of the vascular system. In the examination of sections of lung, liver, kidney, and spleen, one meets everywhere with vessels containing free bacilli, and with white blood corpuscles with bacilli in their interior. The bacilli are not specially accumulated in the glomeruli; strangely enough, they are not more numerous in the greatly enlarged spleen than in other organs.

The whole morbid process has thus a great resemblance to anthrax. In both diseases the infective power of the blood is due to the bacili present in it; as soon as these disappear the disease can be no longer produced by inoculation with the blood. Both diseases are distinguished by the invariable development of exceedingly numerous bacilli. There can thus be no doubt that the bacilli of the septicemia described here possess the same significance as the bacilli of splenic fever, namely, that they are to be regarded as the ccontagium of this disease.

As anthrax can be successfully inoculated on different species of animals, I have also tried to infect other animals with the blood of septicemic mice. Having at my disposal only rabbits and field-mice, in addition to house-mice, I was compelled to limit my experiments to them. In both the attempt had a negative result. At first the rabbits were merely inoculated; afterwards the whole of the blood of a septicemic mouse was injected subcutaneously into one animal and finally, in addition to the blood, the lungs, heart, liver, kidneys, and spleen of a septicemic mouse were introduced under the skin of a rabbit.

These animals did not exhibit the slightest evidence of disease, either locally or constitutionally.

It seems peculiar that even field-mice, which resemble house-mice in size and which can hardly at the first glance be distinguished from them, should possess an immunity from this septicemia. These animals, however, are also much less sensitive to anthrax than house-mice. I attribute this result to differences in the blood of these closely allied animals, which strike one at once on investigation of fresh blood. In the blood of the house-mouse crystals seldom form, and when they do they shoot out only at the border of the drop of blood in the shape of small rectangular tablets and needles. The blood of the field-mouse, on the other hand, always undergoes changes very soon after removal from the body, all the red blood corpuscles becoming transformed into large regular hexagonal plates either immediately or after adjacent corpuscles have run together, and thus the drop becomes in a short time transformed into a crystalline pulp. But although one could not inoculate the septicemia of the house-mice on the two species of animals mentioned, yet it does not at all follow that all other species likewise possess an immunity from this disease. Many animals are in like manner insensible to anthrax, and it would certainly repay one to test as many different animals as possible with regard to their behavior towards this septicemia.

II. Progressive Destruction of Tissue (Gangrene) in Mice.

Occurring along with the septicemia bacillus just described I have sometimes found in mice, after the introduction of putrefying blood, a micrococcus in the neighborhood of the place of injection. This organism attracted my attention by its rapid increase and by its regular formation of chains. As a rule, when the animal dies of septicemia after about two days, none of the numerous forms of bacteria which were injected with the putrid blood can be discovered, except the septicemic bacilli, or it may be a few residual specimens growing with difficulty. It must therefore be supposed that none of the other bacteria injected at the same time find in the body of the living mouse a suitable soil, and that they therefore perish more or less quickly. My attention was thus at once arrested, when in some cases micrococci were found growing in unusual abundance and of constantly characteristic form. They were not present in the blood, and by inoculation with the blood the septicemic bacilli alone were transmitted. In order to test whether they could be inoculated, it was therefore necessary that the material used should be taken from the neighborhood of the place of injection. Inoculations carried out in this way were successful in producing both forms of disease and the virulence of the serum from the subcutaneous cellular tissue containing these micrococci was just as marked as that of the septicemic blood. When the point of a knife which had been well cleaned was merely brought in contact with the subcutaneous tissue at a spot about one centimetre and a half from the place of injection or inoculation, and when with this knife another animal was immediately inoculated, the inoculation was successful on every occasion. Septicemia was of course always produced at the same time, because the serum used contained also septicemic bacilli. The influence of these micrococci on animal tissues and their mode of spreading can be best traced on the ear of a mouse; and it is specially instructive to compare an ear on which only septicemic bacilli have been inoculated with one into which both the bacilli and the chain-like micrococci have been introduced. In the former ear the cellular tissue is full of red blood corpuscles and lymph cells, so that the bacilli can often be recognised only with great difficulty among the numerous cell nuclei. The other ear presents totally different appearances. Spreading out from the place of inoculation one can see extremely delicate and regular micrococcus chains, here pressed together so as to form thick masses, there arranged diffusely, the individual elements of these chains, as can be estimated from measurements of the longer ones having a diameter of .5 mikrm. These can be traced almost to the base of the ear, and throughout the part occupied by them all the tissues are markedly altered. As far as the microccoci extend, neither red blood corpuscles, nor nuclei of lymph or of connective tissue cells, can be seen. Even the extremely resistent cartilage cells, and the plasma cells so richly present in the mouse's ear and which are likewise characterised by great resisting power, are pale and scarcely recognisable. All the constituents of the tissue look as if they had been treated with caustic potash; they are dead, they have become gangrenous. Under these circumstances the bacteria develop all the more vigorously. The micrococci penetrate in numbers into the damaged blood and lymphatic vessels, and here and there they fill them so completely that the vessels appear as if injected. Among these the septicemic bacilli, no longer obscured by nuclei, are seen very distinctly in small groups which at times are very dense and remind one of the "Pilz figures" of the inoculated cornea. While the bacilli can be traced up to the root of the ear, and indeed beyond it, have at the same time increased enormously in the blood, and have ultimately caused the death of the animal, the micrococci, on the other hand, and the destructive process associated with them, have only extended during the same time (within about fifty hours) as far as the vicinity of the root of the ear. Their limit is sharply defined, as can be seen very well on a longitudinal section of the ear examined with a low magnifying power (twenty-five diameters). The upper part (*c*), from the tip to *b*, is gangrenous. The larger dark oval or round spots (*d*) are transverse sections of vessels containing masses of micrococci in their interior. The widely-distributed micrococcus chains cannot of course be recognised with this power. It is only in the lower fourth of the gangrenous region that they occur in denser groups, which can be seen as little dark points. Then all of a sudden at *b* appears a densely agglomerated mass of nuclei, forming as it were a wall against the invasion of the micrococci, and this is the limit up to which these organisms may be found. They do not extend, even in the blood-vessels, beyond this line. This wall of nuclei has no great breadth, and immediately beyond it comes the normal tissue. By the use of high magnifying powers it becomes apparent that the micrococci do not reach quite up to the nuclear layer. On the side directed towards the micrococci the nuclei are undergoing destruction. Numerous fragments of irregular shape, constantly becoming smaller, form the upper limit of the wall of nuclei, and when this region is reached, in examining the preparation, we may be sure that we are in the neighborhood of these organisms. There almost always remains between the last remnants of the nuclei and the micrococci a line of considerable breadth consisting only of gangrenous tissue, in which neither micrococci nor nuclei can be found. It is seldom that the micrococci extend into the disintegrating nuclear layer.

These appearances lead us to the conclusion that the action of these micrococci in causing the gangrene is somewhat as follows:- Introduced by inoculation into living animal tissues, they multiply, and as a part of their vegetative process they excrete soluble substances which get into the surrounding tissues by diffusion. When greatly concentrated, as in the neighborhood of the micrococci, this product of the organisms has such a deleterious action on the cells that these perish and finally completely disappear. At a greater distance from the micrococci the poison becomes diluted and acts less intensely, only producing inflammation and accumulation of lymph corpuscles. Thus it happens that the micrococci are always found in the gangrenous tissue, and that in extending they are preceded by a wall of nuclei which constantly melts down on the side directed towards them, while on the opposite side it is as constantly renewed by lymph corpuscles deposited afresh.

These observations refer to inoculations with fluid containing both micrococci and bacilli, and it might have been supposed that the septicemic bacilli were necessary forerunners of the micrococci, that they must to a certain extent prepare the way for them. I therefore attempted, by various means, to separate these parasites from each other. Thus, at one time a considerable quantity, at another only a little of the fluid was used for inoculation, or again it was taken at different distances from the point of inoculation, or, lastly, the parts of the body to which it was applied were varied as much as possible. But all this was of no avail. Either pure septicemia or septicemia along with progressive gangrene was obtained, never the latter alone. Chance led me to the proper method. A field-mouse—which, as I formerly pointed out, possesses an immunity from septicemia—was inoculated with septicemic bacilli and chain-like micrococci. The experiment was made in the expectation that neither parasite would develop. This expectation, however, was not fulfilled, for, though the bacilli as usual underwent no development, the micrococci increased and spread in exactly the same manner as has been described in the case of the house-mouse. Beginning at the place of inoculation on the root of the tail, the gangrene spread onwards along the back, passing deeply among the dorsal muscles, and downwards on both sides to the abdominal wall. The animal died three days after the inoculation. The parts affected with the gangrene were partially denuded of epidermis and hairs, and contained chain-like micrococci in extraordinary numbers. The same micrococci were also found on the surface of the abdominal organs, although there was no visible peritonitis. The blood and the interior of the organs were, on the other hand, quite free from them. From this animal other field-mice, and from these again house-mice in various successive series were subsequently injected, and always with the like result, *viz.,* that only chain-like micrococci and, in their train, progressive gangrene were obtained.

III. Spreading Abscess in Rabbits.

Coze and Feltz, Davaine, and many others have obtained in rabbits, by the injection of putrid blood, an infective septicemic disease. I have therefore repeated their experiments. I have not, however, succeeded in producing the effects described by Davaine, but I observed—what others who have made similar experiments on rabbits have already noticed—that in these animals the formation of an abscess constantly increasing in extent may occur in the subcutaneous cellular tissue without any general infection taking place. Such animals have at first no symptoms of disease; a flat lentiform hard infiltration at the seat of the injection is all that can be observed. After several days this hardness extends in all directions, chiefly downwards, especially towards the abdomen and anterior extremities. The animal at the same time emaciates and grows feeble, and dies in about twelve to fifteen days after the injection.

The post-mortem examination shows the presence, in the subcutaneous tissue, of extensive flat abscesses with cheesy contents; their walls bulge in various directions, though the whole remains a single cavity. There is also an extreme degree of emaciation, but no alteration in the peritoneum, intestine, kidneys, spleen, liver, heart, or lungs. In the blood the white corpuscles are greatly increased in number, but no bacteria can be found. The cheesy contents consist of a finely granular material, and scattered about in this are nuclei undergoing disintegration, but no bacteria can be definitely made out. Here, then, we have appearances similar to those often found in man, and much used as an argument against the parasitic nature of such morbid processes. I refer to abscesses resulting from phlegmonous inflammation which must be regarded as infective in their origin, but in which no micro-organisms have been found.

When, however, portions of these abscesses are

hardened and examined in sections, the surprising result is obtained that, though bacteria are not present in their contents, their walls are everywhere formed by a thin layer of micrococci united together into thick zooglea masses. These organisms are the smallest pathogenic micrococci which I have as yet observed. In some places I was fortunate enough to find them arranged in rows, and thus was able to measure them; and I ascertained that they were about .15 mikrm. in diameter (this is of course only an approximate measurement). From the form and character of the zooglea masses surrounding the abscesses it follows that these masses stand in the most intimate relation to the contents of the abscesses; that, in fact, the contents are constituted by the zooglea masses and the dead portions of tissue enclosed by them. This process takes place as follows:- The micrococci grow only in masses which, at the periphery of the more or less lentiform abscess, differ in arrangement from that which they assume on its upper, and more especially on its under surface. The margins of the abscess extend into the loose meshes of the subcutaneous cellular tissue, where the micrococci find the least resistance to their extension, and accordingly surround the abscess in thick cloud-like masses. The cellular tissue in the immediate vicinity is more or less richly filled with nuclei (*e*), between which one can see small isolated micrococcus colonies (*b*, *c*)—forerunners, in fact, of the main zooglea masses. The smallest colonies which can be found seem, from their general form and their radiating pointed processes, to be present in the canaliculi of the cellular tissue. I have not been able to demonstrate any connection between these micrococci and the connective tissue corpuscles, such as is observed in the inoculated cornea. On the wall of that part of the abscess which is directed towards the deeper structures, and where the dense fascia opposes the extension of the organisms, thy cannot develop so luxuriantly as at the borders of the abscess. On the contrary, the groups are here small and flattened, and only occasionally send out processes into the layers of the cellular tissue beneath, this tissue being in these situations interspersed with nuclei. An appearance which is quite characteristic can be observed when the zooglea masses are examined more closely. Their outer borders, by which I understand the parts of the zooglea masses which are directed towards the healthy cellular tissue are stained by the aniline fluid of an intense dark color, and the individual micrococci can be distinctly made out. In the small, and apparently young colonies more especially the micrococci are uniformly colored. But on passing towards the interior of the abscess the staining of the zooglea becomes less marked, the individual micrococci can be no longer accurately defined, they become more and more finely granular, and ultimately form an almost homogenous mass which no longer takes the coloring matter. Still nearer the abscess cavity are found pale unrecognisable masses derived from the zooglea intermixed with the detritus of the nuclei; and the cheesy contents of the abscess are composed of these two materials alone—the dead zooglea and the remnants of the nuclei, the former being present in largest amount. I have called these unstained masses *dead* zooglea for the following reasons:- In the first place, this explanation suggests itself so naturally, and seems such a necessary deduction from direct observation and from the comparison of the small micrococcus colonies found in process of growth with the large zooglea masses which have completed their vegetative life, that no special proof is required for it. One might fairly compare this growth of the micrococci on the one side and their death on the other with the vegetation of Sphagnum. Other considerations further indicate that, when bacteria are no longer stained by aniline, it is certain sign of their death. The form of bacteria vegetation described here deserves the greatest attention, for it is evident how easily in similar cases the narrow line of bacteria might be overlooked, even though the latter were still in full growth and easily recognisable. Similar circumstances also apparently occur in human infective diseases. Thus Klebs found in endocarditis that the micrococci deposited on the aortic valves were dark-colored on the surface, while in the deeper parts they became paler, and finally quite disappeared, passing into a homogeneous mass.

In order to ascertain whether the morbid process here designated as progressive abscess formation could be transmitted from one animal to another, rabbits were injected with blood taken from others which had already died of this disease. These injections produced no effect. A small quantity of the cheesy contents of the abscess was now taken, diluted with distilled water, and injected under the skin of a rabbit. There resulted exactly the same abscess-formation in this animal as in the first. The abscesses spread in the same manner as described in the former case, and caused the death of the animal experimented on in a week and a half. From this animal the disease was conveyed to a third, and so on through several in succession.

It was thus demonstrated that the disease is not merely occasioned by the injection of a considerable quantity of putrefying blood, but is of decidedly infective character. The assumption made above that the micrococci in the cheesy contents of these abscesses are dead, does not appear in keeping with this result of inoculation. This apparent contradiction may, however, I think, be cleared up, for it is very probable that these micrococci, like other bacteria, form resting spores after the expiration of their vegetative life, and that these bodies, just like the spores of bacillus, are not stained by aniline, and therefore remain invisible in Canada balsam. The infection in the case referred to would be brought about by such spores.

IV. Pyemia in Rabbits.

Having failed in various attempts to produce a general infection in rabbits by the injection of putrid blood, I tried the effect of other putrid fluids.

A piece of a mouse's skin about a square centimetre in size was macerated for two days in thirty grammes of distilled water, and a syringeful of this fluid was injected subcutaneously into the back of a rabbit. This animal remained for two days free from any noticeable symptoms of disease, then it began to eat less, became gradually weaker, and died one hundred and five hours after the injection. A post-mortem examination was at once made, and there was found a flat, purulent (not cheesy) infiltration in the subcutaneous cellular tissue, extending from the point of injection as far as the hip behind and the linea alba below. In the abdominal wall the yellowish infiltration extended in parts through the abdominal muscles, and even to the peritoneum. The latter was dull and in many places covered with delicate whitish clots. In the peritoneal cavity a small quantity of turbid fluid was found. The intestines were glued together by white fibrinous masses. The liver, stomach, and spleen were covered with thin white layers of fibrin, and the spleen was much enlarged. The liver, after the removal of the deposit on it, presented a greyish mottled appearance, and showed on section grey wedge-shaped patches; its borders were also in parts of a grey color. In the lungs were found some dark red patches about as large as a pea, devoid of air. As regards the remaining organs no alterations could be detected, not even in the heart.

A syringeful of blood taken from the heart of this animal was now injected under the skin of the back of a second rabbit. The latter died in forty hours. The result of the post-mortem examination was essentially the same. The infiltration in the neighborhood of the place of injection was, however, more oedematous, and the cellular tissue was besprinkled with small extravasations of blood; the peritonitis was less advanced; on the small and large intestines a few small subserous extravasations of blood were present; and in the lungs and the liver were metastatic deposits similar to those found in the first rabbit.

I had therefore without doubt a general infective disease to deal with. Indeed it was possible that it might be the same affection as had been obtained by Coze and Feltz, and by Davaine, from injections of putrid fluids into rabbits, and which had led them to their observations on the increasing virulence of septicemic blood when transmitted through a series of animals in succession. I therefore resolved to carry out a series of experiments similar to those already performed by Davaine.

To furnish a general view of the results of these experiments I shall arrange them in a tabular form:-

Rabbits	Fluid Injected	Quantity	Death
I.	Maceration fluid,	10 drops,	in 105 hours.
II.	Blood of I.,	10 drops,	in 40 hours.
III.	Blood of II.,	3 drops,	in 54 hours.
IV.	Blood of III.,	1 drop	in 92 hours.
V.	Blood of IV.,	1/10 drop,	in 125 hours.
VI.	Blood of V.,	1/1000 drop,	remained well.

The blood was diluted in the same manner as had been done by Davaine in his experiments. In order to obtain the one-thousandth of a drop for injection, a drop of blood was mixed with one hundred drops of distilled water; of this mixture one drop was again added to one hundred drops of distilled water, and of the solution so obtained (the blood being now diluted ten thousand times) ten drops were injected. The table comprises only a few experiments, but the relation between the quantity of blood injected and the time which elapsed before death is so constant that it cannot be accidental. There was no indication of increasing virulence of this blood when inoculated into several animals in succession. The less the quantity of blood injected, the longer the time which elapsed before death occurred, and where the quantity was reduced to the one-thousandth of a drop no result followed. I do not say, however, that the infective power of the blood was entirely abolished by reducing the quantity to one-thousandth of a drop, for this experiment was performed on one animal only, and it might very possibly have happened that if several animals had been injected at the same time with the same amount, one or other would have become ill, or even have died. But it follows from the table that when the quantity is small the effect is delayed, and that when very minute the result is uncertain, or even negative. These results can only be explained on the supposition that the blood always contains a like quantity of undissolved infective particles, and that these particles must have increased to a certain number before they can cause death.

For, an infective material in solution, which is active in quantities varying from ten drops to one-tenth of a drop, must also be infective under all circumstances, even when reduced to a thousandth of a drop; but death would take place at a correspondingly later period.

If, however, the infective material be supposed to be insoluble, and if a certain quantity is always necessary to destroy a rabbit, then the explanation of the fact that the result is more and more delayed in proportion as the injected blood is diluted is at once evident. For the more the blood is diluted the fewer bacteria does each drop contain, and if fewer bacteria be introduced into the animal experimented on, longer time must of course elapse before these have attained the number to cause death of a rabbit than when the quantity at first injected was large. If the blood be yet further diluted, a time will finally come when in the quantity of blood used for injection, say ten drops, there will not with certainty be a single bacterium, or at least a number sufficient for infection. Then the result becomes a matter of uncertainty.

Let us now see how the facts furnished by microscopic investigation coincide with this explanation.

But first I must mention that the post-mortem appearances found in the last three rabbits were, with some unimportant variations, the same as in the first two, viz., local purulent oedematous infiltration of the subcutaneous cellular tissue, metastatic deposits in the lungs and liver, swelling of the spleen, and peritonitis. These appearances harmonize so completely with those commonly designated as pyemia, that I do not hesitate to use that term for the disease under consideration.

On microscopic examination micrococci are found in great numbers everywhere throughout the body, and more especially in the parts which have undergone alterations visible to the naked eye. These micrococci are for the most part single or in pairs, and their measurement is therefore difficult. Ten measurements of pairs of micrococci differed but little from each other, and gave .25 mikrm. as the average diameter of a single individual. As regards size, therefore, they stand midway between the chain-like micrococcus of the progressive gangrene of the tissues and the zooglea-forming micrococcus of the cheesy abscesses of rabbits. Their relation to the blood-vessels can be best seen in the renal capillaries, and I have therefore selected a small vessel from the cortex of the kidney for delineation. In the interior of the vessel is a dense deposit of micrococci adherent to the wall, and enclosing in its substance a number of red blood corpuscles. This mass would probably have very soon filled the calibre of the vessel, for fresh blood corpuscles are constantly being deposited upon it, and these become surrounded by delicate offshoots from the mass of micrococci. From this we may conclude, either that the micrococci have of themselves, owing to the nature of their surface, the power of causing the red blood corpuscles, to which they adhere, to stick together, or that these organisms can occasion coagulation of the blood in their vicinity, and thus the formation of thrombi.

The manner in which these micrococci, as it were, spin round the blood corpuscles and enclose them, seems to me to be quite characteristic of this particular form. Such partial or complete thrombus formations occur in the renal vessels in many places, particularly in the glomeruli, where individual capillary loops may be found completely blocked by micrococci. But even in these thick zooglea-like masses one can still recognise the clear circles due to the enclosed red blood corpuscles. As a rule, however, only small groups of micrococci are met with. They were found arranged in this manner surrounding and glueing together a small number of blood corpuscles, in the capillary vascular system of all the organs examined, as, for example, in the spleen and in the lungs. In the larger vessels also groups of considerable size are formed, and I am disposed to believe that the large metastatic deposits in the liver and in the lungs do not arise by gradual growth of a mass of micrococci, but by the arrest of large groups of micrococci and of the clots associated with them formed in the manner described in the circulating blood; in other words, by true embolism. In the metastatic deposits an extensive development of micrococci occurs, and these are not confined to the vessels, but invade the neighboring tissues. Micrococci in pairs are pretty equally distributed over the surface of the abdominal organs. Masses of micrococci do not form in the peritoneal cavity; and the small flakes of pus in the peritoneal fluid and the fibrinous deposits infiltrated with pus cells present on the surface of the abdominal organs, contain micrococci only uniformly distributed, or at most collected into small groups.

In the neighborhood of the place of injection the

subcutaneous cellular tissue is infiltrated with extensive flat collections of pus, which are surrounded by micrococci more or less numerous, but never in the form of zooglea. They also surround the subcutaneous veins of this part, which are much distended with blood corpuscles, and their presence in the walls of the vessels and their passage through these walls into the interior can be seen in many places. No micrococci were found in the lymphatic vessels or in the neighboring lymphatic glands, which were, however, greatly swollen.

Comparing the results of the microscopic investigation with the before-mentioned effects of the injection, we find that they are in complete unison.

In the experiments the blood was taken from the heart, and with reference to the cause of its infecting property we have only to consider the state of the blood in the larger vessels. This, as already mentioned, contains numerous micrococci. The first part of the assumption that the infective particles were bacteria is thus proved. If, however, these underwent the same growth in the blood, as the septicemic and anthracic bacilli, they must become as numerous in the blood as the latter, and the virulence of the blood would thus be much greater than it was in reality found to be. But, as we have seen, the micrococci of pyemia behave differently in this respect from the organisms of septicemia and anthrax. As soon as they come in contact with the red blood corpuscles the latter stick together and form larger or smaller clots in the blood. They can thus no longer pass through the minute capillary networks, like the bacilli which move freely among the red corpuscles, but are arrested in the larger or smaller vessels. From the point of infection fresh micrococci will no doubt constantly pass into the blood, and also individual micrococci will become detached from these small thrombi and emboli and mix with the blood stream. Nevertheless, their total number in the circulating blood cannot exceed a certain point, because they are very soon deposited somewhere. Thus we have a simple explanation of the fact that the number of micrococci present in the body of the animal experimented on constantly increases, and, finally, apart from the disturbances of circulation produced by them, become sufficiently numerous to cause the death of the animal. Nevertheless, the quantity present in the cardiac blood continues pretty uniform, and is so small as to have an uncertain action when the thousandth part of a drop is used.

V. Septicemia in Rabbits.

After injection of putrid infusion of meat into rabbits, I have twice obtained a general infection of another sort in which metastatic deposits do not occur, and which I would therefore describe, in contrast to the foregoing, as septicemia. This infusion, like the putrid fluids used in the earlier experiments, contained numbers of bacteria of the most various forms. When injected under the skin of the back of a rabbit it produces an extensive putrid suppuration of the subcutaneous cellular tissue, and the animal dies in three days and a half. At the ichorous spot, which must, on account of its size, be looked upon as the immediate cause of death (owing to absorption of poisonous materials in solution), the same variety of bacteric forms was present as in the meat infusion. At the border of this spot the cellular tissue was infiltrated with a slightly turbid watery fluid, which contrasted strikingly with the brownish stinking ichor in the vicinity of the place of injection. In this oedema fluid great numbers of micrococci of considerable size and of an oval form were almost the only organism observed. In the blood also similar micrococci were found, though only in small numbers. Further, in the papilli of the kidney and in the greatly-enlarged spleen some of the small veins were completely blocked for short distances with these oval micrococci.

Two drops of this oedematous fluid were now injected under the skin of the back of a second rabbit. The animal died in twenty-two hours, and here, in the neighborhood of the place of injection, not a trace of pus could be observed. On the other hand slight oedema, with a streaky whitish appearance of the subcutaneous cellular tissue, extended from the point of injection to the abdomen. In this oedematous cellular tissue lay numerous flat extravasations of blood half a centimetre in breadth, the vessels around these being very greatly distended. The muscles of the thigh and of the abdominal wall were also interspersed with small extravasations. In the heart and lungs no alterations were found. In the peritoneal cavity no fluid was present, the peritoneum being unaltered and the coils of intestine not glued together. But the surface of the intestine, in consequence of a number of small subserous extravasations presented an appearance as if injected here and there with blood. The spleen was also very considerably enlarged.

In this second animal the oval micrococci were alone present in the oedematous cellular tissue, all the other bacteria having disappeared. The number of these organisms was very considerable, many of the small veins being completely filled with them. In the hemorrhagic spots were small veins, which were here and there distended with micrococci, thus presenting spindle-shaped dilatations, which had at parts burst, the micrococci having thus escaped in large numbers into the surrounding cellular tissue. This appearance could be particularly well seen in the muscles of the thigh.

In the pulmonary capillaries the micrococci were not very numerous; they were scattered through the blood singly or in pairs, and occasionally in small groups. In the kidneys these organisms were present in much larger numbers. The great majority of the glomeruli seemed enlarged, as if swollen; their capillary loops were increased in size and distended with red blood corpuscles. The other glomeruli were smaller than usual, the nuclei of their capillary walls being closer together, so that they presented an appearance as if they had been compressed. In all the enlarged glomeruli, without exception, more or less extensive deposits of oval micrococci were present. These were arranged in longitudinal series and also side by side, so as to form a single layer, covering the inner wall of the capillaries for short distances, but never embracing the whole circumference. The micrococcus colonies thus presented the appearance of short, slightly-curled, trough-like pellicles. In other places the vascular loops were completely distended, and there were also present all transitions from these dense obstructing masses to the small loose colonies and the single micrococci.

In the compressed glomeruli colonies were very exceptionally present, and then only of small size. Isolated obstructing micrococcus masses were also present in the vascular capillary network of the medullary substance. They were also present in an isolated form in almost all the vessels. Accumulations of whitish corpuscles in the neighborhood of the micrococci and alterations in the epithelial cells of the uriniferous tubules were not observed. The micrococci were never seen in the interior of the uriniferous tubules. The spleen contained loosely-arranged micrococcus colonies scattered about in the capillaries in moderate numbers, and also isolated dense deposits which distended the small vessels at the border and in the interior of the Malpighian corpuscles for short distances.

In the capillaries surrounding the intestinal glands numerous obstructing micrococcus masses were present. At many points these were so extensive that branching accumulations were seen consisting entirely of these organisms.

The liver, like the lungs, contained no great accumulation of micrococci.

The largest diameter of an isolated micrococcus was .8 to 1.0 mikrm.

These organisms differ from the micrococci of pyemia very markedly as regards size, and in most other points. Thus they never enclose the blood corpuscles, even when they have accumulated in large numbers in the interior of the blood-vessels. They rather push them on one side. They do not cause coagulation of the blood, and thus emboli do not occur. Only in one point do they resemble the pyemic micrococci, namely, they do not show an increasing virulence when inoculated into a series of animals in succession.

Thus a syringeful (ten drops) of blood taken from the heart of the second rabbit was injected subcutaneously into a third rabbit. This animal died in thirty-six hours, the naked eye and microscopic appearances being exactly the same as in rabbit No.2.

From rabbit No.3 two drops of blood were injected into a mouse, and one drop into a rabbit.

The mouse died in thirty-seven hours; the rabbit remained unaffected.

The blood and all the organs of this mouse contained these oval micrococci, just as in the rabbit. A second mouse was then inoculated with blood taken from this mouse's heart, the operation being performed in the following manner:- The point of a scalpel was dipped in the blood of the heart, and about one-tenth of a drop was put into a small pocket-like wound on the root of the tail. This animal remained healthy.

On a second occasion I have, by injection of putrid meat infusion, obtained in a rabbit the same septicemic process with the same oval micrococci.

Here, also, the disease could only be transmitted to other rabbits when at least five to ten drops of blood were used for inoculation.

VI. Erysipelas in Rabbits.

Not only were large quantities of putrid fluids *injected* into rabbits, but various attempts were also made to produce disease by *inoculation* with different putrefying materials. These were not successful. In one case, however, after inoculation of the ear of a rabbit with mouse's dung softened in distilled water, redness and swelling occurred and spread slowly downwards from the point of inoculation. This redness extended on the fifth day as far as the root of the ear. When held up to the sunlight the ear which had not been inoculated appeared unaltered, only the chief blood-vessels being seen, while the inoculated ear, similarly illuminated, presented a uniformly dark red appearance, the individual vessels being no longer recognisable. It was thicker, and at the same time had become more fluid than the other, its point being bent and hanging down in consequence of its weight. The animal was, moreover, evidently ill, and died on the seventh day.

No effect was produced on another rabbit by injecting into it blood taken from the first. Unfortunately an attempt was not made to transmit the morbid process by inoculation with material from the ear of the affected rabbit to that of another.

Neither in the blood nor in the internal organs of this rabbit were any alterations found worthy of mention, notably no bacteria. The state of matters in the ear was, however, so remarkable, and bore so unmistakably the characters of a parasitic disease, that I have considered it right, although the infective nature of the disease was not directly demonstrated, to give here a description of the affection.

In transverse sections of the ear the blood-vessels were seen to be markedly dilated, full of red corpuscles, and surrounded by the nuclei of numerous white corpuscles. These nuclei were more numerous towards the cartilage of the ear, and on its surface they formed a pretty uniform dense layer. Between this layer and the cartilage cells were seen small fine rods arranged at pretty equal distances, which rods were distributed parallel to the cartilage in the dense cellular tissue which lies immediately outside the cartilage cells. In many places only single rods were seen; in others several were present, being arranged parallel to each other; while again, thickly interwoven clumps of these same rods were found, and that in parts where the white corpuscles were somewhat more thickly accumulated than elsewhere. These rods were present nowhere except close to the cartilage. Longitudinal sections were accordingly prepared which showed very distinctly the distribution of the rods on the surface of the cartilage. Large round bodies are the nuclei of large flat cells, under which lie the cartilage cells. On this layer of flat cells there is a thick network consisting of bacilli, and outside these bacilli, indeed in fact covering them, are the nuclei of the white corpuscles of which, however, only a small portion remains in the section. In many places the bacilli form more or less round dense clumps which look like a pad of hair. From these clumps long rows of bacilli, in which the organisms become fewer and fewer, radiate in all directions. This reminds one of the peculiar, often starlike, figures which the bacillus anthracis forms when inoculated in the cornea of a living rabbit. This network of bacilli extended over the whole cartilage of the ear on both surfaces. As the morbid process could be traced in its extension from its origin at the point of inoculation over the whole ear, and as throughout the whole limit of the process these bacilli were present, and as, further, the signs of inflammatory reaction were most marked in the immediate neighborhood of these organisms, I consider it indubitable that they were the cause of the disease. I have never observed any formation of spores in them. They vary much in length. One rod, in which I could with certainty only distinguish two joints, was 3 mikrm. in length. The longest rod, consisting of six or seven joints, was 9-10 mikrm. in length. They are about .3 mikrm. thick (the bacillus anthracis may be as long as 20 mikrm. and as thick as 1 to 1.25 mikrm.,—that is to say, about twice as long and three or four times as thick as the bacilli of the rabbit's ear).

ANTHRAX

THE numerous investigations which have been made with regard to anthrax have almost all had reference to the behavior of the bacillus anthracis outside the animal body. With regard to their numbers in the blood the conclusions have, as a rule, been drawn from blood taken by chance from any part of the body. No observations have yet been published as to the number of bacilli really present in the body, and as to their distribution in the vascular system.

In order to supply this deficiency, and because the bacillus anthracis behaves so like the septicemic bacilli (thus being useful for comparison with the other pathogenic bacteria here described), I have examined rabbits and mice which have died of inoculated anthrax in the same manner as I did those killed by artificial traumatic infective diseases.

The staining of the bacillus alone, as obtained by treatment of sections stained in methyl violet with carbonate of potash, here proved of the greatest service. The mucous membrane of the stomach and intestine can, for example, be so prepared for examination by this method, that even with low powers the bacilli may be seen in all the vessels. In like manner sections of lung, liver, and kidneys, furnish extremely distinct and instructive preparations.

Although I had often previously examined the blood of animals suffering from anthrax, and had thus formed a high estimate as to the number of bacilli present in the body of an anthracic animal, yet I was quite surprised when I saw for the first time sections and portions of organs stained in this way, as *e.g.*, the intestinal mucous membrane and the iris of a rabbit. When magnified fifty diameters such a preparation presents at the first glance an appearance as if a blue coloring-matter had been injected into the vessels. Each intestinal villus is permeated by an excedingly delicate blue network; in the mucous membrane of the stomach all the capillary network surrounding the gastric glands is stained blue; in the ciliary processes each projection is injected, and a spiral vessel stained of a dark blue color leads from thence to the iris and breaks up into a fine blue network with loops directed towards the edge of the iris. The liver and lungs, and the glandular structures, such as the pancreas and salivary glands, are completely permeated by the same blue vascular network. Indeed there is no organ which is not more or less injected with the blue mass. It is, however, very striking that this injection is only present in the capillary vessels. All the larger vessels, even the arteries and veins of an intestinal villus, are either not at all stained or have but a light blue streak in their interior, and that only here and there. When magnified 250 times one can see that the blue capillary network is composed of numerous delicate rods, and when a power of 700 diameters is used it is found that the apparent injection is nothing more or less than the bacillus anthracis, stained dark blue, and present in incredible numbers in the whole capillary system. In other vessels, especially in the larger ones, often only a single bacillus may be met with at long intervals, or they may be quite absent. Here, therefore, we have a striking proof of how little value are conclusions drawn in traumatic infective diseases from the examination of a drop of blood taken from a blood-vessel by chance; for one might quite well take a drop of blood from the heart and find no micro-organisms in it, or one might readily overlook the few which might be present, and that although the capillary system abounds in them.

The distribution of the bacillus anthracis in the capillaries is not, however, quite uniform. There are fewer in the brain, in the skin, in the capillaries of the muscle, and in the tongue than elsewhere; on the other hand, in the liver, lungs, kidneys, spleen, intestines, and stomach, they are always present in the enormous numbers above described. The spleen, to which the disease owes its name, is not distinguished above the other organs which have been mentioned by a greater number of bacilli. In the capillaries themselves the bacilli accumulate in largest numbers at the point farthest removed from the nearest afferent artery and the efferent vein; that is to say, where the arterial capillaries join the venous, the aggregate diameter of the vessels being there the broadest and the blood stream flowing the slowest. In the intestinal villus this spot is at its apex and the neighboring part of the periphery; in the liver it lies midway between the ultimate twigs of the hepatic vein and of the vena portae. Among the points where the bacilli accumulate in greatest numbers are also the glomeruli of the kidney, which become for the most part transformed into clumps of bacilli. It by no means unfrequently happens that from the presence of the rapidly increasing bacilli at the places mentioned, chiefly in the glomeruli, intestinal villi, mucous membrane of the stomach, salivary glands, and pancreas, individual capillaries become torn, and blood with the contained bacilli is extravasated. This occurs most frequently in the glomeruli. Many of these burst and the bacilli pass into the uriniferous tubules. They do not, however, extend far into these; at least I have only found them in the commencement of the convoluted tubules, in which they form long threads interwoven with each other. I have never seen bacilli in the straight uriniferous tubules.

The facts which I have described are those met with in rabbits. Mice, which I have often investigated, behave essentially in the same manner. In the latter animals, however, the spleen is more especially the seat of the bacilli; then come the lungs, and last of all the kidneys. The contrast between the very large numbers of bacilli in the capillaries and their small quantity in the large vessels is even more striking in the mouse than in the rabbit.

I have also had an opportunity of examining the

lungs, liver, spleen, and kidneys of sheep which had died of anthrax, and I found here also that the bacilli had the same relations as regards numbers and distribution as in the rabbit.

I would recommend the study of organs taken from animals affected with anthrax, and stained in the manner described, to those who, in spite of all the proof already furnished, do not yet regard it as a parasitic disease. The simple fact that death occurs in twenty-four hours after inoculation with the smallest drop of anthracic blood, provided that it contains bacilli or their spores, and that then almost all the capillaries of the lungs, liver, kidneys, spleen, intestine, stomach, etc. (placed in absolute alcohol immediately after death), are found to be filled with enormous numbers of the same bacilli, has so evidently only one interpretation that no commentary is required. The investigator who still considers the presence of these organisms as accidental, quite immaterial, or merely accessory, must, before he can attribute the death of the animal to some other unknown ferment, consider likewise as immaterial the loss of the constituents of the blood which go to build up these innumerable bacilli, the accumulation of waste products which such a rapid interchange of material as the growth of the bacilli must of necessity involve, and also the disturbances in the circulation and in the nourishment of important organs induced by the plugging of most of the capillaries. But in that case there would be no reason why, in the case of trichinosis, scabies, and other parasitic diseases communicated by direct contact, some specific ferments in addition to trichinae, acari, etc., should not also be supposed to be present.

CONCLUSIONS.

I am well aware that the investigations above described are very imperfect. It was necessary, in order to have time for those parts of the investigation which seemed the most important and essential, to omit the examination of many organs, such as the brain, heart, retina, etc., which ought not to pass unnoticed in researches on infective diseases. For the same reason no record was kept of the temperature, although this would undoubtedly have yielded most interesting results. I have intentionally refrained from entering into details of morbid anatomy, as only the etiology interested me, and as I did not feel qualified to undertake a study of the morbid anatomy of traumatic infective diseases. I must therefore leave this part of the investigation to those who are better able to undertake it.

Nevertheless I consider that the results of my researches are sufficiently definite to enable me to deduce from them some well-founded conclusions.

In this summary I shall, however, confine myself to the most obvious conclusions. It has indeed of late become too common to draw the most sweeping conclusions as to infective diseases in general from the most unimportant observations on bacteria. I shall not follow this custom, although the material at my command would furnish rich food for meditation. For the longer I study infective diseases the more am I convinced that generalisations of new facts are here a mistake, and that every individual infective disease or group of closely allied diseases must be investigated for itself.

As regards the artificial traumatic infective diseases observed by me, the conditions, which must be established before their parasitic nature can be proved, were completely fulfilled in the case of the first five, but only partially in that of the sixth. For the infection was produced by such small quantities of fluid (blood, serum, pus, etc.) that the result cannot be attributed to a merely chemical poison.

In the materials used for inoculation bacteria were without exception present, and in each disease a different and well-marked form of organism could be demonstrated.

At the same time, the bodies of those animals which died of the artificial traumatic infective diseases contained bacteria in such numbers that the symptoms and the death of the animals were sufficiently explained. Further, the bacteria found were identical with those which were present in the fluid used for inoculation, and a definite form of organisms corresponded in every instance to a distinct disease.

These artificial traumatic infective diseases bear the greatest resemblance to human traumatic infective diseases, both as regards their origin from putrid substances, their course, and the result of post-mortem examination. Further, in the first case, just as in the last, the parasitic organisms could be only imperfectly demonstrated by the earlier methods of investigation; not till an improved method of procedure was introduced was it possible to obtain complete proof that they were parasitic diseases. We are therefore justified in assuming that human traumatic infective diseases will in all probability be proved to be parasitic when investigated by these improved methods.

On the other hand, it follows from the fact that a definite pathogenic bacterium, *e.g.*, the septicemic bacillus, cannot be inoculated on every variety of animal (a similar fact is also true with regard to the bacillus anthracis); that the septicemia of mice, rabbits, and man are not under all circumstances produced by the same bacterial form. It is of course possible that one or other of the bacteric forms found in animals also play a part in such diseases in the human subject. That, however, must be specially demonstrated for each case; *a priori* one need only expect that bacteria are present; as regards form, size, and conditions of growth, they may be similar, but not always the same, even in what appear to be similar diseases in different animals.

Besides the pathogenic bacteria already found in

animals, there are no doubt many others. My experiments refer only to those diseases which ended fatally. Even these are in all probability not exhausted in the six forms mentioned. Further experiments on many different species of animals, with the most putrid substances and with every possible modification in the method of application, will doubtless bring to light a number of other infective diseases, which will lead to further conclusions regarding infective diseases and pathogenic bacteria.

But even in the small series of experiments which I was able to carry out, one fact was so prominent that I must regard it as constant, and, as it helps to remove most of the obstacles to the admission of the existence of a contagium vivum for traumatic infective diseases, I look on it as the most important result of my work. I refer to the differences which exist between pathogenic bacteria and to the constancy of their characters. A distinct bacteric form corresponds, as we have seen, to each disease, and this form always remains the same, however often the disease is transmitted from one animal to another. Further, when we succeed in reproducing the same disease *de novo* by the injection of putrid substances, only the same bacteric form occurs which was before found to be specific for that disease.

Further, the differences between these bacteria are as great as could be expected between particles which border on the invisible. With regard to these differences, I refer not only to the size and form of the bacteria, but also to the conditions of their growth, which can be best recognised by observing their situation and grouping. I therefore study not only the individual alone, but the whole group of bacteria, and would, for example, consider a micrococcus which in one species of animal occurred only in masses (*i.e.*, in a zooglea form), as different from another which in the same variety of animal, under the same conditions of life, was only met with as isolated individuals.

Attention must also be paid to the physiological effect, of which I scarcely know a more striking example than the case of the bacillus and the chain-like micrococcus growing together in the cellular tissue of the ear; the one passing into the blood and penetrating into the white blood corpuscles, the other spreading out slowly in the tissue in its vicinity and destroying everything round about; or again, the case of the septicemic and pyemic micrococci of the rabbit in their different relations to the blood; or lastly, the bacilli extending only over the surface of the aural cartilage in the erysipelous disease, as contrasted with the bacillus anthracis likewise inoculated on the rabbit's ear, but quickly passing into the blood.

As, however, there corresponds to each of the diseases investigated a form of bacterium distinctly characterised by its physiological action, by its conditions of growth, size, and form, which, however often the disease be transmitted from one animal to another, always remains the same and never passes over into other forms, *e.g.,* from the spherical to the rod-shaped, we must in the meantime regard these different forms of pathogenic bacteria as distinct and constant species.

This is, however, an assertion which will be much disputed by botanists, to whose special province this subject really belongs.

Amongst those botanists who have written against the subdivision of bacteria into species, is Naegeli, who says, "I have for ten years examined thousands of different forms of bacteria, and I have not yet seen any absolute necessity for dividing them even into two distinct species."

Brefeld also states that he can only admit the existence of specific forms justifying the formation of distinct species when the whole history of development has been traced by cultivation from spore to spore in the most diverse nutritive fluids.

Although Brefeld's demand is undoubtedly theoretically correct, it cannot be made a *sine qua non* in every investigation on pathogenic bacteria. We should otherwise be compelled to cease our investigations into the etiology of infective diseases till botanists have succeeded in finding out the different species of bacteria by cultivation and development from spore to spore. It might then very easily happen that the endless trouble of pure cultivation would be expended on some form of bacterium which would finally turn out to be scarcely worthy of attention. In practice only the opposite method can work. In the first place certain peculiarities of a particular form of bacterium different from those of other forms, and in the second place its constancy, compel us to separate it from others less known and less interesting, and provisionally to regard it as a species. And now, to verify this provisional supposition, the cultivation from spore to spore may be undertaken. If this succeeds under conditions which shut out all sources of fallacy, and if it furnishes a result corresponding to that obtained by the previous observations, then the conclusions which were drawn from these observations and which led to its being ranked as a distinct species must be regarded as valid.

On this, which as it seems to me is the only correct practical method, I take my stand, and, till the cultivation of bacteria from spore to spore shows that I am wrong, I shall look on pathogenic bacteria as consisting of different species.

In order, however, to show that I do not stand alone in this view, I shall here mention the opinion of some botanists who have already come to a similar conclusion.

Cohn states that, in spite of the fact that many dispute the necessity of separating bacteria into genera and species, he must nevertheless adhere to the method as yet followed by him, and separate bacteria of different form and fermenting power from each other, so long as complete proof of their identity is not given.

From his investigations on the effects of different temperatures and of decisions on the development of bacterium termo, Eidam came to the conclusion that different forms of bacteria require different conditions of nutriment, and that they behave differently towards physical and chemical influences. He regards these facts as a further proof of the necessity of dividing organisms into distinct species.

I shall bring forward another reason to show the necessity of looking on the pathogenic bacteria which I have described as distinct species. The greatest stress, in investigations on bacteria, is justly laid on the so-called pure cultivations, in whch only one definite form of bacterium is present. This evidently arises from the view that if, in a series of cultivations, the same form of bacterium is always obtained, a special significance must attach to this form: it must indeed be accepted as a constant form, or, in a word, as a species. Can, then, a series of pure cultivations be carried out without admixture of other bacteria? It can in truth be done, but only under very limited conditions. Only such bacteria can be cultivated pure, with the aids at present at command, which can always be known to be pure, either by their size and easily recognisable form, as the bacillus anthracis, or by the production of a characteristic coloring matter, as the pigment bacteria. When, during a series of cultivations, a strange species of bacteria has by chance got in, as may occasionally happen under any circumstances, it will in these cases be at once observed, and the unsuccessful experiment will be thrown out of the series without the progress of the investigation being thereby necessarily interfered with.

But the case is quite different when attempts are made to carry out cultivations of very small bacteria, which, perhaps, cannot be distinguished at all without staining; how are we then to discover the occurrence of contamination? It is impossible to do so, and therefore all attempts at pure cultivation in apparatus, however skillfully planned and executed, must, as soon as small bacteria with but little characteristic appearances are dealt with, be considered as subject to unavoidable sources of fallacy, and in themselves inconclusive.

But nevertheless a pure cultivation is possible, even in the case of the bacteria which are smallest and most difficult to recognise. This, however, is not conducted in cultivation apparatus, but in the animal body. My experiments demonstrate this. In all the cases of distinct disease, *e.g.,* of septicemia of mice, only the small bacilli were present, and no other form of bacterium was ever found with it, unless in the case where that causing the tissue gangrene was intentionally inoculated at the same time. In fact, there exists no better cultivation apparatus for pathogenic bacteria than the animal body itself. Only a very limited number of bacteria can grow in the body, and the penetration of organisms into it is so difficult that the uninjured living body may be regarded as completely isolated with respect to other forms of bacteria than those intentionally introduced. It is quite evident, from a careful consideration of the two diseases produced in mice—septicemia and gangrene of the tissue—that I have succeeded in my experiments in obtaining a pure cultivation. In the putrefying blood, which was the cause of these two diseases, the most different forms of bacteria were present, and yet only two of these found in the living mouse the conditions necessary for their existence. All the others died, and these two alone, a small bacillus and a chain-like micrococcus, remained and grew. These could be transferred from one animal to another as often as was desired, without suffering any alteration in their characteristic form, in their specific physiological action and without any other variety of bacteria at any time appearing. And further, as I have demonstrated, it is quite in the power of the experimenter to separate these two forms of bacteria from each other. When the blood in which only the bacilli are present is used, these alone are transmitted, and thenceforth are obtained quite pure; while on the other hand, when a field-mouse is inoculated with both forms of bacteria, the bacilli disappear, and the micrococcus can be then cultivated pure. Doubtless an attempt to unite these two forms again in the same animal by inoculation would have been successful. In short, one has it completely in one's power to cultivate several varieties of bacteria together, to separate them from each other, and eventually to combine them again. Greater demands can hardly be made on a pure cultivation, and I must therefore regard the successive transmission of artificial infective diseases as the best and surest method of pure cultivation. And it can further claim the same power of demonstrating the existence of specific forms of bacteria, as must be conceded to any faultless cultivation experiments.

From the fact that the animal body is such an excellent apparatus for pure cultivation, and that, as we have seen, when the experiments are properly arranged and sufficient optical aids used, only one specific form of bacterium can be found in each distinct case of artificial traumatic infective diseases, we may now further conclude that when, in examining a traumatic infective disease, several different varieties of bacteria are found, as *e.g.*, chains of small granules, rods, and long oscillating threads (such as were seen together by Coze and Feltz in the artificial septicæmia of rabbits, see p. 5), we have to do with either a combined infective disease,—that is, not a pure one,—or, what in the case cited is more probable, an inexact and inaccurate observation. Where, therefore, several species of bacteria occur together in any morbid process, before definite conclusions are drawn as to the relations of the disease in question to the organisms, either proof must be furnished that they are all concerned in the morbid process, or an attempt must be made to isolate them and to obtain a true pure cultivation. Otherwise we cannot avoid the objection that the cultivation was not pure, and therefore not conclusive. I shall only briefly refer to a further necessary consequence of the admission of the existence of different species of pathogenic bacteria. The number of the species of these bacteria is limited; for, of the numerous diverse forms present in putrid fluids, one or but few can in the most favourable cases develop in the animal body. Those which disappear are, for that species of animal at least, not pathogenic bacteria. If, however, as follows from the foregoing, there exist hurtful and harmless bacteria, experiments performed on animals with the latter, *e.g.*, with bacterium termo, prove absolutely nothing for or against the behaviour of the former—the pathogenic forms. But almost all the experiments of this nature have been carried out with the first mixture of different species of bacteria which came to hand without there being any certainty that pathogenic bacteria were in reality present in the mixture. It is therefore evident that none of these experiments can be regarded as furnishing evidence of any value for or against the parasitic nature of infective diseases.

In all my experiments, not only have the form and size of the bacteria been constant, but the greatest uniformity in their actions on the animal organism has been observed, though no increase in virulence, as described by Coze and Feltz, Davaine, and others. This leads me to make some remarks on the supposed law of the increasing virulence of blood when transmitted through successive animals, discovered or confirmed by the investigators just mentioned.

The discovery of this law has, as is well known, been received with great enthusiasm, and it has excited no little interest owing to its intimate bearing on the doctrine of natural selection (Anpassung und Vererbung). Some investigators, who are in other things very exact, have allowed themselves to be blinded by the seductive theory that the insignificant action of a single putrefactive bacterium may, by continued natural selection in passing from animal to animal, be increased in virulence till it becomes deadly though a drop of the infective liquid be diluted a quadrillion times. They have founded thereon the most beautiful practical applications, not suspecting that the bacteria in question have never been with certainty demonstrated.

The original works of Coze and Feltz, as also that of Davaine, are not at my disposal for reference; and I cannot therefore enter into a complete criticism of them. So far, however, as I can gather from the references accessible to me, especially from the detailed notices in Virchow and Hirsch's 'Jahresbericht,' no complete proof that the virulence of septicemic blood increases from generation to generation seems to have been furnished. Apparently blood more and more diluted was injected, and astonishment was felt when this always acted, the effect being then ascribed to its increasing virulence. But controlling experiments to ascertain whether the septicemic blood were not already as virulent in the second and third generations as in the twenty-fifth, do not seem to have been made. My experiments so far support and are in accordance with those of Coze, Feltz, and Davaine in that for the first infection of an animal relatively large quantities of putrid fluids are necessary; but in the second generation, or at the latest in the third, the full virulence was attained, and afterwards remained constant.

Of my artificial infective diseases the septicemia of the mouse has the greatest correspondence with the artificial septicemia described by Davaine. If we were to experiment with this disease in the same manner as Davaine experimented, we would, if no controlling experiments were employed, find the same increase in virulence of the disease. It would only be necessary to use blood in slowly decreasing quantities in order to obtain in this way any progressive increase of the virulence that might be desired. I, however, took from the second or third animal the smallest possible quantity of material for inoculation, and thus arrived more quickly at the greatest degree of virulence. Till, therefore, I am assured that, in the septicemia observed by Davaine, such controlling experiments were made, I can only look on an increase in virulence as holding good for the earlier generations. In order to explain this we do not, however, require to have recourse to the magical wand of natural selection; a feasible explanation can be very naturally furnished. Let us take again the septicemia of mice, as being the most suitable example.

If two drops of putrefying blood be injected into such an animal there is introduced not only a number of totally distinct species of bacteria, but also a certain amount of dissolved putrid poison (sepsin), not sufficient to produce a fatal effect, but yet certainly not wihout influence on the health of the animal. Different factors must therefore be considered as affecting the health of the animal. On the one hand there is the dissolved poison, on the other the different species of bacteria, of which, however, perhaps only two, as in the example before us, can multiply in the body of the mouse and there exert a continuous noxious influence. Only one of these two species can penetrate into the blood, and if the blood alone be used for further inoculations, only this one variety will come victorious out of the battle for existence. The further development of the experiment depends entirely on the quantity of the putrid poison, and on the relation of the two forms of bacteria to each other in point of numbers. If one injects a large amount of the septic poison and a large number of that variety of bacteria which increases locally (in this case the chain-like micrococci causing the gangrene of the tissue), but only a very small number of the bacteria which pass into the blood (here the bacilli), the first animal experimented on will die, as a result of the preponderating influence of the first two factors before many bacilli can have got into the blood and multiplied there.

Of the blood of this first animal, containing, as it does proportionately very few bacilli, one-fifth to one-tenth of a drop must be inoculated in order to convey the disease with certainty. In the second animal, however, only the bacilli are introduced, and these develop undisturbed in the blood. For the infection of the third animal the smallest quantity of this blood which can produce an effect is then sufficient, and after this third generation the virulence of the blood remains uniform.

We may also imagine another case in which the increase of the virulence may go on through more than two generations without any modification resulting from natural selection and transmission from animal to animal. This would take place if several species of bacteria capable of passing into the blood were introduced into the animal at the first injection. Let us suppose, for example, that in the same putrefying blood which served for the foregoing experiment, the bacilli of anthrax were also present, there would be then contained in the blood of the first animal not only the septicemic bacillus, but also bacillus anthracis, and of each only a small number; of the anthrax bacillus there would be fewer than of the other, because in mice they are deposited chiefly in the spleen, lungs, etc.; while in the blood of the heart they are, even in the most favourable cases, only sparsely distributed. On the other hand, the anthrax bacilli have this advantage, that, provided they be inoculated in considerable numbers, they kill even within twenty hours, while the septicemic bacilli only destroy life after fifty hours. In the blood of the second animal, therefore, both species of bacilli would be present in larger numbers than in the first, although not yet so numerous as if either organism had been inoculated singly. Hence a larger quantity of blood is necessary to ensure transmission to a third animal. Perhaps this might be the case even in the fourth generation, till finally one or other variety of bacillus would alone be present in the blood injected. Probably this would be the septicemic bacillus.

In this way the experiments of Coze, Feltz, and Davaine may admit of simple explanation and be brought into harmony with my results.

THE END

The
ANTISEPTIC
SYSTEM

THE ANTISEPTIC SYSTEM

ON A NEW METHOD OF TREATING COMPOUND FRACTURE, ABSCESS, ETC.

WITH OBSERVATIONS ON THE CONDITIONS OF SUPPURATION.

(Lancet, 1867, vol. i, pp. 326, 357, 387, 507; vol. ii, p. 95.)

ON COMPOUND FRACTURE

THE frequency of disastrous consequences in compound fracture, contrasted with the complete immunity from danger to life or limb in simple fracture, is one of the most striking as well as melancholy facts in surgical practice.

If we inquire how it is that an external wound communicating with the seat of fracture leads to such grave results, we cannot but conclude that it is by inducing, through access of the atmosphere, decomposition of the blood which is effused in greater or less amount around the fragments and among the interstices of the tissues, and, losing by putrefaction its natural bland character, assuming the properties of an acrid irritant, occasions both local and general disturbance.

We know that blood kept exposed to the air at the temperature of the body, in a vessel of glass or other material chemically inert, soon decomposes; and there is no reason to suppose that the living tissues surrounding a mass of extravasated blood could preserve it from being affected in a similar manner by the atmosphere. On the contrary, it may be ascertained as a matter of observation that, in a compound fracture, twenty-four hours after the accident the coloured serum which oozes from the wound is already distinctly tainted with the odour of decomposition and during the next two or three days, before suppuration has set in, the smell of the effused fluids becomes more and more offensive.

This state of things is enough to account for all the bad consequences of the injury.

The pernicious influence of decomposing animal matter upon the tissues has probably been underrated, in consequence of the healthy state in which granulating sores remain in spite of a very offensive condition of their discharges. To argue from this, however, that fetid material would be innocuous in a recent wound would be to make a great mistake. The granulations being composed of an imperfect form of tissue, insensible and indisposed to absorption, but with remarkably active cell-development, and perpetually renovated as fast as it is destroyed at the surface, form a most admirable protective layer, or living plaster. But before a raw surface has granulated, an acrid discharge acts with unrestrained effect upon it, exciting the sensory nerves, and causing through them both local inflammation and general fever, and also producing by its caustic action a greater or less extent of sloughs, which must be thrown off by a corresponding suppuration, while there is at the same time a risk of absorption of the poisonous fluids into the circulation.

This view of the cause of the mischief in compound fracture is strikingly corroborated by cases in which the external wound is very small. Here, if the coagulum at the orifice is allowed to dry and form a crust, as was advised by John Hunter, all bad consequences are probably averted, and, the air being excluded, the blood beneath becomes organized and absorbed, exactly as in simple fracture. But if any accidental circumstance interferes with the satisfactory formation of the scab, the smallness of the wound, instead of being an advantage, is apt to prove injurious, because, while decomposition is permitted, the due escape of foul discharges is prevented. Indeed, so impressed are some surgeons with the evil which may result from this latter cause, that, deviating from the excellent Hunterian practice, they enlarge the orifice with the knife in the first instance and apply fomentations, in order to mitigate the suppuration which they render inevitable.

Turning now to the question how the atmosphere produces decomposition of organic substances, we find that a flood of light has been thrown upn this most important subject by the philosophic researches of Pasteur, who has demonstrated by thoroughly convincing evidence that it is not to its oxygen or to any of its gaseous constituents that the air owes this property, but to minute particles suspended in it, which are the germs of various low forms of life, long since revealed by the microscope, and regarded as merely accidental concomitants of putrescence, but now shown by Pasteur to be its essential cause, resolving the complex organic compounds into substances of simpler chemical constitution, just as the yeast plant converts sugar into alcohol and carbonic acid.

A beautiful illustration of this doctrine seems to me to be presented in surgery by pneumothorax with emphysema, resulting from puncture of the lung by a fractured rib. Here, though atmospheric air is perpetually introduced into the pleura in great abundance, no inflammatory disturbance supervenes; whereas an external wound penetrating the chest, if it remains open, infallibly causes dangerous suppurative pleurisy. In the latter case the blood and serum poured out into the pleural cavity, as an immediate consequence of the injury, are decomposed by the germs that enter with the air, and then operate as a powerful irritant upon the serous membrane. But in case of puncture of the lung without external wound, the atmospheric gases are filtered of the causes of decomposition before they enter the pleura, by passing through the bronchial tubes, which, by their small size, their tortuous course, their mucous secretion, and ciliated epithelial lining, seem to be specially designed to arrest all solid particles in the air inhaled. Consequently the effused fluids retain their original characters unimpaired, and are speedily absorbed by the unirritated pleura.

Applying these principles to the treatment of compound fracture, bearing in mind that it is from the vitality of the atmospheric particles that all the mischief arises, it appears that all that is requisite is to dress the wound with some material capable of killing these septic germs, provided that any substance can be found reliable for this purpose, yet not too potent as a caustic.

In the course of the year 1864 I was much struck with an account of the remarkable effects produced by carbolic acid upon the sewage of the town of Carlisle, the admixture of a very small proportion not only preventing all odour from the lands irrigated with the refuse material, but, as it was stated, destroying the entozoa which usually infest cattle fed upon such pastures.

My attention having for several years been much directed to the subject of suppuration, more especially in its relation to decomposition, I saw that such a powerful antiseptic was peculiarly adapted for experiments with a view to elucidating that subject, and while I was engaged in the investigation the applicability of carbolic acid for the treatment of compound fracture naturally occurred to me.

My first attempt of this kind was made in the Glasgow Royal Infirmary in March 1865, in a case of compound fracture of the leg. It proved unsuccessful, in consequence, as I now believe, of improper management; but subsequent trials have more than realized my most sanguine anticipations.

Carbolic acid proved in various ways well adapted for the purpose. It exercises a local sedative influence upon the sensory nerves; and hence is not only almost painless in its immediate action on a raw surface, but speedily renders a wound previously painful entirely free from uneasiness. When employed in compound fracture its caustic properties are mitigated so as to be unobjectionable by admixture with the blood, with which it forms a tenacious mass that hardens into a dense crust, which long retains its antiseptic virtue, and has also other advantages, as will appear from the following cases, which I will relate in the order of their occurrence, premising that, as the treatment has been gradually improved, the earlier ones are not to be taken as patterns.

CASE I.—James G., aged eleven years, was admitted into the Glasgow Royal Infirmary on the 12th of August, 1865, with compound fracture of the left leg, caused by the wheel of an empty cart passing over the limb a little below its middle. The wound, which was about an inch and a half long, and three-quarters of an inch broad, was close to, but not exactly over, the line of fracture of the tibia. A probe, however, could be passed beneath the integument over the seat of fracture and for some inches beyond it. Very little blood had been extravasated into the tissues.

My house surgeon, Dr. Macfee, acting under my instructions, laid a piece of lint dipped in liquid carbolic acid upon the wound, and applied lateral pasteboard splints padded with cotton wool, the limb resting on its outer side, with the knee bent. It was left undisturbed for four days, when, the boy complaining of some uneasiness, I removed the inner splint and examined the wound. It showed no signs of suppuration, but the skin in its immediate vicinity had a slight blush of redness. I now dressed the sore with lint soaked with water having a small proportion of carbolic acid diffused through it; and this was continued for five days, during which the uneasiness and the redness of the skin disappeared, the sore meanwhile furnishing no pus, although some superficial sloughs caused by the acid were separating. But the epidermis being excoriated by this dressing, I substituted for it a solution of one part of carbolic acid in from ten to twenty parts of olive oil, which was used for four days, during which a small amount of imperfect pus was produced from the surface of the sore, but not a drop appeared from beneath the skin. It was now clear that there was no longer any danger of deep-seated suppuration, and simple water dressing was employed. Cicatrization proceeded just as in an ordinary granulating sore. At the expiration of six weeks I examined the condition of the bones, and, finding them firmly united, discarded the splints; and two days later the sore was entirely healed, so that the cure could not be said to have been at all retarded by the circumstance of the fracture being compound.

This, no doubt, was a favourable case, and might have done well under ordinary treatment. But the remarkable retardation of suppuration, and the immediate conversion of the compound fracture into a simple fracture with a superficial sore, were most encouraging facts.

CASE 2.—Patrick F., a healthy labourer, aged thirty-two, had his right tibia broken on the afternoon of the 11th of September, 1865, by a horse kicking him with its full force over the anterior edge of the bone about its middle. He was at once taken to the infirmary, where Mr. Miller, the house surgeon in charge, found a wound measuring about an inch by a quarter of an inch, from which blood was welling profusely.

He put up the fracture in pasteboard splints, leaving the wound exposed between their anterior edges, and dressing it with a piece of lint dipped in carbolic acid, large enough to overlap the sound skin about a quarter of an inch in every direction. In the evening he changed the lint for another piece, also dipped in carbolic acid, and covered this with oiled paper. I saw the patient next day, and advised the daily application of a bit of lint soaked in carbolic acid over the oiled paper; and this was done for the next five days. On the second day there was an oozing of red fluid from beneath the dressing, but by the third day this had ceased entirely. On the fourth day, when, under ordinary circumstances, suppuration would have made its appearance, the skin had a nearly natural aspect, and there was no increase of swelling, while the uneasiness he had previously felt was almost entirely absent. His pulse was 64, and his appetite improving. On the seventh day, though his general condition was all that could be wished, he complained again of some uneasiness, and the skin about the still adherent crust of blood, carbolic acid, and lint was found to be vesicated, apparently in consequence of the irritation of the carbolic acid. From the seventh day the crust was left untouched till the eleventh day, when I removed it, disclosing a concave surface destitute of granulations, and free from suppuration. Water dressing was now applied, and by the sixteenth day the entire sore, with the exception of one small spot where the bone was bare, presented a healthy granulating aspect, the formation of pus being limited to the surface of granulations.

I now had occasion to leave Glasgow for some weeks, and did so feeling that the cure was assured. On my return, however, I was deeply mortified to learn that hospital gangrene attacked the sore soon after I went away, and made such havoc that amputation became necessary.

While I could not but feel that this case, by its unfortunate issue, might lose much of its value in the minds of others, yet to myself it was perfectly conclusive of the efficacy of carbolic acid for the object in view. At the same time it suggested some improvement in matters of detail. It showed that the acid may give rise to a serous exudation apt to irritate by its accumulation, and therefore that a warm and moist application would be advantageous to soothe the part, and also ensure the free exit of such exuded fluid. At the same time it appeared desirable to protect the crust with something that would retain the volatile organic acid more effectually than oiled silk or gutta-percha, through which it makes its way with the utmost facility. For this purpose a metallic covering naturally suggested itself, and as ordinary tin-foil is unsuitable from its porosity, I employed thin sheet-lead, and afterwards block-tin, such as is used for covering the jars of anatomical preparations, superior to lead on account of the facility with which it can be moulded to any shape that is desired.

For a long time, however, I had no opportunity of giving this improvement a trial, the compound fractures admitted into my wards during the next eight months being merely two cases with small wounds. One of these was a fracture of the ulna into the elbow-joint in a woman so old that suppuration, had it occurred, would probably have proved fatal. The orifice in the integument was extremely small, and all would most likely have gone on well had the bit of dry lint applied to check the free bleeding from the interior been left undisturbed, instead of being saturated with carbolic acid as it was. This, however, could not but be an additional safeguard, and at the same time it was satisfactory to find that the caustic application did not interfere with the usual healing by scabbing, cicatrization being found complete when the crust was removed.

The other case was a fracture of the humerus a little above the elbow in a young man, caused by a fall from a height of thirty-five feet, the wound, which was not quite half an inch in length, being situated at the inner side of the limb, where it must necessarily be covered by a splint. Dr. Watson, then my house surgeon, applied lint dipped in carbolic acid covered with a slightly concave piece of sheet-lead about as large as a shilling, and put the limb in pasteboard padded with cotton. At the end of ten days the inner side of the limb was uncovered for the first time, and merely as a matter of curiosity, when the lead, with the lint adhering to it, dropped off, disclosing a small superficial granulating sore without the slightest suppuration, just as in ordinary healing by scabbing. This case is interesting, not so much because the compound fracture was converted into a simple one, for this might have occurred under ordinary treatment, but because it showed that in any case of fracture complicated with a small wound, we have in carbolic acid a means which enables us to disregard the wound altogether after the splints have been applied, instead of being under the necessity of daily disturbing the apparatus to change the dressing.

At length a case presented itself well calculated to test the value of carbolic acid in compound fracture.

Case 3.—John H., aged twenty-one, a moulder in an iron foundry, was admitted on the 19th of May, 1866, with compound fracture of the left leg, produced in the following manner. He was superintending the raising by crane of an iron box containing sand ready for a casting, the box and its contents weighing about 12 cwt., when one of the chains by which it was suspended slipped, and the box fell from the height of four feet with unbroken force upon the inner side of his leg, which was planted obliquely beneath it. Both bones were fractured, the tibia about its middle, and a wound an inch and a half in length, and three-quarters of an inch broad, was made at the inner aspect of the limb, on a level with the fracture of the tibia, and obviously communicating with it. At the same time the soft parts generally were much contused, as was evident from the great distension of the limb with extravasated blood. Dr. A. Cameron, my house surgeon, finding, on manipulating the limb, that bubbles escaped along with the blood, implying that air had been introduced during the movements of the leg as the patient was being carried to the infirmary, thought it best that I should see the case, which I did at three p.m., three hours and half after the accident. In order to expel the air I squeezed out as much as I could of the clotted and fluid blood which lay accumulated beneath the skin, and then applied a bit of lint dipped in carbolic acid slightly larger than the wound, and over this a piece of sheet-tin about four inches square. Finally the limb was placed in pasteboard splints, resting on its outer side with the knee bent. At eight p.m. some more acid was added with another piece of lint, so that the crust of clots, carbolic acid, and lint was about one-third of an inch in thickness. A hot fomentation also was applied over the inner aspect of the leg, the crust being protected by the tin. Next day he was pretty easy, and had passed a quiet night, though occasionally awakened by starting pains; the pulse was 90, but he took some food with relish. The surface of the crust was touched again with carbolic acid, and the fomentation was continued, and in place of the internal pasteboard splint, a large sheet of tin was applied over the flannel from the knee to the ankle, being retained in position by looped bandages. This proved a very satisfactory arrangement, the tin having sufficient firmness to answer the purpose of a splint, while it most effectually retained the moisture of the flannel, which, again, served as an excellent padding. The fomentation was changed night and morning, and gave great comfort to the patient, and once a day carbolic acid was applied lightly to the crust.

Two days after the accident the limb was easier, but the circumferential measurement of the calf continued the same, and the pulse was 96, though soft. On the fourth day—the critical period with reference to suppuration—the limb was free from pain, and the calf less tense, and distinctly reduced in dimensions; while the pulse had fallen to 80, and the patient had enjoyed his food after a good night's rest. After this the swelling steadily subsided, the skin remaining, as it had been from the first, free from the slightest inflammatory blush, and his general health was in all respects satisfactory. Seven days after the receipt of the injury there was some puriform discharge from the surface of the skin where the carbolic acid, confined by the smaller piece of tin that covered the crust, had produced excoriation by its caustic action; and to prevent needless irritation from this cause, the tin was reduced so as to leave only a narrow flat rim round a bulging part which corresponded to the crust.

About a fortnight after the accident a sense of fluctuation was experienced over the seat of fracture, but, as all was going on favourably otherwise, I hoped that this was due simply to serum from the effused blood; and in a few days it had completely disappeared, not a drop of pus meanwhile having escaped from beneath the crust. About this time the edges of the crust became softened by the superficial discharge from the surrounding parts, and these softened portions were daily clipped away with scissors. Thus the circumferential part of the crust which had overlapped the skin was removed, and that which lay over the extravasated blood in the wound was also reduced to smaller and smaller size.

On the 7th of June, nearly three weeks after the accident, an observation of much interest was made. I was detaching a portion of the adherent crust from the surface of the vascular structure into which the extravasated blood beneath had been converted by the process of organization, when I exposed a little spherical cavity about as big as a pea, containing brown serum, forming a sort of pocket in the living tissues, which, when scraped with the edge of a knife, bled even at the very margin of the cavity. This appearance showed that the deeper portions of the crust itself had been converted into living tissue. For cavities formed during the process of aggregation, like those with clear liquid contents in a Gruyere cheese, occur in the grumous mass which results from the action of carbolic acid upon blood; and that which I had exposed had evidently been one of these, though its walls were now alive and vascular. Thus the blood which had been acted upon by carbolic acid, though greatly altered in physical characters, and doubtless chemically also, had not been rendered unsuitable for serving as pabulum for the growing elements of new tissue in its vicinity. The knowlede of this fact is of importance; as it shows that, should circumstances appear to demand it, we may introduce carbolic acid deeply among the blood extravasated in a limb, confident that all will nevertheless be removed by absorption. A few days later all traces of the little cavity had become obliterated by the granulating process.

At the close of the third week the application of carbolic acid to the crust was discontinued, and the original internal pasteboard splint padded with cotton was again employed, instead of the tin and fomentation. What remained of the crust was still kept protected with the tin cap, with the view of ascertaining how long it would continue to adhere; and at length, nearly four weeks after the accident, I tore it off from the vascular surface beneath, which bled as I did so. The crust had preserved the subjacent parts from disturbance as effectually as if it had been a piece of living integument; and it is worthy of remark that the vascular surface below had not the pulpy softness of granulations, but was comparatively firm and substantial. The bit of crust still smelt of carbolic acid, though none had been applied for five days.

At the expiration of six weeks from the receipt of

the injury the fragments were found firmly united in good position, just as if the fracture had been a simple one, though the cicatrization of the rather extensive sore was not complete till a later period.

Case 4.—James W., aged ten, was engaged in a turner's factory worked by steam power on the 8th of June, 1866, when his right arm was drawn in between a strap and a shaft turned by it. He called out for assistance, but thinks two minutes must have e-elapsed before the machinery was stopped, and during the whole of this time the strap, which was still moving when he held the arm steady, was cutting into the ulnar side of the forearm, breaking through the ulna about its middle, while the radius was bent with 'green-stick' fracture. He was taken at once to the infirmary, where the wound was found to be about an inch and a half in depth, occupying more than half the circumference of the limb, chiefly at the dorsal aspect, but extending round also to the palmar side. The upper fragment of the ulna was protruding about an inch, and two strips of muscle, about a quarter of an inch in thickness and from two to three inches in length, were hanging out; the lacerated state of the parts confirming the boy's account of the accident.

On seeing him about two hours afterwards, I sawed off the protruding portion of the ulna, and the tags of muscle having been previously clipped away, I applied carbolic acid freely to the whole interior of the wound, including the exposed surface of the bone; and having straightened the radius, which gave way during the process, placed the limb upon a wooden palmar splint. Avoiding any attempt to approximate the lips of the wound, I covered it with a piece of sheet-tin, sufficiently large to overlap the sound skin about a quarter of an inch in every direction. The limb was fixed to the splint by a bandage, so arranged as to permit the removal of the tin without disturbing the apparatus; and hot fomentations were applied over the whole. A few minutes after the carbolic acid was applied he said he was perfectly easy. At seven o'clock he asked for food, and took it. His pulse was then 84. At eight p.m. I saw him again, and applied beneath the tin a piece of lint dipped in carbolic acid, about as large as the wound. Noticing some distortion in the upper arm, I found that the humerus also was broken in its lower third, and applied splints accordingly, the limb being kept supported upon a pillow beside him. He slept a good deal during the night, though moaning and starting occasionally. Next day his pulse was 108; but he took his breakfast heartily, and the tongue was healthy, while he complained only of a little uneasiness about the elbow, and even this disappeared on changing the fomentation cloth. A piece of sheet-tin was now arranged so as to form a sort of cover for the forearm, including the hand. Being retained in position by looped bandages, it increased the steadiness of the limb, while it ensured efficiency of the fomentation.

Two days after the accident the oozing of blood and serum, which had been considerable during the previous twenty-four hours, had nearly ceased; but he still experienced comfort from the fomentation, though any pain which he felt was connected with the simple fracture of the humerus. His pulse was 88; his tongue clean and appetite good after a sound sleep at night; and from this time onward his general health continued perfectly satisfactory. On the fourth day a small quantity of pale, grey, slimy discharge was observed from beneath the crust at one part; and thinking that this might, perhaps, have occurred for want of proper action of the carbolic acid, I applied the latter with unusual freedom to the surface of the crust. This was repeated at night; and the same energetic use of the carbolic acid, twice in the twenty-four hours, was continued on the fifth day. Yet, on the sixth day, the discharge from beneath the crust, instead of being diminished, was increased, and more puriform to the naked eye; while, under the microscope, there was clear indication of new cell-formation, whereas, on the day before, nothing but fibrinous material, with granular and other debris, had been discoverable. On the seventh day the discharge was still greater in amount; yet the limb remained free from pain, and was steadily diminishing in circumference, and pressure in the neighbourhood of the crust failed to induce any increase of the discharge, which appeared to be merely superficial.

In the course of the next few days it became apparent that this discharge, so far from being the result of insufficient action of the carbolic acid, was caused by the stimulating influence of the acid itself, applied with greater freedom over a crust much thinner than that of Case 3. Suppuration from this cause is, however, productive of no mischief, as will be better understood from the sequel. That such was the case in this instance was manifest on the fourteenth day, when the crust, which was nearly detached, was removed, disclosing an appearance for which I confess I had not been prepared. In place of the deep and ragged wound was a granulating sore, nearly on a level with the skin, and pretty uniform in surface, except at one part about its middle, where there was a depression about half an inch in depth, at the bottom of which a small portion of the outer surface of the ulna was visible, bare, but of pink colour. Not only had the compound of blood and carbolic acid which had existed in the depths of the wound been organized, but the portions of tissue killed by the violence to which they had been subjected in the accident, and also those destroyed by the caustic action of the carbolic acid, had been similarly acted on, and all had been, so to speak, fused together into a living mass, without the occurrence of any deep-seated suppuration.

By the nineteenth day the exposed part of the bone was covered, and the depression in the sore obliterated by granulation, without any exfoliation occurring; and two days short of seven weeks after the accident the sore was entirely healed.

The extensive loss both of bone and of the soft parts made osseous union of the ulna a matter of difficulty, and on the 5th of August the limb was placed in a starched apparatus, to promote complete consolidation, and he was soon after discharged from the hospital.

About six weeks later he presented himself at the infirmary, and the bandage was removed in my absence, when, the bone appearing firm, he was allowed to dispense with the apparatus, and was unfortunately not directed to show himself again. In the course of a few weeks, however, he appeared with the fragments again movable. The starched bandage was therefore reapplied, but when I last saw him, some weeks ago, bony union had not yet occurred. A good deal of osseous formation had, however, taken place, so that the fragments now overlapped each other; and should the cure be still incomplete when he next shows himself, the case will be a fair subject for Bickersteth's method of treating ununited fracture by drilling. Meanwhile, the radius being firm, and the injured extensors of the fingers having completely regained their powers, he will, in any event, have a very useful hand.

This case indicated a greater range of applicability of the treatment by carbolic acid than I had anticipated, and encouraged me to employ it under the almost desperate circumstances of the following case.

Case 5.—Charles F., a fine, intelligent boy, seven years of age, was knocked down at eight p.m. on the 23rd of June, 1866, by an omnibus crowded with passengers inside and out, and one if not both wheels passed over his right leg, breaking both the bones and inflicting a frightfully extensive wound. The person who brought him to the infirmary said that he had lost a great deal of blood, and the presence of a compress in the ham, placed there by the medical man who saw him at the time of the accident, corroborated this statement. When I saw the child, after an unavoidable delay of three hours, he was greatly prostrated by shock as well as haemorrhage, so much so that amputation appeared likely to afford but a slender chance of life, although the state of the injured parts seemed at first sight to admit of no alternative. The tibia, which was broken about its middle, lay exposed in a wound occupying almost the entire length and breadth of the inner aspect of the leg, reaching from the inner condyle of the femur to within an inch and a quarter of the tip of the internal malleolus; the skin having been stripped back so as to lay bare the gastrocnemius as well as the bone. The large flap of integument was perforated about two inches from its edge opposite to the seat of fracture, and there was also an opening in the skin on the outer side of the leg, implying that the violence had acted with full effect upon the wohle thickness of the limb. Yet the bone was not comminuted, and the muscles, though evidently severely contused, were not much lacerated, while the anterior tibial artery was felt beating in the foot; and, hopeless as would have been the idea of trying to save the limb by ordinary treatment, I determined to make the attempt by the help of carbolic acid.

Chloroform having been administered, the acid of full strength was applied with great freedom, the contused mass being repeatedly squeezed, to induce the liquid to insinuate itself into all its interstices, including that between the riding fragments of the tibia. The flap of skin was then brought towards its natural position, and lint soaked in the acid was placed upon the wide raw surface which still remained exposed, and over the lint a piece of sheet-tin. The other openings in the integument were similarly treated; and, the riding of the fragments having been corrected by extension, the limb was laid on its outer side, with the knee bent, upon an external pasteboard splint, moulded to the leg and foot, and strengthened by a temporary wooden splint. A porous cloth was applied over the tin to absorb the blood and serum which must escape from beneath its edges; and the whole apparatus was secured with a roller. At the conclusion of the dressing the pulse was 112.

He passed a restless night, though occasionally dozing, and the pulse next morning was 120. The bandage having been cut away sufficiently to enable the tin to be removed, the wound was found to have gaped so that the lint no longer covered the whole of it. Pieces of the cloth, which had become soaked with the exuded blood, were placed upon the exposed part, and also over the lint so as to make the crust more substantial, and the whole was freely treated with carbolic acid. The tin was then bulged out so as to be accommodated to the thickened crust, while overlapping the neighbouring skin to a slight extent; being retained in position by a couple of turns of bandage. A hot fomentation was then placed upon the inner aspect of the limb, and the whole leg enveloped in a large sheet of block-tin secured by looped bandages.

In the evening the pulse was 136, and on the following morning, thirty-six hours after the accident, it had risen to 168, and was very weak. He lay talking to himself in a rambling manner, unable to understand what was said to him. He was extremely restless, and had taken no food whatever since his admission. During the next night, however, he became composed, and took a little milk; and on the morning of the third day he was found to be again intelligent, while the pulse had fallen to 140, and was of fair strength. The skin in the vicinity of the injury, both at the knee and ankle, was free from discoloration or swelling; but part of the large flap of skin over the calf was of purple tint, and had evidently lost its vitality. This dead part was touched with carbolic acid, to preserve it from decomposition, and convert it into a crust for the protection of the subjacent textures, and an additional piece of tin was applied to cover it. A good deal of brown transparent fluid escaped from beneath the crust.

On the fourth day the pulse was 120; he was quite bright and tranquil, and said he felt no pain. There was still no odour about the injured part, except that of carbolic acid. The discharge was much diminished, and was principally serous.

By the sixth day the pulse was as low as 108. He had a hearty appetite, and also took with avidity the six ounces of port wine allowed him during the twenty-four hours. His tongue, which had previously been dry, was moist. He had slept well at night, though waking occasionally with a scream. The discharge from beneath the crust, trifling in amount, was chiefly serous.

On the eighth day the splint was removed for the first time, and was covered with sheet-tin in order to prevent the discharge from softening the pasteboard. The leg had become slightly bent inwards through the yielding of the splint; and when it was now straightened, the upper margin of the crust became detached, exposing a deep granulating cavity. A bit of lint, dipped in carbolic acid, was applied lightly over this opening, and the tin was readjusted so as to cover it. Pressure in the neighbourhood of the injured part, about the knee, ankle, and calf, failed to induce the slightest increase of the discharge, which was thus shown to come merely from the surface beneath the crust, and was still for the most part transparent.

At the close of the second week his state was on the whole very favourable. His general health was much improved; and although he still suffered occasionally, especially at night, from restless movements of the limb, these had been much restrained by a new splint, extending from half-way up the thigh to the toes. The wound was certainly very large, measuring eight inches in length by six in greatest width; but it was healing round almost the entire circumference. In order to permit cicatrization, which carbolic acid tends to check, the detached edges of the crust had been clipped away, and the exposed narrow ring of granulations was dressed with lint dipped in a solution of sulphite of potash—five grains to an ounce of water. The crust, however, was still touched daily as before with carbolic acid, while the tin still covered the whole of the injured part. By this means it was intended that cicatrization should be allowed to go on, and yet decomposition of the discharge be prevented; and this seemed to be to a great extent, if not entirely, attained.

There was, however, one unfavourable circumstance. The little sore on the outer side of the leg, which had been dressed separately without carbolic acid, and had for some time been observed to be increasing rather than diminishing, now assumed unmistakably the appearance of a mild form of hospital gangrene, and became blended with the main sore. For two days an attempt was made to correct the disease by touching the affected part with nitric acid; but on the eighteenth day it was clear that some more effectual measures must be adopted, as the skin in the vicinity had become insidiously undermined to a very serious extent. Accordingly I placed the boy under chloroform, and scraped away with a spoon all the soft grey sloughs, slitting up the skin in order to gain access to them, and in some parts clipping portions of it away, and then applied the strongest nitric acid thoroughly to the bleeding surface. As the disease extended up to the anterior edge of the crust, I thought it right to examine the state of the parts beneath, and as it was pretty loose I removed it. And now a sight presented itself which filled me with horror. There was, indeed, no appearance of hospital gangrene in the parts which the crust had covered, the granulations there having the florid aspect of perfect health; but in the large sore lay the lower fragment of the tibia, freely exposed to the extent of two inches and a half in length, bare and white like a macerated bone. At the upper end of this fragment, and apparently for a considerable distance from it, the bone was thus denuded round its entire circumference; and, judging from previous experience, there was reason to expect that, even if the patient should survive the profuse suppuration which was to be anticipated, about two inches of the whole thickness of the tibia must exfoliate, an amount of loss which in the child's small limb, would of necessity render it utterly useless. The upper fragment was also bare for about half an inch just above its extremity, but the end itself was covered with prominent granulations.

Though despairing of any good result, I resolved to watch for a while the progress of events, prepared to amputate as soon as the boy's health should show signs of failing; and comforting myself with the reflection that he had been brought into a state greatly more favourable for the operation than on his admission. In order to keep down the amount of the discharge the sore was dressed with the sulphite-of-potash lotion, a poultice being applied to the part which had been treated with nitric acid. When the sloughs caused by the caustic separated a healthy surface appeared, which in the course of the next ten days was nearly healed. In other parts of the sore, however, grey patches occasionally showed themselves, assuming healthy characters after being touched with carbolic acid, which, when efficient, has the advantage over other caustics of being painless. But at length spots of hospital gangrene appeared in a form no longer amenable to this mild treatment, in spite of which they began to extend rapidly, and on the 26th of July it became necessary to put the child again under chloroform and apply nitric acid in the same thorough manner as before. This had the effect of producing a perfectly healthy state of the whole sore, which proceeded to heal with great rapidity; so that by the 8th of August it was found to measure an inch less in length and two inches less in greatest breadth than at the time when the crust was removed.

In the meantime his general health, instead of deteriorating, had improved, and he was evidently regaining flesh, while the discharge of pus was astonishingly little considering the state of the limb, being barely sufficient to soak the single layer of lint that covered the sore.

The explanation of this satisfactory state of things was afforded by an observation of much interest made at this period. Since the removal of the crust the granulations had been growing up on all sides about the bone, so that the bare part of the upper fragment was almost entirely covered in, and even the lower fragment, which projected beyond the level of the upper, was to a great extent embedded in the new growth. It had been noticed before the end of this fragment was so much covered up, that granulations were sprouting from the medullary canal, showing that the bone was not dead in its entire thickness. Nevertheless, as the superficial parts had certainly lost their vitality, I had not doubted that a thin layer at least must exfoliate from the whole. Now, however, I observed that some of the surface which remained exposed had assumed a pink colour, implying that the layer of dead bone, whatever its thickness might have originally been, had become so thin as to be transparent, through absorption by new tissue growing in the interior. Further, on attempting to pass the eyed end of a probe between the tibia and the granulations which had enveloped it, I found to my surprise that the instrument could only be introduced for a very short distance, the granulations, with the exception of a narrow free border, being everywhere adherent. The new tissue outside the bone had coalesced with that within, after complete absorption of the intervening dead stratum. Hence the remarkable absence of discharge from around the bone.

During the following month I was absent from home, but was informed that the same process was for some time continued; the granulations gradually encroaching more and more on the exposed bone, and adhering to it as they advanced. The upper fragment was thus entirely covered without any exfoliation occurring, and the bare surface of the lower fragment was reduced to comparatively small dimensions. On the 10th of September the remainder of the dead part, being loose, was removed without difficulty as an exfoliation. It was about an inch in greatest length; but was of extremely irregular shape, full a quarter of the circumference of the tibia being deficient. At the upper end, where it had been most prominent and had become discoloured, it had nearly the full thickness of the dense tissue; but towards the lower end it became thinned away, so as to be in some places as delicate as tissue-paper. The outer surface presented near the margin an appearance of especial interest, being at some parts, even where the bone had considerable thickness, variously scooped and bevelled in a manner that admitted of no other explanation than that the granulations overlapping the dead bone externally had been engaged in its absorption. On applying a magnifier to these excavations in the external surface, they were seen to present a peculiar velvety aspect, differing from the rest of the exterior, but resembling the internal parts of the exfoliation.

The only observation at all analogous to this with which I am acquainted is that of the effects produced upon the ivory pegs used in Dieffenbach's method of treating ununited fracture, the parts of the pegs driven into the bone having been observed, when removed, to have suffered diminution in size. This has hitherto remained as an isolated fact, and it has been regarded as an axiom in surgery that a piece of bone once dead must all come away as an exfoliation. Why it was that in the case before us the osseous tissue destroyed by external violence, aided by the action of carbolic acid, was so exceptionally affected by surrounding parts, the granulations in its vicinity discharging the office of absorbents of the dense tissue, instead of forming pus like those around an ordinary exfoliation, I will reserve for future discussion, when I shall have occasion to point out the great importance of the fact in its bearing both on pathology and practice. Meanwhile I may remark that it illustrates beautifully the function of absorption, which, even where solid substances are taken up, does not require any special set of absorbent vessels, but may be effected even by granulations, the most rudimentary of all tissues, each cell feeding upon any suitable substance in its vicinity.

We also see at once the value of the observation with reference to the treatment of compound fracture with carbolic acid; for it shows that in cases in which the bone is exposed, the acid may be applied so freely as to cause death of its tissue without necessarily inducing exfoliation.

The case was now reduced to one of simple fracture with a large granulating sore, and this was greatly diminished and healing rapidly, while the union of the fragments was becoming very firm; and the limb would doubtless soon have been entirely sound had it not been for that cruel scourge, hospital gangrene. This, however, had shown itself ten days before the removal of the exfoliation, not in the sore, but about an inch from its edge, as a pustule in the cicatrix, which on bursting disclosed a grey slough that soon showed its characters unmistakably, producing considerable destruction of the scar, although the original sore continued to heal kindly.

I will not enter into the history of this and numerous subsequent attacks of the disease further than to state that they were partial in their effect, the unaffected parts still healing with rapidity, and that they continued to yield to the treatment with nitric acid; so that at one time the whole sore was very nearly healed.

But in the early part of October the disease assumed a more intractable form, and in spite of the most energetic use of nitric acid on several occasions, which produced illusory appearances of temporary improvement, by the 27th of the month the sore had become enlarged to nearly its original dimensions, while the limb had swollen greatly through inflammation caused by the irritation, and the boy's general health was rapidly giving way under the increased discharge and nervous excitement.

The question of amputation now again presented itself, but a good airy room in a different department of the hospital being happily now at my disposal, I determined to give the limb one last chance. Before he was taken to the new ward, nitric acid was once more thoroughly applied. His nurse was directed to change the poultice every three hours, and he continued to take wine and some tonic medicine. His general health immediately improved, and when the slough separated, the sore looked healthy. It was now dressed with lint dipped in a solution of sulphate of copper, five grains to an ounce of water, and over this a poultice, the whole being changed every three or four hours night and day; and under this treatment cicatrization proceeded rapidly. Yet when the scar had attained a certain width, a tendency to vesication again showed itself, threatening recurrence of the disease, and in order to prevent the newly formed epidermis from acquiring poisonous qualities as it seemed to do,

I ordered the lint with the lotion, as well as the poultice, to be extended over the whole cicatrix. From the time this dressing was adopted the progress was uninterruptedly satisfactory till the 9th of January, when the sore was at length entirely healed, and he was allowed for the first time to put his foot to the ground. The contraction of the large cicatrix, involving at one part the gastrocnemius muscle, had caused some bending of the knee and pointing of the toes. The former has since become corrected spontaneously by his habitual attitude, sitting in bed with the legs extended before him. The pointing of the toes has also become diminished, and will probably soon pass off entirely, without the division of the tendo Achillis, which I had in view. The tibia, which has long been firm, is of precisely the same length as the other, and the contour of the limb is natural. His general health also is excellent; but he was detained in the hospital till the 9th inst. (March 1867), on account of an obstinate eczematous eruption on the integument of the leg irritated by the long-continued poulticing.

Case 6.— The following case terminated fatally, but from circumstances of an accidental nature; and I trust that the instruction to be derived from it will not be interfered with by the unhappy ultimate result.

John C——, aged fifty-seven, a labourer, was working in a quarry at Row, near Helensburgh, on the Clyde, at nine a.m. on the 26th of October, 1866, when, striking with a crowbar an overhanging part, he brought down an enormous mass of stone weighing six or seven tons, which fell in large blocks on and about him. His right thigh-bone was broken in its lower third, and, as afterwards appeared, the end of the upper fragment was driven through the skin at the inner aspect of the limb a little above the knee. The right collar-bone was fractured at the same time, and he was severely contused in other parts. It was long before his only companion in the quarry could extricate him from his position, and the procuring of a conveyance involved further delay; so that a considerable period elapsed, during which he lost much blood from the thigh, before he could be taken to Helensburgh. Here he was placed on a litter, with a warm moist blanket round the limb, with the object, as he said, of checking the bleeding, which, however, it could not but tend to encourage. He was then conveyed by train to Glasgow, where he reached the infirmary six hours after the occurrence of the accident.

Dr. Archibald Cameron, the house surgeon, seeing the case to be a very grave one, at once sent for me, but without any delay introduced carbolic acid into the wound by means of a piece of lint held in a pair of dressing forceps, passing it about an inch in every direction beneath the integument, after squeezing out a considerable quantity of extravasated blood from the orifice, which was large enough to admit the tip of the finger.

On arriving, an hour after the patient's admission, I found him in a state of prostration sufficiently explained by the severity of his injuries and by the blood lost to the circulation, including a large amount extravasated in the limb, and distending, not only the whole thigh, but the calf, the tenseness of which contrasted strikingly with the flaccidity of the other.

Under these circumstances decomposition of the blood effused among the tissues would have been necessarily fatal. And yet, considering the length of time that had elapsed since the receipt of the injury, and the fact that a reeking flannel had been for two hours in contact with the wound, and had already a somewhat offensive odour when removed from it, there seemed but a poor chance for the treatment with carbolic acid. On the other hand, taking into account the man's time of life and general condition, I believed that to amputate through the thigh infiltrated with blood would be certainly to kill him. And therefore, as it was impossible to say that the other treatment had no chance, while, if it should prove successful, it would have the immeasurable superiority of saving limb as well as life, I determined to persevere with it.

Having removed from the wound the dressings placed on it by Dr. Cameron, I forcibly squeezed out a further large amount of blood, and applied carbolic acid in lint and also mixed with blood, so as to provide for a crust of considerable thickness overlapping the skin by about half an inch every way. This was covered with a circular piece of tin, two inches across, well bulged out except a flat margin about a quarter of an inch wide, which rested on the surrounding integument. This tin cap was retained in position by a single turn of bandage tied round the limb.

The lower end of the upper fragment was much displaced downwards in the vicinity of the wound, but returned towards its natural position on extension of the limb. There still remained considerable depression anteriorly over the seat of fracture; but the lower fragment did not seem to project towards the ham so much as to forbid the use of the long splint. This I accordingly employed with two interior splints to support the muscles of the thigh, one of Gooch's material on the outer aspect, the other a large sheet of stout block-tin, embracing the anterior, inner, and posterior aspects of the limb to a little below the knee, padded in the first instance with a dry towel, for which a hot fomentation should be substituted when all tendency to haemorrhage should have ceased. The object of having the tin extend round the back of the thigh was that it might prevent the discharges from soaking into the bed beneath; and in this way it proved extremely useful.

He passed an uneasy though not entirely sleepless night, suffering more from his shoulder and bruised side than from the thigh. Next morning his aspect was favourable, the pulse 76, and tongue natural; he took a little tea for his breakfast, but nothing solid. The tin cap having been removed, care being taken to avoid detaching the crust along with it, carbolic acid was applied to the surface of the latter. A hot fomentation cloth was then placed on the inner side and front of the thigh and gave him great comfort, and when the dressing was completed he was quite easy. The interior splints being kept in position by looped bandages, and the long splint by the usual folded sheet fixed by pins, along with the perineal band and handkerchief round the foot, the fomentations could be changed night and morning without any disturbance of the limb.

The following night he had a good deal of sleep, the thigh not causing him any inconvenience; and next day, the third after the accident, he took solid food with relish. His pulse was 72, and his tongue continued moist, though he was somewhat thirsty. The crust was touched again with carbolic acid, and covered with a circular piece of calico to prevent the tin cap from adhering to it. He still found comfort in the fomentations.

On the fourth day he made a substantial breakfast after a good night's rest, and was not so thirsty. There was, however, now seen for the first time a slight blush of redness on the front of the thigh over the seat of injury. This was on the fifth day somewhat increased, and the thigh and calf were both more swollen. The tongue also was slightly furred at the base, and his appetite was not quite so good.

On the sixth day the dimensions and appearance of the limb were unaltered, but on the seventh both the redness and swelling were distinctly diminished.

By the end of the second week his appetite was improved and his pulse was 76; while there had not been a drop of discharge from beneath the crust, which had been still touched daily with carbolic acid, the fomentations also having been continued. The swelling, however, had not subsided, and the redness, though varying in extent and degree, had never disappeared from over the seat of fracture. On the fifteenth day a defined prominence made its appearance at this part in a space about as large as the palm of the hand, a little further forward than the crust, and a sense of fluctuation was to be perceived in it. In the evening Dr. Cameron, on changing the fomentation, saw more pus than he thought could be accounted for by the superficial excoriation round the crust, and next morning, on removing the flannel, I found it soaked with similar discharge; a considerable quantity also lying between the tin splint and the limb. On raising the tin cap, the matter was seen welling out from beneath the lower edge of the crust. It was perfectly free from odour, confirming the conclusion I had previously arrived at that this abscess was not in any way caused by decomposition from atmospheric influence. The long period that elapsed before it made its appearance, together with the absence of any serious constitutional disturbance, clearly showed that the carbolic acid had effectually answered the purpose for which it was applied, the constant oozing of blood from the small wound having doubtless been in the patient's favour, by preventing decomposition from penetrating far into the interior before he came under treatment. We know that a mass of extravasated blood occasionally becomes the seat of suppuration without the existence of any external wound. A curious instance of this occurred lately in my practice, in a boy who fell down the hold of a ship upon his head, and, besides serious cerebral symptoms, exhibited at once remarkable prominence of the right eyeball, evidently due to extravasation of blood into the orbit. There being no wound, I expected that the blood would be absorbed; but after the lapse of several days, the prominence of the eye showed increase rather than diminution, and the boy began to complain of supraorbital pain. Fluctuation then became perceptible, and pus was evacuated by incision, after which the eyeball gradually resumed its natural position.

Such I supposed to be the nature of the abscess in C.'s case, and previous experience made me fear that, if decomposition of its contents should occur, the irritation of the fetid pus might cause very serious consequences from rapid extension of suppuration among the imperfect and feeble products of the organization of the blood in the yet swollen limb.

Hence I had intended to evacuate the matter by aid of carbolic acid in such a way as to prevent decomposition. As the abscess was not near the surface at the part where it appeared to be pointing, I had reckoned on having plenty of time for my operations, and was greatly disappointed to find that it had discharged itself spontaneously.

Nevertheless, as the pus was proceeding from beneath the crust impregnated with carbolic acid and was still quite odourless, I did not altogether despair of attaining my object. In order to make the crust more effectual, I extended it for about three-quarters of an inch at the part from which the pus was escaping, by a piece of lint dipped in carbolic acid, which, when mixed with pus, forms a sort of curdy mass which answered pretty well for a crust. A considerable quantity of matter, of moderate consistence and greenish-white colour, was then pressed out from the limb. A new tin cap having been made, large enough to cover the whole of the extended crust, the fomentation was continued as usual.

Next day it was evident, from the sense of fluctuation, that reaccumulation had occured in the abscess, but no further discharge had taken place. On removing the tin cap, however, pus was seen to well out from a new situation at the upper edge of the crust. A piece of lint dipped in carbolic acid was at once placed on this part, and the matter was pressed out and carefully collected measuring 3 oz., of moderate consistence and yellowish-white colour, still without odour except that of carbolic acid. The crust having been somewhat extended at the situation of the new opening, the whole was freely treated with carbolic acid, the tin cap readjusted, and fomentation continued.

During the rest of the week that followed the first evacuation of the abscess the same treatment was pursued with the most satisfactory results. Some pus was usually seen on the fomenting flannel both morning and evening, and some was pressed out of the limb from the orifice last formed, but the amount rapidly diminished in quantity, and also became thinner and more transparent, while it continued free from odour. It may be worth while to mention in detail the quantities obtained from the limb in the morning of each of these days. On the seventeenth day it was an ounce and a half, somewhat thinner than before; in the eighteenth, two drachms and a half, decidedly thinner; on the nineteenth, half a drachm, much thinner and more transparent; on the twentieth, a quarter of a drachm, similar in quality; and on the twenty-first, six drops only, and almost free from opacity. Finally, in the evening of that day no discharge was seen on the flannel, nor could any be squeezed out from the limb. Meanwhile the calf, which had increased markedly in circumference just before the abscess opened, steadily diminished, and in the thigh all swelling disappeared from over the seat of fracture, so that the end of the upper fragment, previously quite obscured, could be distinctly defined. His general heatlh, too, had improved; his tongue had become quite clean, and he had acquired for the first time since his admission a genuine appetite, the pulse continuing about 72.

I suspect, however, that this success made us relax a little our vigilant care in guarding against decomposition. But be this as it may, the method which we pursued in order to avoid it was not, as experience has since shown, thoroughly trustworthy. Would that I had at that time known of the mode of proceeding which will be found described in a future section of this communication. Very different then might have been the issue of the case!

On the twenty-second day pus was again found in the flannel, and some bubbles of gas were observed to escape along with the two or three drops that could be squeezed from the limb, and these had a distinctly offensive odour. Judging it now useless to retain the crust any longer, I removed it, and found the original wound still sealed by the original clot, the openings by which the pus had escaped being new apertures in the skin overlapped by the crust. In the after-part of the day he had a good deal of uneasiness, and in the evening half an ounce of pus, with numerous air-bubbles, was pressed out of the limb by Dr. Cameron. After this the patient passed a comfortable night, and in the morning only two drachms of matter could be procured from the thigh, but this was thicker and more opaque than it had been, with decidedly offensive odour, and contained bubbles of gas; there was also pus in the flannel. There was, further, some return of swelling over the seat of fracture.

But though the plan of dealing with the abscess had failed to accomplish all that I desired, its essential object appeared to have been attained. For during the week in which decomposition was prevented, the thigh had become so much consolidated and strengthened that all danger of serious consequences semed to have been tided over. No extension of the suppuration took place beyond the trifling degree above described, and his constitution did not suffer. Any further use of carbolic acid being obviously uncalled for, the sore was simply dressed with a lotion, the lint being so arranged as to allow free escape for the pus, and afterwards, to promote this more effectually, a small perforated caoutchouc tube was introduced, a dry cloth being substituted for the fomentation. Under this management the discharge gradually diminished in quantity, and became again thinner and more transparent, and the swelling of the calf became steadily reduced.

Still the opening did not close, and on the 2nd of December, more than a fortnight having passed in this way, I introduced a probe, and found that it passed downwards to bare bone, including a considerable extent of surface in the lower fragment. Here, then, was presented the prospect of a tedious process of exfoliation; whereas if decomposition of the pus had not occurred, the granulations would probably have closed upon the dead bone, and absorbed it, as in the last case, and the fact that any part had lost its vitality would then never have been known. That there is a reasonable ground for this belief will, I trust, appear from the discussion in the succeeding section.

For a long time the progress of the patient continued satisfactory, the process of union of the fragments advancing steadily, till in the early part of February, the bone being firm, the splints were entirely discarded, and the case was reduced from one of fracture to one of limited exfoliation. It was satisfactory also to find that the knee-joint continued movable, so that I confidently anticipated recovery, with a perfectly useful limb.

At this period, however, a new symptom presented itself—viz., haemorrhage from the sinus. Mr. Hector Cameron, my present house surgeon, who saw the first appearance of bleeding, supposed it to proceed from the surface of the granulations; for it was then small in amount, and ceased spontaneously. Some days later, however—viz. on the 11th of February—a very profuse haemorrhage occurred, the blood soaking through the bed, and dropping upon the floor beneath, before it was observed, and the gentleman who was summoned to see the patient in Mr. Cameron's absence, found him pulseless. He afterwards rallied to some extent, but remained utterly prostrated, and unable to retain the slightest nourishment. As the popliteal artery could be felt beating in the lower part of the ham, I hoped that the source of the blood might be some minor branch, which might possibly close. But it afterwards appeared that a circular opening existed in the main vessel, occasioned no doubt by the pressure of an irregular projection of the lower fragment. It would be irrelevant to relate particularly the history of his yet further exhaustion by recurrent haemorrhages after delusive temporary cessations, or of my attempts to restore him by tying the popliteal artery, and making arrangements for transfusion, to which he declined to submit. He died on the 25th of February.

The next four cases occurred in the practice of my colleagues in the infirmary, who have kindly placed them at my disposal.

CASE 7.—Mary M., aged sixty-two, was admitted under the care of Dr. Morton on the 13th of August, 1866, at eleven p.m., when she stated that about five o'clock in the afternoon of that day she missed her footing when going downstairs, and fell with violence, and on getting up found that her right forearm was broken and bleeding. A medical man was called in, who made various applications in order to stop the haemorrhage, but failed to do so, and she was advised to go to the infirmary. Mr. A. T. Thomson, the house surgeon (to whom I am indebted for notes of the case), on removing the bandage, from which blood was trickling, found both bones of the forearm broken a little above the wrist, and a detached fragment of the radius projecting from a wound about as large as a fourpenny-piece, on the outer aspect of the limb. Having extracted this fragment, he applied liquid carbolic acid thoroughly to the interior of the wound. This rather increased the bleeding, which, however, he arrested completely by plugging the orifice with a bit of lint dipped in the acid. Over this he placed a mixture of blood and carbolic acid, covering it with a piece of dry lint. He then put up the limb in two well-padded Gooch's splints, retained in position with a continuous bandage. The apparatus was left undisturbed for five days, when, on removal of the splints, it was found that the piece of dry lint over the wound, though it had been saturated with blood, was quite dry, having become incorporated with the crust beneath. It was not interfered with except that the surface was touched with carbolic acid, and the splints were reapplied as before, the part being quite free from uneasiness.

On the twelfth day the splints were again removed and the crust was detached, when it was found that the piece of lint with which the wound had been plugged had become partly pushed out of the orifice. The plug also was now removed, when the surface beneath was observed to be granulating, but entirely free from pus. The sore was dressed with one part of carbolic acid to seven parts of olive oil applied on lint every second day, the use of the splints being continued till the 8th of September, when she was discharged, with the sore healed and both bones firmly united, two days less than four weeks after the accident.

This case is valuable as an example of a mode in which troublesome bleeding in compound fracture may sometimes be advantageously arrested. The entire absence of pus about the plug on the twelfth day after its introduction contrasts strikingly with the suppuration invariably caused within four days by a piece of lint inserted without carbolic acid into a wound.

CASE 8.—Samuel B., aged thirteen, was admitted under Dr. Morton's care, on the 30th of August, 1866, with a compound fracture of the left femur, about the junction of the upper and middle thirds of the shaft, and a simple fracture of the right thigh in a similar situation. He stated that about four hours previously he was engaged in some work about a steam-engine, when he was struck by one of the balls of the 'governor', and hurled with great force against an iron pillar. The men who brought him to the infirmary said that when he was raised from the ground a piece of bone was seen to protrude from a wound in the left thigh, but was restored to its natural position by a medical man who was called in to see him, and who applied a long splint and bandage to each limb. Mr. A. T. Thomson, on examining the boy, found a lacerated wound about three inches long at the upper part of the left thigh, running transversely from the middle of the inner side of the limb to its posterior aspect, and in this wound the upper fragment of the femur was visible, somewhat displaced, but not protruding. There was some bleeding, but not to any serious extent. He sponged out the wound thoroughly with a solution of one part of carbolic acid in three parts of olive oil, and then covered its lips with a mixture of blood and the undiluted acid spread upon lint, and over this a piece of sheet-tin, retained in position by means of a looped bandage. He next corrected the faulty position of the fragments and applied lateral splints of Gooch's material to the thigh, maintaining gentle extension by means of plasters applied to the integument of the leg after the American plan, and fixed to the foot of the bed, a perineal band being attached to the bed-head. While the left limb was thus kept readily accessible for changing the dressings, the long splint was employed as usual for the simple fracture on the right side.

Next day the surface of the crust was touched with carbolic acid, and a hot fomentation applied to the limb.

On the third day the crust was removed through a misunderstanding, but it was resolved to follow out the treatment on the same principle, and with this view the wound was dressed twice a day with lint dipped in the mixture of carbolic acid and oil (one part to three), covered with the tin, as the crust had been before, while the fomentations also were continued. Meanwhile the limb remained free from pain, redness, or swelling, and there was a complete absence of constitutional disturbance.

On the sixth day, however, he was a little feverish, and remained so, though without any apparent local symptoms, till the twelfth day, when Mr. Thomson noticed that the central part of the wound, which had become covered with a whitish crust, was somewhat prominent, and, on careful examination, perceived a distinct sense of fluctuation. He therefore removed the white layer from that part, when eight ounces of perfectly odourless pus escaped. A probe introduced failed to detect any bare bone. Mr. Thomson now sponged out the cavity of the abscess with the mixture of carbolic acid and oil, and left in it a strip of lint dipped in the same, continuing the other dressings as before. The constitutional disturbance now at once subsided, and under the same dressing the cavity of the abscess quickly contracted, and in a little more than a fortnight closed entirely. Six weeks after the accident the wound was completely healed, and both the thigh-bones were firmly united, with the limbs of equal length. In another week he was able to stand.

This case, which, I cannot avoid remarking, reflects great credit on the house surgeon in charge, is interesting as another instance of the occurrence of abscess in compound fracture, independently of atmospheric influence. That it was so in this instance is clearly shown by the entire absence of constitutional symptoms for the first five days, the circumscribed character of the suppuration, and the odourless nature of the pus. The injured part suppurated, probably from the same cause as a severe bruise may without any breach of the integument. The satisfactory results obtained by treating the wound with carbolic acid diluted with oil, instead of the undiluted acid, will naturally suggest the inquiry whether this would not always be the better practice. And I may mention that my former house surgeon, Dr. A. Cameron, met with similar success in two cases in which he pursued the same treatment —one of them a compound fracture of the ulna at the elbow, the other a severe contused wound of the back of the hand communicating with a fractured metatarsal bone. But considering how much is at stake, and that the patient's life may depend upon entire destruction of the septic germs that lie in the wound, I am inclined to think it wiser to avail ourselves of the full energy of the pure acid, more especially since we have had sufficient evidence that any caustic effects it may have are not productive of serious consequences.

CASE 9.—William C., aged thirty-three, was admitted on the 29th of September, 1866, under the care of Dr. Eben. Watson, with a compound fracture of the left tibia, produced by an omnibus passing over the limb at eight o'clock p.m. The broken part of the bone was exposed in a wound six and a half inches in length, a little above the ankle. The skin in the vicinity was detached from the subjacent tissues for about two inches, and there was ecchymosis reaching some distance up the leg, with other evidence of severe contusion.

An hour and half after the accident Dr. A. Forsyth, the house surgeon, from whose notes these particulars are obtained, sponged out the wound thoroughly with undiluted carbolic acid, and placed over it layers of calico soaked with the acid; and, in order to provide for a sufficiently substantial crust, spread over the calico some paste composed of starch moistened with carbolic acid, covering the whole with a piece of block-tin secured with a bandage, the fracture being treated with a suitable apparatus. After the dressing, the patient, though unable to express his feelings, being dumb, appeared entirely free from uneasiness.

Next day the tin was carefully removed from the crust, the surface of which was touched with carbolic acid, and, the tin having been readjusted, hot fomentations were applied to the leg and foot. The pulse was now 96, the tongue clean, and appetite good. The same treatment was pursued till the thirteenth day, when the fomentations were discontinued, and the edges of the crust which were loose were clipped away, and lint moistened with water was applied to the granulating surface thus exposed, the remainder of the crust being still touched daily with carbolic acid. Meanwhile there had been no suppuration beneath the crust, and the patient had remained free from constitutional symptoms.

On the seventeenth day the crust, which had separated from the wound at its lower third, was removed, disclosing a healthy granulating surface, the bone being nowhere visible, while there was no appearance of pus, except a trifling amount towards the lower part. The sore, which was entirely superficial, was now treated like an ordinary ulcer, and healed quickly. The bone also united as in a simple fracture, and he was discharged eight weeks after the receipt of the injury, having been kept longer in the hospital than would otherwise have been necessary, on account of a head affection to which he was subject.

The above case, besides being a good example of the effects of the treatment of compound fracture with carbolic acid, affords an illustration of a practice which I have on several occasions found useful when there has been but little bleeding from the wound, a dough or paste composed of flour or starch, moistened with the acid, being employed in lieu of the compound with blood to render the crust sufficiently substantial.

CASE 10.—Thomas M'B., a labourer, who gave his age as fifty-two, but had the appearance of a much older person, was admitted at noon on the 2nd of January, 1867, under the care of Dr. G. Buchanan, having been knocked down an hour before by the shaft of a luggage wagon, the wheel of which passed over his left leg, producing a compound fracture in the lower third of the limb. Mr. James Robinson, the house surgeon, who has given me notes of the case, found a wound from which blood was oozing, about an inch and a half in length, exposing part of the tibia, and communicating with the seat of fracture. The tissues were pretty severely contused. Undiluted carbolic acid was applied freely to the interior of the wound by means of lint held in a pair of dressing-forceps, and a crust was formed of blood mingled with the acid, covered with lint, over which a cap of tin was placed, well bulged out to correspond to the substantial crust, and large enough to overlap to a slight extent the sound skin in the vicinity. The fragments having been brought into proper position, the limb was put up with lateral wooden splints, with a hot fomentation. At the conclusion of the dressing the patient expressed himself as greatly relieved. The pulse was then 65.

Next day he was free from pain after a fair night's rest. The pulse was 74, and the tongue clean and moist. The surface of the crust was touched with carbolic acid, the limb being still fomented; and the same treatment was continued daily for the following fortnight, during which the limb was entirely free from pain, redness, or suppuration, while his constitution was quite unaffected by the injury, the tongue remaining clean, and the pulse varying only between 72 and 85.

I was present when the crust was removed, eighteen days after the accident. Not a drop of pus existed beneath it. On the contrary, the superficial sloughs of the cutis occasioned by the caustic action of the acid first applied remained still undetached. The exposed surface was treated with water dressing, and in two days presented the appearance of an ordinary granulating sore, which healed without interruption.

Six weeks and three days after the receipt of the injury the splints were removed, the bones being satisfactorily united.

This is an excellent example of the effects of the carbolic-acid treatment in a compound fracture of the leg of average severity. No simple fracture could have caused less disturbance, either local or constitutional.

Case II.—The following case, though incomplete, is given on account of the conclusive evidence it affords regarding a complication of compound fracture of much interest both practically and theoretically—viz. emphysema of the limb in consequence of air being introduced into the wound, and diffused among the interstices of the tissues by a pumping action of the fragments of the broken bone when freely moved through restlessness of the patient or carelessness of his attendants before he comes under the surgeon's care. Such a state of things may seem at first sight to render it impossible to prevent decomposition of the extravasated blood, since it would be out of the question to attempt to apply carbolic acid to all the emphysematous tissues. But I have long indulged the hope that, the air entering in small successive portions, its floating organisms might be arrested by the first blood with which they came in contact, and remain for some time confined to the vicinity of the external wound, in which case, by squeezing out as much blood as possible from the orifice in the integument, and introducing carbolic acid freely, we might get rid of all causes of decomposition in the limb, the mere atmospheric gases diffused more remotely, however abundant, being entirely innocuous. This hope, it now appears, was not ill-founded.

John D.,—aged fifty-five, a calico-printer, of intemperate habits, was admitted under my care in the Royal Infirmary at six p.m. on the 4th of April, 1867, having broken both bones of his right leg about an hour before by jumping out of a window into the street, from a height of between fifteen and twenty feet, while in a state of intoxication. He was carried upstairs to his lodgings, kicking about in his drunken frenzy. A cloth was then put round the leg, but no efficient means were employed to steady it, and he was conveyed to the hospital from a distant part of the city in a cab, moving the limb recklessly during the whole journey. His friends stated that he had lost a great deal of blood, and the cloth which was round the limb on his admission was saturated. Mr. H. Cameron, the house surgeon, found a wound about half an inch in length, situated over the spine of the tibia, at the junction of the middle and lower thirds of the bone, the fracture being half an inch lower down, and obviously communicating. The wound was bleeding very freely, and the leg was considerably swollen through extravasation of blood into it. On manipulation, Mr. Cameron found the tissues about the seat of fracture emphysematous, the characteristic cracking sensation being experienced fully four inches above the wound and two inches below it, and also on the opposite side of the limb, over the fibula; and as a result of the handling, a frothy mixture of blood and air, in larger and smaller bubbles, escaped from the orifice. The fragments were much displaced, the foot being greatly everted.

Mr. Cameron, having squeezed out as much blood as possible from the wound, introduced melted crystallized carbolic acid in a piece of calico held in dressing-forceps, which he passed in various directions for more than two inches beneath the integument and about an inch and a half among the deeper structures of the limb, using three different pieces of calico soaked with the acid, and leaving the last in the wound as a plug to check the very free haemorrhage, which the treatment had considerably increased. He then applied several layers of calico steeped in carbolic acid and smeared with blood, so as to make a pretty thick crust overlapping the skin by about half an inch, and adapted to the crust a cap of block-tin of slightly larger dimensions, pressing it down upon the skin by means of a looped bandage encircling the leg. Having next corrected the displacement of the fragments, he moulded a pasteboard splint to the outer side of the leg and foot, strengthening it with a temporary Gooch's splint, and laid the limb on its outer side upon a pillow with the knee bent. The patient now stated that the pain he had suffered was greately relieved. His pulse was 100. Two hours later, as a good deal of oozing of blood was still going on, a folded cloth was placed upon the tin cap and pressed down upon it with a bandage. The limb meanwhile was considerably more swollen, from bleeding into its interior, kept up, no doubt, by the sudden jerking movements which in his unreasoning condition he could not be prevented from making. The pressure employed greatly diminished the external haemorrhage, but did not entirely arrest it; and when two hours more had elapsed Mr. Cameron asked my advice. I recommended the use of a well-fitting internal splint, to procure greater steadiness of the fragments, and so get rid of the irritation which perpetuated the bleeding. Mr. Cameron, however, on removing the compress, found that all tendency to oozing of blood had ceased. The patient was now sober, but continued very restless. The internal splint was therefore applied, and thirty drops of solution of muriate of morphia were administered.

During the night he suffered a good deal, and got no sleep at all. Next morning, however, he complained rather of a general sense of weariness and sickness, the consequences of his debauch, than of pain; the pulse had fallen to 76; and he took his breakfast pretty well. The surface of the crust was touched with carbolic acid, and this was repeated in the afternoon, when a hot fomentation was applied to the inner side of the leg, and over this a sheet of stout block-tin, to serve, as in some previous cases, the double purpose of ensuring the efficiency of the fomentation, and acting as an internal splint. The limb was now quite easy. At night the pulse was still 76. He had made a pretty hearty supper, and felt only occasional twinges in the limb. The fomentation was changed, and the crust again touched with carbolic acid, and the opiate repeated.

He passed the following night like the preceding, without getting any sleep whatever; and in the morning his pulse was 90, although the limb was free from pain or inflammatory blush, and he made a hearty breakfast. Fearing the approach of traumatic delirium, I ordered a larger opiate to be given at night. Fifty drops of the morphia solution were accordingly administered; and after this dose he slept for about five hours. Nevertheless, he grew more restless and was found in the morning with the leg fully extended and resting on the calf instead of on its outer side. His pulse continued at 90; and although the state of the limb and his appetite were all that could be wished, he exhibited in the afternoon unmistakable signs of delirium tremens, jerking out his tongue when asked to show it, twitching his hands in an excited manner, and declaring that his bedclothes were creeping away from him, while the restless movements of the limb were continued. I ordered a dose of castor oil, to be followed, as soon as it should have operated, by a drachm of the solution of muriate of morphia, to be repeated if necessary. He took the opiate about eight o'clock p.m., and soon afterwards dozed a little; and at eleven his pulse had fallen to 82. After this he fell into a sound sleep, from which he did not wake till six a.m.; and from this time forth he was perfectly tranquil and rational.

It is needless to enter into particulars regarding his subsequent progress further than to say that it has been in all respects satisfactory; and on the tenth day after the accident, when I saw him last, his pulse was 76, his appetite excellent, and he had the appearance of a man in perfect health. The limb was still free from pain, while the swelling due to extravasation of blood had disappeared, and the skin was of natural aspect. After the second day from the accident, there had not been even any discharge of serum from beneath the crust, which had been daily touched with carbolic acid, the fomentations being also continued, as he found them comfortable.

I need not hesitate to say that all danger in this case is over; and that the compound fracture is already converted into a simple one under circumstances which, even for a simple fracture, would have been trying.

In revising the proof, after nine days more have elapsed, I may add that all has continued to go on well.

PRELIMINARY NOTICE ON ABSCESS

I will now give a description of a new method of treating abscess, which has afforded results so satisfactory that it does not seem right to withhold it longer from the profession generally.

It is based, like the treatment of compound fracture, on the antiseptic principle, and the material employed is essentially the same—namely, carbolic acid, but differently applied in accordance with the difference of the circumstances. In compound fracture there is an irregular wound, which has probably been exposed to the air before it is seen by the surgeon, and may therefore contain in its interstices the atmospheric germs which are the causes of decomposition, and these must be destroyed by the energetic application of the antiseptic agent. In an unopened abscess, on the other hand, as a general rule, no septic organisms are present, so that it is not necessary to introduce the carbolic acid into the interior. Here the essential object is to guard against the introduction of living particles from without, at the same time that a free exit is afforded for the constant discharge of the contents. The mode in which this is accomplished is as follows:—

A solution of one part of crystallized carbolic acid in four parts of boiled linseed oil having been prepared, a piece of rag from four to six inches square is dipped in the oily mixture, and laid upon the skin where the incision is to be made. The lower edge of the rag being then raised, while the upper edge is kept from slipping by an assistant, a common scalpel or bistoury dipped in the oil is plunged into the cavity of the abscess, and an opening about three-quarters of an inch in length is made, and the instant the knife is withdrawn the rag is dropped upon the skin as an antiseptic curtain, beneath which the pus flows out into a vessel placed to receive it. The cavity of the abscess is firmly pressed, so as to force out all existing pus as nearly as may be (the old fear of doing mischief by rough treatment of the pyogenic membrane being quite ill-founded); and if there be much oozing of blood, or if there be a considerable thickness of parts between the abscess and the surface, a piece of lint dipped in the antiseptic oil is introduced into the incision to check bleeding and prevent primary adhesion, which is otherwise very apt to occur. The introduction of the lint is effected as rapidly as may be, and under the protection of the antiseptic rag. Thus the evacuation of the original contents is accomplished with perfect security against the introduction of living germs. This, however, would be of no avail unless an antiseptic dressing could be applied that would effectually prevent the decomposition of the stream of pus constantly flowing out beneath it. After numerous disappointments, I have succeeded with the following, which may be relied upon as absolutely trustworthy. About six teaspoonfuls of the above-mentioned solution of carbolic acid in linseed oil are mixed up with common whitening (carbonate of lime) to the consistence of a firm paste, which is in fact glazier's putty with the addition of a little carbolic acid. This is spread upon a piece of sheet block-tin about six inches square; or common tinfoil will answer equally well if strengthened with adhesive plaster to prevent it from tearing, and in some situations it is preferable, from its adapting itself more readily to the shape of the part affected. The putty forms a layer about a quarter of an inch thick; it may be spread with a table-knife, or pressed out with the hand, a towel being temporarily interposed to prevent the putty from sticking to the hand or soiling the coat-sleeve. The tin thus spread with putty is placed upon the skin so that the middle of it corresponds to the position of the incision, the antiseptic rag used in opening the abscess being removed the instant before. The tin is then fixed securely by adhesive plaster, the lowest edge being left free for the escape of the discharge into a folded towel placed over it and secured by a bandage. This dressing has the following advantages: The tin prevents the evaporation of the carbolic acid, which escapes readily through any organic tissue such as oiled silk or gutta-percha. The putty contains the carbolic acid just sufficiently diluted to prevent its excoriating the skin, while its substance serves as a reservoir of the acid during the intervals between the dressings. Its oily nature and tenacity prevent it from being washed away by the discharge, which all oozes out beneath it as fast as it escapes from the incision; while the extent of the surface of the putty renders it securely antiseptic. Lastly, the putty is a cleanly application, and gives the surgeon very little trouble; a supply being daily made by some convalescent in a hospital, or in private practice by the nurse or a friend of the patient; or a larger quantity may be made at once, and kept in a tin canister. The dressing is changed, as a general rule, once in twenty-four hours; but if the abscess be a very large one, it is prudent to see the patient twelve hours after it has been opened, when, if the towel should be much stained with discharge, the dressing should be changed, to avoid subjecting its antiseptic virtues to too severe a test. But after the first twenty-four hours, a single daily dressing is sufficient. The changing of the dressing must be methodically done as follows: A second similar piece of tin having been spread with the putty, a piece of rag is dipped in the oily solution, and placed on the incision the moment the first tin is removed. This guards against the possibility of mischief occurring during the cleansing of the skin with a dry cloth and pressing out any discharge which may exist in the cavity. If a plug of lint was introduced when the abscess was opened, it is removed under cover of the antiseptic rag, which is taken off at the moment when the new tin is to be applied. The same process is continued daily till the sinus closes.

The results of this treatment are such as correct pathological knowledge might have enabled us to predict. The pyogenic membrane has no innate disposition to form pus, but does so only because it is subjected to some preternatural stimulus. In an ordinary abscess, whether acute or chronic, the original cause that led to suppuration is no longer in operation, and the stimulus that determines the continued pus-formation is derived from the presence of the pus pent up in the interior. When an abscess is opened in the ordinary way this cause of stimulation is removed, but in its place is substituted the potent stimulus of decomposition. If, however, the abscess be opened antiseptically, the pyogenic membrance, freed from the operation of the previous stimulus without the substitution of a new one, ought, according to theory, to cease to suppurate, while the patient should be relieved from any local or general disturbance caused by the abscess, without the risk of irritative fever or hectic.

Such, accordingly, is the fact. Abscesses of large size have, after the original contents have been evacuated, furnished no further pus whatever, the discharge being merely serum, which in a few days has amounted only to a few drops in the twenty-four hours. Whether the opening be dependent or not is a matter of perfect indifference, the small amount of unirritating fluid being all evacuated spontaneously by the rapidly contracting pyogenic membrane. At the same time, we reckon with perfect certainty on the absence of all constitutional disturbance.

As an illustration, I may mention the last case which has come under my care. It is that of a young woman, twenty-five years old, with psoas abscess, which had of late been rapidly on the increase, and caused a large swelling below Poupart's ligament, communicating with a fluctuating mass, dull on percussion, reaching to a considerable distance up the abdomen, the femoral vessels being raised over the communication between them. Six days ago I opened, in the manner above described, the swelling in the thigh at the anterior part of the limb where it was nearest the surface, giving exit to twenty-seven ounces of pus, thin, but containing numerous large curdy masses. I introduced a piece of lint, dipped in the carbolic acid and oil, into the incision; and this prevented any discharge from escaping during the next twenty-four hours, when, on removal of the plug of lint under an antiseptic rag, three ounces of turbid serum escaped. For the next three days there was scarcely any discharge, the deeper parts of the incision having cohered. On firm pressure, however, the product of seventy-two hours escaped, and amounted to four drachms of serum. Meanwhile the girl's general health, which had not been interfered with by the abscess, continued perfectly good, neither pulse, tongue, appetite, nor sleep having been disturbed.

In this case, though there is no deformity of the spine, there is great probability that caries of the vertebræ is present. But even though such be the case, there is good reason to hope for a favourable issue. Regarding caries as merely the suppurative stage of chronic inflammation in a weak form of tissue, I have been not surprised, though greatly rejoiced, to find that it exhibits the tendency of inflammatory affections generally—viz. a disposition to spontaneous cure on the withdrawal of irritation. Hitherto, in surgical practice, caries has had to contend against the formidable irritation of decomposing matter, which, under circumstances of weakness, is often sufficient to cause ulceration, even in the soft parts; yet, in spite of this irritation, caries is often recoverable in the child where the vital powers of all the tissues are stronger. If, therefore, this serious complication can be avoided, there seems nothing in theory against the probability that caries may prove curable in the adult. And even should portions of necrosed bone be present, as is not infrequently the case, our experience of the treatment of compound fracture with carbolic acid has taught us that dead bone, if undecomposed, not only fails to induce suppuration in its vicinity, but is liable to absorption by the granulations around it.

Such were the hopes which I ventured to express several months ago to my winter class. Since that time I have opened numerous abscesses connected with caries of the vertebræ, the hip, knee, ankle, and elbow, and in all cases I have found the discharge become in a few days trifling in amount, and in many it has ceased to be puriform after the first twenty-four hours. Finally, three days ago—viz. on the 4th inst. (July 1867)—I had the inexpressible happiness of finding the sinus soundly closed in a middle-aged man, in whom I opened in February last a psoas abscess, proved to be connected with diseased bone by the discharge, on one occasion, of an osseous spiculum. For months past we had persevered with the antiseptic dressing, although the discharge did not amount to more than a drop or two of serum in the twenty-four hours, well knowing by bitter experience that so long as a sinus existed the occurrence of decomposition might produce the most disastrous consequences; and at length our patience has been crowned with success.

Hence I no longer feel any hesitation in recommending the early opening of such abscesses, because, while they remain unopened, the disease of the bone is necessarily progressive, whereas when opened antiseptically, there is good ground to hope for their steady, though tedious, recovery.

The putty of the strength above recommended, though it generally fails to excoriate the skin, sometimes produces this effect when long continued. In such case it may be reduced in strength so that the oil contains only one part to five or six without disadvantage when the discharge is very small in amount.

The application prevents the occurrence of cicatrization in the little sore caused by the incision, and perpetuates a trifling discharge from it. Hence it is impossible to judge whether or not the sinus has closed, except by examining it from time to time with a probe, which should be dipped in the antiseptic oil, and passed in between folds of the antiseptic rag. This may seem a refinement, but if we could see with the naked eye a few only of the septic organisms that people every cubic inch of the atmosphere of a hospital ward, we should rather wonder that the antiseptic treatment is ever successful than omit any precautions in conducting it.

The putty used in treating abscesses has proved very valuable in simplifying the treatment of compound fracture, and enlarging the range of its applicability, and also in dealing with incised wounds on the antiseptic principle. But I must defer a notice of these matters to a future occasion.

ON THE ANTISEPTIC PRINCIPLE IN THE PRACTICE OF SURGERY

A paper read before the British Medical Association in Dublin on August 9, 1867.

(*British Medical Journal,* 1867, vol. ii, p. 246.)

In the course of an extended investigation into the nature of inflammation, and the healthy and morbid conditions of the blood in relation to it, I arrived, several years ago, at the conclusion that the essential cause of suppuration in wounds is decomposition, brought about by the influence of the atmosphere upon blood or serum retained within them, and, in the case of contused wounds, upon portions of tissue destroyed by the violence of the injury.

To prevent the occurrence of suppuration, with all its attendant risks, was an object manifestly desirable; but till lately apparently unattainable, since it seemed hopeless to attempt to exclude the oxygen, which was universally regarded as the agent by which putrefaction was effected. But when it had been shown by the researches of Pasteur that the septic property of the atmosphere depended, not on the oxygen or any gaseous constituent, but on minute organisms suspended in it, which owed their energy to their vitality, it occurred to me that decomposition in the injured part might be avoided without excluding the air, by applying as a dressing some material capable of destroying the life of the floating particles.

Upon this principle I have based a practice of which I will now attempt to give a short account.

The material which I have employed is carbolic or phenic acid, a volatile organic compound which appears to exercise a peculiarly destructive influence upon low forms of life, and hence is the most powerful antiseptic with which we are at present acquainted.

The first class of cases to which I applied it was that of compound fractures, in which the effects of decomposition in the injured part were especially striking and pernicious. The results have been such as to establish conclusively the great principle, that *all the local inflammatory mischief and general febrile disturbance which follow severe injuries are due to the irritating and poisoning influence of decomposing blood or sloughs.* For these evils are entirely avoided by the antiseptic treatment, so that limbs which otherwise would be unhesitatingly condemned to amputation may be retained with confidence of the best results.

In conducting the treatment, the first object must be the destruction of any septic germs which may have been introduced into the wound, either at the moment of the accident or during the time which has since elapsed. This is done by introducing the acid of full strength into all accessible recesses of the wound by means of a piece of rag held in dressing-forceps and dipped in the liquid. This I did not venture to do in the earlier cases; but experience has shown that the compound which carbolic acid forms with the blood, and also any portions of tissue killed by its caustic action, including even parts of the bone, are disposed of by absorption and organization, provided they are afterwards kept from decomposing. We are thus enabled to employ the antiseptic treatment efficiently at a period after the occurrence of the injury at which it would otherwise probably fail. Thus I have now under my care in the Glasgow Infirmary a boy who was admitted with compound fracture of the leg as late as eight and a half hours after the accident, in whom nevertheless all local and constitutional disturbance was avoided by means of carbolic acid, and the bones were firmly united five weeks after his admission.

The next object to be kept in view is to guard effectually against the spreading of decomposition into the wound along the stream of blood and serum which oozes out during the first few days after the accident when the acid originally applied has been washed out, or dissipated by absorption and evaporation. This part of the treatment has been greatly improved during the last few weeks. The method which I have hitherto published consisted in the application of a piece of lint dipped in the acid, overlapping the sound skin to some extent, and covered with a tin cap, which was daily raised in order to touch the surface of the lint with the antiseptic. This method certainly succeeded well with wounds of moderate size; and, indeed, I may say that in all the many cases of this kind which have been so treated by myself or my house surgeons, not a single failure has occurred. When, however, the wound is very large, the flow of blood and serum is so profuse, especially during the first twenty-four hours, that the antiseptic application cannot prevent the spread of decomposition into the interior unless it overlaps the sound skin for a very considerable distance, and this was inadmissible by the method described above, on account of the extensive sloughing of the surface of the cutis which it would involve. This difficulty has, however, been overcome by employing a paste composed of common whitening (carbonate of lime) mixed with a solution of one part of carbolic acid in four parts of boiled linseed oil, so as to form a firm putty. This application contains the acid in too dilute a form to excoriate the skin, which it may be made to cover to any extent that may be thought desirable, while its substance serves as a reservoir of the antiseptic material. So long as any discharge continues, the paste should be changed daily; and, in order to prevent the chance of mischief occurring during the process, a piece of rag dipped in the solution of carbolic acid in oil is put on next the skin, and maintained there permanently, care being taken to avoid raising it along with the putty. This rag is always kept in an antiseptic condition from contact with the paste above it, and destroys any germs that may fall upon it during the short time that should alone be allowed to pass in the changing of the dressing. The putty should be in a layer about a quarter of an inch thick, and may be advantageously applied rolled out between two pieces of thin calico, which maintain it in the form of a continuous sheet, that may be wrapped in a moment round the whole circumference of a limb, if this be thought desirable, while the putty is prevented by the calico from sticking to the rag which is next the skin. When all discharge has ceased, the use of the paste is discontinued, but the original rag is left adhering to the skin till healing by scabbing is supposed to be complete. I have at present in the hospital a man with severe compound fracture of both bones of the left leg, caused by direct violence, who, after the cessation of the sanious discharge under the use of the paste, without a drop of pus appearing, has been treated for the last two weeks exactly as if the fracture were a simple one. During this time the rag, adhering by means of a crust of inspissated blood collected beneath it, has continued perfectly dry, and it will be left untouched till the usual period for removing the splints in a simple fracture, when we may fairly expect to find a sound cicatrix beneath it.

We cannot, however, always calculate on so perfect a result as this. More or less pus may appear after the lapse of the first week; and the larger the wound the more likely is this to happen. And here I would desire earnestly to enforce the necessity of persevering with the antiseptic application, in spite of the appearance of suppuration, so long as other symptoms are favourable. The surgeon is extremely apt to suppose that any suppuration is an indication that the antiseptic treatment has failed, and that poulticing or water dressing should be resorted to. But such a course would in many cases sacrifice a limb or a life. I can not, however, expect my professional brethren to follow my advice blindly in such a matter, and therefore I feel it necessary to place before them, as shortly as I can, some pathological principles, intimately connected not only with the point we are immediately considering, but with the whole subject of this paper.

If a perfectly healthy granulating sore be well washed and covered with a plate of clean metal, such as block-tin, fitting its surface pretty accurately, and overlapping the surrounding skin an inch or so in every direction, and retained in position by adhesive plaster and a bandage, it will be found, on removing it after twenty-four or forty-eight hours, that little or nothing that can be called pus is present, merely a little transparent fluid, while at the same time there is an entire absence of the unpleasant odour invariably perceived when water dressing is changed. Here the clean metallic surface presenting no recesses, like those of porous lint, for the septic germs to develop in, the fluid exuding from the surface of the granulations has flowed away undecomposed, and the result is absence of suppuration. This simple experiment illustrates the important fact, that granulations have no inherent tendency to form pus, but do so only when subjected to a preternatural stimulus. Further, it shows that the mere contact of a foreign body does not of itself stimulate granulations to suppurate; whereas the presence of decomposing organic matter does. These truths are even more strikingly exemplified by the fact, which I have elsewhere recorded, that a piece of dead bone, free from decomposition, may not only fail to induce the granulations around it to suppurate, but may actually be absorbed by them; whereas a bit of dead bone soaked with putrid pus infallibly induces suppuration in its vicinity.

Another instructive experiment is to dress a granulating sore with some of the putty above described, overlapping the sound skin extensively, when we find in the course of twenty-four hours that pus has been produced by the sore, although the application has been perfectly antiseptic; and, indeed, the larger the amount of carbolic acid in the paste the greater is the quantity of pus formed, provided we avoid such a proportion as would act as a caustic. The carbolic acid, though it prevents decomposition, induces suppuration—obviously by acting as a chemical stimulus; and we may safely infer that putrescent organic materials (which we know to be chemically acrid) operate in the same way.

In so far, then, carbolic acid and decomposing substances are alike—namely, that they induce suppuration by chemical stimulation, as distinguished from what may be termed simple inflammatory suppuration, such as that in which ordinary abscessses originate, where the pus appears to be formed in consequence of an excited action of the nerves, independently of any other stimulus. There is, however, this enormous difference between the effects of carbolic acid and those of decomposition—viz. that carbolic acid stimulates only the surface to which it is first applied, and every drop of discharge that forms weakens the stimulant by diluting it. But decomposition is a self-propagating and self-aggravating poison; and if it occurs at the surface of a severely injured limb, it will spread into all its recesses so far as any extravasated blood or shreds of dead tissue may extend, and, lying in these recesses, it will become from hour to hour more acid till it acquires the energy of a caustic, sufficient to destroy the vitality of any tissues naturally weak from inferior vascular supply, or weakened by the injury they sustained in the accident.

Hence it is easy to understand how, when a wound is very large, the crust beneath the rag may prove here and there insufficient to protect the raw surface from the stimulating influence of the carbolic acid in the putty, and the result will be, first, the conversion of the tissues so acted on into granulations, and subsequently the formation of more or less pus. This, however, will be merely superficial, and will not interfere with the absorption and organization of extravasated blood or dead tissues in the interior; but, on the other hand, should decomposition set in before the internal parts have become securely consolidated, the most disastrous results may ensue.

I left behind me in Glasgow a boy, thirteen years of age, who between three and four weeks previously met with a most severe injury to the left arm, which he got entangled in a machine at a fair. There was a wound six inches long and three inches broad, and the skin was very extensively undermined beyond its limits, while the soft parts generally were so much lacerated that a pair of dressing-forceps introduced at the wound, and pushed directly inwards, appeared beneath the skin at the opposite aspect of the limb. From this wound several tags of muscle were hanging, and among them there was one consisting of about three inches of the triceps in almost its entire thickness; while the lower fragment of the bone, which was broken high up, was protruding four and a half inches, stripped of muscle, the skin being tucked in under it. Without the assistance of the antiseptic treatment, I should certainly have thought of nothing else but amputation at the shoulder-joint; but as the radial pulse could be felt, and the fingers had sensation, I did not hesitate to try to save the limb, and adopted the plan of treatment above described, wrapping the arm from the shoulder to below the elbow in the antiseptic application, the whole interior of the wound, together with the protruding bone, having previously been freely treated with strong carbolic acid. About the tenth day the discharge, which up to that time had been only sanious and serous, showed a slight admixture of slimy pus, and this increased till, a few days before I left, it amounted to about three drachms in twenty-four hours. But the boy continued, as he had been after the second day, free from unfavourable symptoms, with pulse, tongue, appetite, and sleep natural, and strength increasing, while the limb remained, as it had been from the first, free from swelling, redness, or pain. I therefore persevered with the antiseptic dressing, and before I left, the discharge was already somewhat less, while the bone was becoming firm. I think it likely that in that boy's case I should have found merely a superficial sore had I taken off all the dressings at the end of three weeks, though, considering the extent of the injury, I thought it prudent to let the month expire before disturbing the rag next the skin. But I feel sure that if I had resorted to ordinary dressing when the pus first appeared, the progress of the case would have been exceedingly different.

The next class of cases to which I have applied the antiseptic treatment is that of abscesses. Here, also, the results have been extremely satisfactory, and in beautiful harmony with the pathological principles indicated above. The pyogenic membrane, like the granulations of a sore, which it resembles in nature, forms pus, not from any inherent disposition to do so, but only because it is subjected to some preternatural stimulation. In an ordinary abscess, whether acute or chronic, before it is opened, the stimulus which maintains the suppuration is derived from the presence of the pus pent up within the cavity. When a free opening is made in the ordinary way, this stimulus is got rid of; but the atmosphere gaining access to the contents, the potent stimulus of decomposition comes into operation, and pus is generated in greater abundance than before. But when the evacuation is effected on the antiseptic principle, the pyogenic membrane, freed from the influence of the former stimulus without the substitution of a new one, ceases to suppurate (like the granulations of a sore under metallic dressing), furnishing merely a trifling amount of clear serum, and, whether the opening be dependent or not, rapidly contracts and coalesces. At the same time any constitutional symptoms previously occasioned by the accumulation of the matter are got rid of without the slightest risk of the irritative fever or hectic hitherto so justly dreaded in dealing with large abscesses.

In order that the treatment may be satisfactory, the abscess must be seen before it has opened. Then, except in very rare and peculiar cases, there are no septic organisms in the contents, so that it is needless to introduce carbolic acid into the interior. Indeed, such a proceeding would be objectionable, as it would stimulate the pyogenic membrane to unnecessary suppuration. All that is necessary is to guard against the introduction of living atmospheric germs from without, at the same time that free opportunity is afforded for the escape of discharge from within.

I have so lately given elsewhere a detailed account of the method by which this is effected, that is needless for me to enter into it at present, further than to say that the means employed are the same as those described above for the superficial dressing of compound fractures—namely, a piece of rag dipped in the solution of carbolic acid in oil, to serve as an antiseptic curtain, under cover of which the abscess is evacuated by free incision; and the antiseptic paste, to guard against decomposition occurring in the stream of pus that flows out beneath it: the dressing being changed daily till the sinus has closed.

The most remarkable results of this practice in a pathological point of view have been afforded by cases where the formation of pus depended upon disease of bone. Here the abscesses, instead of forming exceptions to the general class in the obstinacy of the suppuration, have resembled the rest in yielding in a few days only a trifling discharge; and frequently the production of pus has ceased from the moment of the evacuation of the original contents. Hence it appears that caries, when no longer labouring, as heretofore, under the irritation of decomposing matter, ceases to be an opprobrium of surgery, and recovers like other inflammatory affections. In the publication before alluded to, I have mentioned the case of a middle-aged man with psoas abscess depending on diseased bone, in whom the sinus finally closed after months of patient perseverance with the antiseptic treatment. Since that article was written I have had another instance of success, equally gratifying, but differing in the circumstance that the disease and the recovery were both more rapid in their course. The patient was a blacksmith who had suffered four and a half months before I saw him from symptoms of ulceration of cartilage in the left elbow. These had latterly increased in severity, so as to deprive him entirely of his night's rest and of appetite. I found the region of the elbow greatly swollen, and on careful examination discovered a fluctuation point at the outer aspect of the articulation. I opened it on the antiseptic principle, the incision evidently penetrating to the joint, giving exit to a few drachms of pus. The medical gentleman under whose care he was (Dr. MacGregor of Glasgow) supervised the daily dressing with the carbolic-acid paste till the patient went to spend two or three weeks at the coast, when his wife was entrusted with it. Just two months after I opened the abscess he called to show me the limb, stating that the discharge had for at least two weeks been as little as it then was—a trifling moisture upon the paste, such as might be accounted for by the little sore caused by the incision. On applying a probe guarded with an antiseptic rag, I found that the sinus was soundly closed, while the limb was free from swelling or tenderness; and, although he had not attempted to exercise it much, the joint could already be moved through a considerable angle. Here the antiseptic principle had effected the restoration of a joint which on any other known system of treatment must have been excised.

Ordinary contused wounds are of course amenable to the same treatment as compound fractures, which are a complicated variety of them. I will content myself with mentioning a single instance of this class of cases. In April last a volunteer was discharging a rifle, when it burst, and blew back the thumb with its metacarpal bone, so that it could be bent back as on a hinge at the trapezial joint, which had evidently been opened, while all the soft parts between the metacarpal bones of the thumb and fore-finger were torn through. I need not insist before my present audience on the ugly character of such an injury. My house surgeon, Mr. Hector Cameron, applied carbolic acid to the whole raw surface, and completed the dressing as if for compound fracture. The hand remained free from pain, redness, or swelling, and, with the exception of a shallow groove, all the wound consolidated without a drop of matter, so that if it had been a clean cut, it would have been regarded as a good example of primary union. The small granulating surface soon healed, and at present a linear cicatrix alone tells of the injury he had sustained, while his thumb has all its movements and his hand a firm grasp.

If the severest forms of contused and lacerated wounds heal thus kindly under the antiseptic treatment, it is obvious that its application to simple incised wounds must be merely a matter of detail. I have devoted a good deal of attention to this class, but I have not as yet pleased myself altogether with any of the methods I have employed. I am, however, prepared to go so far as to say that a solution of carbolic acid in twenty parts of water, while a mild and cleanly application, may be relied on for destroying any septic germs that may fall upon the wound during the performance of an operation; and also that for preventing the subsequent introduction of others, the paste above described, applied as for compound fractures, gives excellent results. Thus I have had a case of strangulated inguinal hernia, in which it was necessary to take away half a pound of thickened omentum, heal without any deep-seated suppuration or any tenderness of the sac or any fever; and amputations, including one immediately below the knee, have remained absolutely free from constitutional symptoms.

Further, I have found that when the antiseptic treatment is efficiently conducted, ligatures may be safely cut short and left to be disposed of by absorption or otherwise. Should this particular branch of the subject yield all that it promises, should it turn out on further trial that when the knot is applied on the antiseptic principle, we may calculate as securely as if it were absent on the occurrence of healing without any deep-seated suppuration; the deligation of main arteries in their continuity will be deprived of the two dangers that now attend it—namely, those of secondary haemorrhage and an unhealthy state of the wound. Further, it seems not unlikely that the present objection to tying an artery in the immediate vicinity of a large branch may be done away with; and that even the innominate, which has lately been the subject of an ingenious experiment by one of the Dublin surgeons on account of its well-known fatality under the ligature from secondary haemorrhage, may cease to have this unhappy character, when the tissues in the vicinity of the thread, instead of becoming softened through the influence of an irritating decomposing substance, are left at liberty to consolidate firmly near an unoffending though foreign body.

It would carry me far beyond the limited time which, by the rules of the Association, is alone at my disposal, were I to enter into the various applications of the antiseptic principle in the several special departments of surgery.

There is, however, one point more that I cannot but advert to—namely, the influence of this mode of treatment upon the general healthiness of a hospital. Previously to its introduction, the two large wards in which most of my cases of accident and of operation are treated were amongst the unhealthiest in the whole surgical division of the Glasgow Royal Infirmary, in consequence, apparently, of those wards being unfavourably placed with reference to the supply of fresh air; and I have felt ashamed, when recording the results of my practice, to have so often to allude to hospital gangrene or pyemia. It was interesting, though melancholy, to observe that, whenever all, or nearly all, the beds contained cases with open sores, these grievous complications were pretty sure to show themselves; so that I came to welcome simple fractures, though in themselves of little interest either for myself or the students, because their presence diminished the proportion of open sores among the patients. But since the antiseptic treatment has been brought into full operation, and wounds and abscesses no longer poison the atmosphere with putrid exhalations, my wards, though in other respects under precisely the same circumstances as before, have completely changed their character; so that during the last nine months not a single instance of pyemia, hospital gangrene, or erysipelas has occurred in them.

As there appears to be no doubt regarding the cause

of this change, the importance of the fact can hardly be exaggerated.

ILLUSTRATIONS OF THE ANTISEPTIC SYSTEM OF TREATMENT IN SURGERY

(*Lancet,* 1867, vol. ii, p. 668.)

I.

Decomposition or putrefaction has long been known to be a source of great mischief in surgery, and antiseptic applications have for several years been employed by many surgeons. But the full extent of the evil, and the paramount importance of adopting effectual measures against it, are far from being generally recognized.

It is now six years since I first publicly taught in the University of Glasgow that the occurrence of suppuration in a wound under ordinary circumstances, and its continuance on a healthy granulating sore treated with water dressing, are determined simply by the influence of decomposing organic matter. The subject has since received a large share of my attention, resulting in the system of treatment which I have been engaged for the last three years in elaborating. The benefits which attend this practice are so remarkable that I feel it incumbent upon me to do what I can to diffuse them; and with this view I propose to present to the readers of the *Lancet* a series of illustrative cases, prefacing them with a short notice of the principles which it is essential to bear in mind in order to attain success.

The cases in which this treatment is most signally beneficial are divisible into three great classes—incised wounds, of whatever form; contused or lacerated wounds, including compound fractures; and abscesses, acute or chronic—a list, indeed, which comprises the greater part of surgery. In each of these groups our aim is simply to prevent the occurrence of decomposition in the part, in order that its reparatory powers may be left undisturbed by the irritating and poisoning influence of putrid materials. In pursuing this object we are guided by the 'germ theory,' which supplies us with a knowledge of the nature and habits of the subtle foe we have to contend with; and without a firm belief in the truth of that theory, perplexity and blunders must be of frequent occurrence. The facts upon which it is based appear sufficiently convincing. We know from the researches of Pasteur that the atmosphere does contain among its floating particles the spores of minute vegetations and infusoria, and in greater numbers where animal and vegetable life abound, as in crowded cities or under the shade of trees, than where the opposite conditions prevail, as in unfrequented caves or on Alpine glaciers. Also, it appears that the septic energy of the air is directly proportioned to the abundance of the minute organisms in it, and is destroyed entirely by means calculated to kill its living germs—as, for example, by exposure for a while to a temperature of 212 degrees Fahr., or a little higher, after which it may be kept for an indefinite time in contact with putrescible substances, such as urine, milk, or blood, without producing any effect upon them. It has further been shown, and this is particularly striking, that the atmosphere is deprived of its power of producing decomposition as well as organic growth by merely passing in a very gentle stream through a narrow and tortuous tube of glass, which, while it arrests all its solid particles, cannot possibly have any effect upon its gases; while conversely, 'air-dust' collected by filtration rapidly gives rise simultaneously to the development of organisms and the putrefactive changes. Lastly, it seems to have been established that the character of the decomposition which occurs in a given fermentable substance is determined by the nature of the organism that develops in it. Thus the same saccharine solution may be made to undergo either the vinous or the butyric fermentation, according as the yeast plant or another organism, described by Pasteur, is introduced into it. Hence we cannot, I think, refuse to believe that the living beings invariably associated with the various fermentative and putrefactive changes are indeed their causes. And it is peculiarly in harmony with the extraordinary powers of self-diffusion and penetration exhibited by putrefaction that the chief agents in this process appear to be 'vibrios' endowed with the faculty of locomotion, so that they are able to make their way speedily along a layer of fluid such as serum or pus.

Admitting, then, the truth of the germ theory, and proceeding in accordance with it, we must, when dealing with any case, destroy in the first instance once for all any septic organisms which may exist within the part concerned; and after this has been done, our efforts must be directed to the prevention of the entrance of others into it. And provided that these indications are really fulfilled, the less the antiseptic agent comes in contact with the living tissues the better, so that unnecessary disturbance from its irritating properties may be avoided.

The simplest conditions are presented by an unopened abscess. Here, as no septic particles are present in the contents, it is needless to apply the antiseptic directly to the part affected. All that is requisite is to guard securely against the possibility of the penetration of living germs from without, at the same time that free escape is afforded for the discharge from within. When this is done we witness an example of the unaided curative powers of Nature as beautiful as it is, I believe, entirely new. The pyogenic membrane, freed from the operation of the stimulus derived from the presence of the pus pent up within it, without the substitution of the powerful stimulus of decomposition as has heretofore been the case after the opening of abscesses, ceases at once to develop pus-corpuscles, and, exuding merely a little clear serum, rapidly contracts and coalesces discharging meanwhile its unirritating contents completely, whether the outlet be dependent in position or otherwise. At the same time the irritative fever and hectic hitherto so much dreaded in large abscesses are, with perfect security, entirely avoided.

In suppurations of the vertebrae or of the joints the results of this system are such as I ventured with trembling hope to anticipate; patient perseverance being rewarded by a spontaneous cure in cases where excision, amputation, or death must have resulted from any other known system of treatment. In short, the element of incurability has been eliminated from caries.

In compound fractures and other severe contused wounds the antiseptic agent must in the first instance be applied freely and energetically to the injured parts themselves, the conditions being the opposite of those in unopened abscesses. The wound being of complicated form, with its interstices loaded with extravasated blood, into which septic organisms may have already insinuated themselves during the time that has elapsed before the patient is seen by the surgeon, mere guarding of the external orifice, however effectually, is not sufficient. After squeezing out as much as possible of the effused blood, a material calculated to kill the septic particles must be introduced into the recesses of the wound; and if the substance employed is of sufficient strength to operate to a certain extent as a caustic, this is regarded as a matter of little moment in comparison with the terrible evil of inefficiency in its antiseptic action. For experience has abundantly shown that parts killed in this way, including even portions of bone, become disposed of by absorption and organization, provided that the subsequent part of the treatment is properly managed.

Sloughs, as ordinarily observed, are soaked with the acrid products of decomposition, and therefore produce disturbance upon the tissues around them, leading first to their gradual tranformation into the rudimentary structure which, when met with at the surface of a sore, is termed 'granulations', and afterwards to the formation of pus by the granulations. But a dead portion of tissue, if not altered by adventitious circumstances, in in its proper substance perfectly bland and unirritating, and causes no more disorder in its neighbourhood than a bullet or a piece of glass, which may remain imbedded in the living body for an indefinite period without inducing the formation of pus; while the dead tissue differs from the foreign bodies alluded to in the circumstance that the materials of which it is composed are susceptible of absorption.

Antiseptic substances, being, like the products of decomposition, chemically stimulating, will, like them, induce granulation and suppuration in tissues exposed for a sufficient length of time to their influence; but there is this all-important difference, that an antiseptic merely stimulates the surface to which it is applied, becoming diluted and weakened by the discharge which it excites; but the acrid salts which result from putrefaction are perpetually multiplied and intensified by self-propagating ferments, so that every drop of serum or pus effused through their agency becomes a drop of poison, extending its baleful influence both in the injured part and in the system generally.

These pathological considerations indicate the after-treatment in compound fracture, and explain the progress of the case. The antiseptic introduced into the wound is soon washed out by the discharge or carried away by the circulation, so that the blood and sloughs at first imbued with it become unstimulating and amenable to absorption, while at the same time they are prone to decomposition should any living atmospheric germs gain access to them. The further treatment, therefore, must consist in maintaining an efficient antiseptic guard over the orifice of the wound until sufficient time has elapsed to ensure complete consolidation of the injured parts.

The sanious and serous discharge which occurs at the outset will give place in a few days to a small amount of pus, if the wound is dressed in such a way that the antiseptic continues to act upon the raw surface. This discharge, due to the stimulating nature of the application, being merely superficial, and involving no inflammatory or febrile disturbance, will occasion no anxiety to one who understands its cause; and I venture to repeat the caution given in a previous communication, that the surgeon must on no account be induced to explore the wound and pry into the source of the suppuration, so long as all is going on well otherwise; for such a course, by admitting germs into the interior, may produce the most disastrous consequences in an otherwise promising case.

But although suppuration resulting from the stimulating influence of the antiseptic is no cause for anxiety, it is more convenient that it should be avoided; and this may often be done entirely by leaving the lower layers of the dressing permanently on the limb and changing only its superficial parts—a plan which, while it protects the wound against the introduction of mischievous particles, permits the foreign body in contact with the tissues to part with its antiseptic material and become an unstimulating crust, under which complete healing by scabbing may occur in wounds of a size hitherto regarded as inconsistent with this process in the human subject.

Upon these principles a really trustworthy treatment for compound fractures and other severe contused wounds has been established for the first time, so far as I am aware, in the history of surgery. In a hospital which receives an unusually large number of patients suffering from machinery accidents, and in wards which, from circumstances to which I need not here allude, were peculiarly unhealthy, my experience of compound fracture in the lower limb was formerly far indeed from satisfactory, even in the selected cases in which alone I attempted to save the limb. But since the antiseptic principle has guided us, not only have ordinary cases of this formidable injury been treated by my successive house surgeons with unvarying success, but limbs such as I should once have condemned without hesitation have gone on to complete recovery without either local or constitutional disturbance: a statement which might be suspected of exaggeration were it not that it refers to proceedings in a public hospital, witnessed not only by students, but by gentlemen once my pupils, and now practitioners in Glasgow.

In the next article I propose, after a few words regarding the principles applicable to simple incised wounds to describe in detail the methods of procedure, illustrated by cases.

AN ADDRESS ON THE ANTISEPTIC SYSTEM OF TREATMENT IN SURGERY

Delivered before the Medico-Chirurgical Society of Glasgow.

(*British Medical Journal,* 1868, vol. ii, pp. 53, 101, 461, 515; 1869, vol. i, p. 301.)

MR. PRESIDENT AND GENTLEMEN :- In order that the antiseptic system of treatment may confer upon mankind all the benefits of which it is capable, three things appear to be indispensably requisite. First, that every surgeon should be convinced of the reality and greatness of those benefits, so that he may be induced to devote to the antiseptic dressing of a case the same kind of thought and pains as he now, if at all worthy of the name of surgeon, bestows upon planning and execution of an operation; secondly, that these efforts on his part should be directed on sound priciples; and thirdly, that, for carrying out these principles, he should have thoroughly trustworthy practical means at his disposal. I venture to hope that the illustrations which I propose to bring before you this evening may promote in some degree each of these essentials.

In speaking of the antiseptic system of treatment, I refer to the systematic employment of some antiseptic substance, so as entirely to prevent the occurrence of putrefaction in the part concerned, as distinguished from the mere use of such an agent as a dressing. The latter has long been practised in many parts of the world. The former originated rather more than three years ago in this city (Glasgow). The material which I have generally used for the purpose is carbolic (or phenic) acid, which, when I first published on the subject, was new to most British surgeons as an external therapeutic agent. This circumstance, while it had the effect of attracting greater notice to the matter than might otherwise have been the case, was perhaps on the whole a misfortune, since it tended to distract attention from the essential principles of the treatment which I advocated, and to lead many in this country to look upon carbolic acid in the light of a specific. On the other hand, continental surgeons visiting our infirmary, familiar with the use of carbolic acid as an ordinary antiseptic dressing, have invariably formed a just estimate of the advantages derived from its employment upon the system to which I have alluded.

So far from carbolic acid being a specific, it owes its virtues to properties which it possesses in common with various other substances; and results similar in kind to those obtained by its means might be got by disinfectants long familiar to British surgery, provided always that the same principles guided their employment. This statement is not made on theoretical grounds alone. About nine months after I had first treated compound fracture with carbolic acid, Mr. Campbell De Morgan published a paper 'On the Use of Chloride of Zinc in Surgical Operations and Injuries', and was kind enough to send me a copy of it. By means of this salt he had obtained highly satisfactory results, though led to employ it with a very different object in view. Mr. De Morgan used chloride of zinc in the first instance in cases of cancer, upon the idea that the frequency of return of the disease after operation might depend on the dissemination of its germs on the cut surface, and he hoped that, by applying a strong solution of the chloride to the wound so as to destroy any cancer-germs that might be scattered over it, he might diminish the chance of recurrence. Having treated cases of cancer in this way, he found that the wounds healed unusually kindly, while there was, at the same time, an absence of 'animal odour', and he expressed his surprise at the small amount of 'action' in the part. To myself it appeared perfectly natural that, if chloride of zinc prevented animal odour, implying that putrefaction was avoided, the wound, protected from the irritating influence of the products of decomposition, should exhibit little inflammatory disturbance. But it struck me as very remarkable that a single application of chloride of zinc to the raw surface should have the effect of preventing all odour of putrefaction for days afterwards; for I knew that in the case of carbolic acid a renewal of the antiseptic to the exterior was essential in order to prevent decomposition. Hence it appeared likely that chloride of zinc would answer better for my purpose than carbolic acid, and I determined, on the first suitable occasion, to give it a trial. It was not long before an opportunity presented itself.

Case of Compound Fracture Treated with Chloride of Zinc.—A labourer was admitted into the infirmary with compound depressed fracture of the *os frontis,* caused by violent impact of the handle of a winch. I applied chloride-of-zinc solution thoroughly to the interior of the wound, and, with the view of preventing the spreading of decomposition inwards, adapted to the forehead a plate of clean block-tin overlapping the sound skin for a considerable distance, a means which, as I had before ascertained, prevents the occurrence of putrefaction in the discharge from a healthy granulating sore. The tin plate was kept in position by a piece of strapping, and over all was laid a damp folded rag to absorb discharge, with directions that it should be frequently changed. The tin was not disturbed till about a week had expired, the patient meanwhile remaining free from any unfavourable symptoms, and not a drop of pus appearing. On removing the plate of metal, I found that the wound, instead of being hollow as when I had last seen it, was on a level with the surface of the forehead, being occupied by a chocolate-coloured mass which I supposed to be a clot, altered by the action of chloride of zinc. But when I scraped the surface of this material it bled, showing that it was in reality alive and vascular. This exactly corresponded to the most striking and peculiar of the results I had seen to follow the use of carbolic acid in compound fracture, and the most likely to be mistaken for the effect of a specific action of that substance, viz., that the blood acted on by the antiseptic, though greatly altered by that action, remained susceptible of organization. Or, speaking more strictly, the product of the action of chloride of zinc upon the blood, like that of the operation of carbolic acid upon it, so soon as the irritating antiseptic material with which it was at first imbued had been withdrawn from it by diffusion into the surrounding circulation, proved a suitable pabulum for the growing elements of living tissue in the vicinity, which accordingly absorbed and appropriated it.

In the case just related, nothing could be more satisfactory than the effects of chloride of zinc. Subsequent trials, however, proved it to be very inferior to carbolic acid except in one class of cases, those, viz., in which, from the circumstances of the part concerned, it is impossible to maintain an efficient external antiseptic dressing, so that the application must be made once for all at the time of the operation. Here the permanence of the effects of chloride of zinc renders it highly valuable, as, for example, after the removal of portions of the maxillary bones. Eevery surgeon is familiar with the highly offensive character of the discharge for the first few days after such operations; and there can be no doubt that the fetid state of the wound, besides being a great inconvenience to the patient and his attendants, involves a certain amount of danger. By means of chloride of zinc this complication is nearly, if not entirely avoided. In the first case of this kind in which I used it, I had to remove a considerable portion of both superior maxillary bones, on account of epithelial cancer which had spread to them from the face. I applied the chloride-of-zinc solution freely to the raw surfaces at the time of the operation, and afterwards examined the breath daily, when the only smell perceptible from first to last was an occasional odour of tobacco. (Since this address was delivered, I have used chloride of zinc with great advantage after the removal of the tongue by Mr. Syme's method, in a case of epithelial cancer.)

But in ordinary cases carbolic acid is very superior to chloride of zinc, and, so far as I am able to judge, to any other antiseptic agent with which we are at present acquainted. It presents, indeed, a remarkable combination of advantages. In the first place, it possesses the essential requisite of being a most potent poison for the low forms of life which determine putrefaction, and it retains this power even though diluted to such a degree as to be almost entirely unirritating to the tissues of the human body. In the second place, it is volatile, and its vapour is quite efficacious as an antiseptic. This gives it a great advantage over chloride of zinc or any other non-volatile substance, enabling the dressings impregnated with the acid to exert their influence not only upon objects in actual contact with them, but also upon the air in their vicinity. Again, carbolic acid is a local anaesthetic, and exercises a most soothing influence upon a painful wound. Lastly, carbolic acid is soluble in a variety of liquids of very different properties, so different, for example, as water and the fixed oils; and each of these solutions has its own special value in practice, a point to which I shall have occasion to allude further on in this communication.

And now, before speaking of some cases treated with carbolic acid on the antiseptic system, I wish to direct your attention to an experiment illustrating the germ theory of putrefaction. It is on this theory that the antiseptic system of treatment is based; and I venture to say that, without a belief in the truth of that theory, no man can be thoroughly successful in the treatment. If any one believe that putrefaction, through atmospheric influence, is due to the operation of the atmospheric gases alone upon the putrescible materials, he will be perpetually meeting with the most perplexing anomalies, and will be liable to commit the most serious practical blunders; the truth being that, on the one hand, the complete exclusion of the gases of the air affords no security against the occurrence of putrefaction, and that, on the other hand, the freest admixture of air with the putrescible contents of a wound or abscess will fail to induce putrefactive changes, if the germs of that air have been removed by filtration or deprived of vitality by a germ-poison. Of this I might, if time permitted, give several very striking illustrations from practical surgery.

The experiment which I wish to bring under your notice is a modification of one described by Pasteur, not, indeed, as originated by himself, but by M. Chevreul. It is so simple, and, at the same time so conclusive, that it should, I think, if believed, carry conviction to the minds of all. To myself the statement of Pasteur, confirmed as it is by the report of the Commission of the French Academy, before whom this, as well as various others of his experiments was performed, was perfectly satisfactory. But there was one reason that made me anxious to repeat the experiment as bearing upon the antiseptic system of treatment; and this was that, so far as I read Pasteur's papers, he had performed it only with reference to the fermentation of a saccharine solution, and I wished to make sure that it applied equally to putrefaction. The experiment was performed in the following manner:

Experiment in support of the Germ Theory of Putrefaction.

On the 26th of October, just half a year ago, I introduced portions of the same specimen of fresh urine into four flasks, of which these are two. (The flasks, which were capable of containing about six fluid ounces each, were about one-third filled.) After washing the urine from their necks, which were then wide and straight, I drew out the necks by means of a spirit-lamp into tubes about a line in diameter, and in three of the flasks bent these elongated and attenuated necks at various acute angles, as you will see in one of the two before you. In the remaining flask, the neck was cut short and left vertical in position as you see it here, but its orifice was reduced to even smaller calibre than in the others. Each flask was then boiled over the lamp, and the fluid maintained in a state of ebullition for five minutes, the steam issuing freely from the orifice. The lamp was then withdrawn, and atmospheric air was permitted to rush into the flask to supply the place of the condensed steam. The flasks were then left undisturbed in the same room, the ends of their necks being stilll open so as to permit free exit and entrance of air as a consequence of the diurnal changes of temperature which, of course, involved alternate expansions and condensations of the contained gases. Sometimes on a cold night I have raised the temperature of the apartment considerably, and then putting the fire out, have thrown open the windows so as to occasion a depression of temperature of twenty degrees, involving the entrance of about a cubic inch of fresh air into the body of each flask. But, independently of any such exceptional treatment, a perpetual daily interchange took place between the air inside the flasks and that of the room in which they stood. And what has been the result of the action of the air upon the urine? In the flask with straight and short, though narrow neck, I observed after ten days a minute filamentous object at the bottom of the glass. It grew larger from day to day, and was evidently a kind of minute vegetation; and on applying a pocket-magnifier, it was seen to consist of delicate branching threads. Four days after this growth first appeared, I observed an object floating on the surface of the liquid, evidently also a minute fungus; but this in the course of a few days clearly showed itself to be of a different kind, consisting of straight radiating filaments much more closely packed, whille to the naked eye its appearance was much denser than the other, which was beautifully feathery and delicate, and its colour bluish-grey instead of perfectly colourless like the first. The two differed also remarkably in their rate of growth, that at the bottom of the vessel springing up with rapidity, so that a month after the commencement of the experiment it occupied about half the mass of the fluid, while the floating kind, though it had been steadily enlarging, had attained only about the size of a pea. Meanwhile the urine had been undergoing a change in chemical constitution, as was indicated by an alteration of its colour from a pale straw to a deep amber tint. But in the meantime, what was the condition of the urine in the three other flasks, with bent necks, of which this is a sample? You observe it is perfectly clear and bright, free from cloud, scum, or sediment, and it retains its original straw colour, contrasting strikingly with the amber tint of the other. In short, it has precisely the same appearance as it had at the outset. I may add that, on the day after these flasks were prepared, having another similar one at my disposal, I introduced into it some fresh urine from the same source, drew out the neck and bent it into angular form, and treated it like the others, so that I have thus four flasks of boiled urine communicating with the air through bent tubes; and in all of these the urine has remained with unchanged colour and undiminished transparency. It can hardly be doubted that this completely unaltered appearance of the fluid is associated with absence of putrefaction. I shall take an early opportunity of ascertaining whether such is the fact or not; but in the meantime, suppose we assume that it is so. (Since the delivery of this address, namely on the 2nd inst., May 1868, I poured out about half an ounce of urine from one of the flasks with bent neck into a wine-glass, and examined it. Its odour was perfectly sweet, and its reaction faintly acid to litmus paper, while under the microscope it showed not the slightest appearance of anything possessing vitality. I then covered the wine-glass with a piece of sheet gutta-percha to prevent evaporation, and left it at a temperature of about seventy degrees. Three days later it had already lost its brilliant transparency, and a distinct change had occurred in its odour, which had assumed something of the smell that urine has when evaporated to dryness. And under the microscope, organic forms of different kinds were present in abundance, some of them motionless delicate elongated rods (bacteria?), others with wriggling movements, apparently of vibrionic nature, while there were also numerous amorphous and faint granules, probably also organic. Nine days after the urine had been placed in the glass, two little woolly balls of fungus were visible in it to the naked eye. In correcting the proof, I may add that the urine is now thronged with fungous growths of at least three different species; while the odour is highly offensive. But the hot summer weather of the last two months has produced no change in the contents of either of the flasks with bent necks.) Observe, then, what inference is to be drawn from this remarkable fact. There has been nothing in the bent tubes that could by possibility interfere with the transit of any of the gases of the atmosphere. At first, indeed, they contained some drops of condensed aqueous vapour; but these in a few days disappeared, the tubes being dried by the air passing through them, and I beg you particularly to observe that, in the instance before you, the tube is open and dry from end to end. Every atmospheric gas, therefore, in whatever proportion it may exist, must have daily passed unchanged into the flasks to exert upon the putrescible urine any influence of which it was capable; yet no putrefaction has occurred. The urine has remained absolutely free from putrefactive changes for half a year, though exposed during the whole of that time to the action of all the gases of the atmosphere, perpetually renewed. Surely we are safe in drawing the inference that, in the case of this putrescible substance at least, the atmospheric gases alone are incapable of inducing putrefaction. What is it, then, that is essential to putrefaction of urine by atmospheric influence which the bent tubes have arrested? It cannot be any of the gases; but it may be, it must be, some particles suspended in them, some dust, which the angles of the tubes might arrest mechanically. And this conclusion, inevitable as it is from the consideration of the flasks with bent necks, is confirmed by comparison with the other in which the orifice, though narrower, was purposely so arranged as to afford a better chance for the introduction of particles of dust, and in which accordingly chemical changes soon declared themselves in the contained liquid.

This experiment has an equally clear bearing upon the question of equivocal generation, essentially involved in the germ theory of putrefaction. It illustrates strikingly what appears to be the truth; namely that even the lowest and most minute forms of life with which we are conversant, do not arise spontaneously in organic substances as the result of the operation of the atmospheric gases upon them, but take their origin from definite particles or germs, the offspring of pre-existing ogranisms. For, on the one hand, we have seen that this liquid, which is a most favourable nidus for such development, has remained for half a year free from any change in its appearance such as even microscopic organisms would produce, though exposed freely during that long period to the influence of air unchanged except in the circumstance that it has been filtered of suspended particles. And, on the other hand, this same liquid similarly situated in every respect, except in the fact that particles floating in the atmosphere might gain access to it, soon presented, even to the naked eye, two distinct kinds of vegetation, each springing from a definite point, and growing steadily from that point, but incapable of taking origin in any other part of the liquid. (The facts subsequently ascertained, of the absence of any living organism which the microscope could detect in the liquid from one of the flasks with bent neck, and the speedy appearance of abundance of such minute objects as well as of others visible to the naked eye, when the liquid had been removed from its protecting chamber, afford, of course, most satisfactory confirmation.)

There is one circumstance in this experiment which may appear difficult to comprehend. Admitting that the angles of a narrow bent tube might arrest the progress of even the finest dust of air when in very gentle motion, is it conceivable that such particles could fail to be driven into the flasks during the first rush of air into them on the withdrawal of the lamp at the time of the original boiling? This difficulty is met by Pasteur in the following way. He says doubtless germs are carried in, but they pass into a liquid so hot as at once to destroy their vitality. Now, though I feel much diffidence in expressing dissent from so high an authority, I must say I do not feel satisfied with this explanation; inasmuch as Pasteur has himself related experiments which show that the mere raising of urine to the temperature of 212 degrees Fahr. is not sufficient to ensure the destruction of the vitality of the tough-lived germs which it may contain; but that it is essential for that purpose to maintain the liquid for some minutes at the boiling-point. But, if this be so, the germs introduced on the withdrawal of the lamp, being under the same circumstances as those in urine simply raised to 212 degrees Fahr., and at once allowed to cool, should retain their vitality and give rise to organic development. The explanation which has occurred to myself is as follows. Immediately that the steam ceases to issue from the tube on the removal of the lamp, moisture is deposited upon its interior from the condensation of the aqueous vapour in it; and this moisture remains clinging to the interior of the tube, and tending to form drops at its angles, however rapidly the air be driven through it. And it seems to me natural that this water in the tube should arrest the particles in the air transmitted through it. Conversely, I am inclined to think that the germs of the two growths visible to the naked eye in the flask with straight and short neck entered with the first rush of air, but retained their vitality in the hot liquid, as in Pasteur's experiments with urine heated to 212 degrees Fahr., and at once cooled. These two fungi had already grown to a sufficient size to be distinguishable by the naked eye, within a few days of the commencement of the experiment, but no other points of growth appeared during the ensuing month; implying that the germs of such fungi, though admitted at first, when the air entered rapidly, were excluded by the narrow though straight neck during the slow movements caused by the gradual diurnal changes of temperature.

Believing that there must be germs of various organisms adhering to the interior of the narrow neck near its orifice, I thought that if I were to seal the orifice, and then allow some of the liquid to pass up to its immediate vicinity, I might wash down some of them into the body of the flask, and so induce other growths in the urine. Accordingly, on the 20th of November, nearly a month after the commencement of the experiment, I sealed the end of the tube with the blow-pipe, protecting the neighbouring parts of the neck from the flame as well as I could with a bit of wet lint wrapped round it. I then tilted the flask so as to cause some of the urine to pass into the neck and back again; and you will observe that there is still a drop in the immediate vicinity of the sealed extremity. A few days later, I imagined that I had attained my object, as several minute points of growth were seen upon the surface of the liquid, distinct from the original floating mass, which by this time had assumed a really beautiful appearance, its upper surface being a circle of three-quarters of an inch in diameter, composed of concentric rings of blue mould. But, in the course of a few more days, it became evident that the new growths were of identically the same species as the original floating one; and, on the other hand, that the drop near the end of the neck remained perfectly transparent, instead of exhibiting fungous developments as I had anticipated. Hence I inferred that the germs, which I could not doubt must have existed near the orifice, had been arrested so close to it as to be destroyed by the heat of the flame. Whence, then, did the new growths in the body of the flask take their origin? The answer is obvious enough. The blue mould covering the surface of the original growth teemed with myriads of sporules of the fungus, and, like larger plants, was ready to shed its ripe seeds when shaken; and the tilting of the flask, which had up to that time been carefully kept from disturbance, scattered some of these ripe germs, which grew into organisms like their parent. About a month after the sealing of the tube, all further growth of the fungi in the flask ceased, and its contents have remained unchanged for the last four months, except that the fungi have become shrunk and unhealthy in aspect. This I attribute to the cutting off of the supply of oxygen by the sealing of the tube. (This view has since been verified. On the 2nd inst., May 1868, I broke off the sealed end of the neck after scratching it with a file, leaving the flask otherwise undisturbed. In four days, I detected the first indications of return of the growth which had been so long suspended; and, a few days later, the dwindled and discoloured original growths were abundantly covered with fresh vegetations of the same nature as before, while the surface of the fluid presented multitudes of new points of development of the same species; the unavoidable motion of the liquid in conveying the flask to and from the meeting, which indeed greatly marred the beauty of the fungi, having evidently scattered other germs about, which remained latent till fresh air was admitted.)

Looking at this experiment as a whole, we see that the atmosphere was rendered incapable of inducing in that specimen of urine either putrefaction or the formation of even the lowest and most minute known organisms, by merely depriving it of its suspended particles; or, conversely, that the 'air-dust' is the essential cause both of organic development and of putrefactive changes in such a liquid; while the experiment further illustrates what seems to be a general law; viz., that the low forms of life to which the atmospheric particles give rise, so far as we are able to observe them, resemble higher plants or animals in springing only from pre-existing organisms. Any one who bears these facts in mind will have little difficulty in admitting the truth of the germ theory of putrefaction; and I venture to recommend to any of you who may hereafter feel perplexed by the contradictory and bewildering statements of various authors upon this subject, and be tempted to regard it as hopelessly obscure, that he should recall to his memory the clear evidence respecting it which has been brought before you this evening.

Emphysema and Pneumothorax from Simple Fracture of the Ribs.

This mode of experimenting, as described by Pasteur, besides charming me by its simplicity and conclusiveness, had a further special interest for myself, because, before knowing of it, I had explained to my own mind on the same principle the remarkable fact, previously quite inexplicable, that in simple fracture of the ribs, if the lung be punctured by a fragment driven inwards upon it, the blood effused into the pleural cavity from the wound in the highly vascular organ, though freely mixed with air which enters the pleura through the same orifice, undergoes no decomposition, as is clearly implied by the absence of any symptoms of pleurisy in such cases. The air is sometimes pumped into the pleural cavity in such abundance that, making its way through the wound in the pleura costalis, it inflates the cellular tissue of the whole body; yet this occasions no alarm to the surgeon, unless the opening in the parietal pleura becomes pent up in the serous cavity, and, distending it far beyond its natural dimensions, encroaches on the other lung so seriously as to embarrass or even abolish its functions. Thirteen years ago, I had the opportunity of making a post mortem examination of the body of a man who had died under such circumstances ten days after the receipt of the injury which caused his symptoms; and I was much struck to find the enormously distended pleura free from effusion, and perfectly smooth and healthy. Why air introduced into the pleura through a wounded lung should have such totally different effects from that entering through a permanently open penetrating wound from without, was to me a complete mystery till I heard of the germ theory of putrefaction, when it at once occurred to me that, though we could not suppose the gases of the atmosphere to be in any way altered in chemical composition by passing through the trachea and bronchial tubes on their way into the pleura, it was only natural that they should be filtered of germs by the air-passages, one of whose offices it is to arrest inhaled particles of dust, and prevent them from entering the air-cells. In truth, this fact in practical surgery, when duly considered, affords as good evidence in support of the germ theory of putrefaction as any experiment that can be performed artificially.

Another remarkable example of the same thing, though brought about by different circumstances, occurred recently in my practice at the infirmary.

Case of Penetrating Wound of the Thorax and Abdomen.—On the 1st of October last, a butcher, aged 18, was admitted on account of a most serious wound of the chest, inflicted by a comrade who, angry at having a dirty bladder thrown at him by the patient, threw in return his knife, with a blade nine inches long, and keen-edged, half of which buried itself in the patient's infra-axillary region, between the ninth and tenth ribs. He himself drew out the knife, which was followed by a fearful gush of blood. Being accustomed to see blood flow, he said 'there was a spout of four inches before the fall'. He was immediately taken to the hospital, where my then house surgeon, Mr. Hector Cameron, found him blanched, his clothes drenched with blood, which was still pouring from the wound, venous in colour, and with a tendency to regurgitate during inspiration, implying that it proceeded from a wound in the lung, which was further indicated by the occurrence of haemoptysis. There was also protruding from the external wound a piece of omentum five inches long, showing that the knife had passed through the diaphragm into the abdominal cavity. No time was to be lost, as death from haemorrhage was imminent; and Mr. Cameron judged it best to plug the wound, but at the same time to introduce an antiseptic as in compound fracture, in order to destroy any atmospheric germs that might have been drawn in during inspiration. With this object, after cutting off the protruding piece of omentum, which he kept to show me, he soaked a piece of lint with a solution of carbolic acid in four parts of boiled linseed oil, and by means of dressing-forceps passed it as far as he could in every direction in the pleural cavity, repeating the application several times. He then took two strips of lint steeped in the same solution, each about a foot long and an inch in breadth, and pushed them into the pleura, one upwards, the other downwards, as far as possible consistently with keeping their ends protruding externally; and, the wound being thus plugged antiseptically, he applied a sheet of paste composed of whitening mixed with the oily solution of carbolic acid before mentioned, taking care that it was large enough to overlap the skin around the orifice by several inches in every direction, retaining it in position by strapping and bandage. It may, perhaps, be said by some of you, 'Surely it was heroic practice to introduce irritating carbolic acid so freely into that important serous cavity. Would it not have been a milder and more prudent course to have plugged the wound with a piece of dry lint?' But any one who argues in this way forgets what would have been the inevitable result of such a procedure. The mass of blood accumulated in the pleura would necessarily have been soon decomposed through the agency of the germs contained in the lint; and the putrefying mass, growing from day to day more acrid in the cavity in which it was confined, would undoubtedly have soon caused the death of the already prostrated patient. On the other hand, carbolic acid, being a local anaesthetic, is much less irritating, even when first applied, than the products of decomposition; and it also differs from the latter in this all-important point, that it soon becomes dissipated by diffusion and removed by the surrounding circulation, when, the blood on which it has acted being still amenable to organization and absorption, the part is as favourably situated as if affected only with a subcutaneous injury. Next day, when I saw the patient for the first time, I cautiously withdrew the plugs, under the protection of a large piece of lint dipped in the oily solution of carbolic acid, and continued the use of the paste. For about ten days the patient progressed admirably, the pulse descending, the laboured rapid respirations growing less laboured and less rapid, and altogether his condition becoming so much improved that he could not be prevented from sitting up in bed, singing songs, and conducting himself otherwise in an imprudent manner. Meanwhile, examination of the thorax disclosed signs of the presence of both blood and air in the pleura, such as dullness of the base and preternatural resonance of the upper and anterior part of that side of the chest, and metallic tinkling, which was well marked. And to such an extent had this accumulation of blood and air proceeded, that the heart had been pushed over towards the right side, so that its apex beat below the right nipple. And yet this mass of blood, freely exposed to the influence of air, had not decomposed. Any putrefactive germs introduced through the external wound had been destroyed by the carbolic acid, and the air, entering the pleura through the wounded bronchial tubes, had deposited its floating organisms upon the slimy mucous secretion of those tortuous canals. Hence the patient remained free from any symptoms of irritation, and suffered only from loss of blood and the embarrassment of the respiration which was the mechanical result of the injury. But, thirteen days after the accident, profuse haemoptysis appeared, which I was disposed to attribute to tearing open of the wound in the lung through his imprudent exertions; and this, continuing for several days, threatened entirely to exhaust his weakened frame. The expectorated blood assumed also a putrid odour, like that from gangrene of the lungs; and I was apprehensive that the putrescence might spread to the mass in the pleura. Fortunately, however, this did not occur. The bloody expectoration gradually became purulent, and then diminished in quantity till it ceased entirely. With regard to the external wound, it furnished no pus so long as the original mode of dressing was continued. In the first twenty-four hours, there was a free discharge of bloody serum; but this grew less from day to day, till, six days after the receipt of the injury, it amounted to less than a minim in forty-eight hours; and when the piece of lint, which had been kept permanently on the wound beneath the paste, was removed, between three and four weeks after the accident, a superficial sore was found, which afterwards cicatrized kindly. On the 18th of November, seven weeks after his admission, the apex of the heart was observed to be again beating below the left mammilla; and, finally, I may add, that he was seen a few days ago by Mr. Cameron, engaged with another butcher in driving a herd of unruly cattle through the streets, when our former patient, though still pale from anemia, proved the more vigorous of the two in turning the animals; while his lusty exclamations, though not couched in the most decorous language, gave satisfactory evidence of the soundness of his lungs.

Ligature of Arteries.

I have now to show you a preparation illustrating the effects of the application of a ligature upon an artery on the antiseptic system. The theory of such a procedure is simple. A foreign body introduced among the tissues does not exert any disturbing influence upon them, unless it be either mechanically or chemically irritating. Thus, it is well known that a needle or a spiculum of glass may lie for an indefinite period embedded in the living textures without inducing suppuration; and any irritation which may result is due simply to the rigidity and form of the foreign solid. Now, a bit of silk or linen thread being composed of materials of soft sonsistence and as unstimulating chemically as glass or steel, its presence among the tissues cannot of itself occasion any disturbance. But, unlike the glass or metal, the thread is porous, and contains in its interstices putrefactive germs, which, developing in the serum that bathes the ligature, give rise to the acrid products of decomposition, and these, in their turn, stimulate the surrounding tissues to granulation and suppuration. If, however, the thread were steeped in some liquid calculated to destroy the life of the germs in its interstices, and the wound by which it was introduced were dressed antiseptically, the ends of the ligature being cut short, it might be felt with confidence that its presence would not interfere with primary union, or occasion any disorder in the surrounding parts. The traction exercised on the external coat by the noose of the ligature is no doubt a temporary cause of mechanical irritation, but this does not appear to have any considerable influence. Before applying these principles upon the human subject, I thought it right to test them on one of the lower animals.

Ligature of the Carotid Artery in the Horse, on the Antiseptic System.— On the 12th of December last, I tied the left carotid of a horse about the middle of the neck, using fine but strong 'purse-silk', unwaxed, but steeped for some time in a saturated watery solution of carbolic acid. (The product of the action of carbolic acid upon blood serves the purpose of wax in preventing the first half of the knot from slipping during the tying of the second half.) The ligature having been tightly tied, so as to rupture the internal and middle coats, its ends were cut short, and the wound was freely treated with carbolic acid dissolved in forty parts of water. Seven stitches of the coarse soft wire used by veterinary surgeons for the purpose were introduced into the long wound, the most dependent part being left free for the escape of discharge. The hair around the wound was well rubbed with a solution of carbolic acid in four parts of olive oil, and cloths saturated with the same antiseptic oil were applied overlapping the surrounding skin freely, and retained in position by means which I need not describe; and similar oil was poured daily upon the cloths for the first six days. Ten days after the operation I removed the dressings, and found the wound perfectly united throughout, except at the part purposely left open, which was covered with a sort of cheesy material, and as each stitch was removed there was absence of even serous exudation. The wound was now left exposed, and in three days more the lower part had healed by scabbing, no suppuration having occurred from first to last. At the same time, there was none of the swelling and induration that usually attend the application of a ligature to a vessel in the horse's neck, and the animal showed no signs of uneasiness when the part was freely handled.

Five weeks and four days after the tying of the artery, the creature, though it had improved greatly in condition under its superior diet in the veterinary establishment, died, as the groom believed, of exhaustion from struggling ineffectually to rise from the recumbent posture. I had thus an opportunity of inspecting the parts concerned in the operation, some of which are now before you. In the first place, here is a portion of the skin containing the scar; and you will observe that it is a perfectly sound linear cicatrix, barely traceable among the hair. Here is the artery, slit up to show the condition of the interior. At the cardiac side of the place where the ligature was applied there was, as you see, an adherent coagulum, an inch and a quarter in length. But at the distal side there was no adherent clot, doubtless in consequence of the circulation through a large branch, about as big as the human vertebral, which came off, you will observe, as close to the situation of the ligature as was possible.

The cul-de-sac formed by the distal end, though it showed indications of the puckering of the divided internal and middle coats, was completely cicatrized, the smooth lining membrane of the artery being continuous over the irregular surface. Why it was that the immediate vicinity of so large a branch did not lead to secondary hæmorrage, was clear from the state of things beside the ligature, which lay embedded in a firm fibrous structure, with not only no pus, but no granulations, no softening of tissue around it. The portion of the external coat included in the noose, though doubtless killed by the violence with which it was pinched, had not been thrown off as a slough, but, being unstimulating, because undecomposing, it had been absorbed and reproduced by the living parts near it; while the thread had been bridged over externally by dense fibrous tissue, so that the vessel showed but little appearance of constriction where it had been tied, and it appears to be as strong at this part as at any other. You may form some estimate of its strength from the manner in which it resists the traction to which I now subject it. Here is the ligature with its short cut ends, apparently unchanged, except that it was divided in my search for it in its fibrous bed.

This case confirms the hope I ventured to express at the meeting of the British Medical Association in Dublin last autumn, that the antiseptic system would free the deligation of a large artery in its continuity of the two essential elements of danger to which it is now liable, viz. an unhealthy condition of the wound, and secondary hæmorrhage. Thus encouraged, I felt justified in carrying a similar practice into human surgery.

The success of these cases of ligature depends, as we have seen, upon the circumstance that not only a neutral foreign body, but a portion of dead tissue, if simply protected from putrefaction, is entirely devoid of irritating properties. A good example of this fact is presented by a case at present under my care.

Case of Acute Necrosis on the Antiseptic System.—The patient is a boy, eight years of age, who was admitted into the infirmary on the 25th of January, 1868, having, five days previously, received a violent blow upon the left leg with a heavy pair of tongs, resulting in intense inflammation in the limb, which was red and swollen from the knee to the ankle. Fluctuation being distinctly perceptible over the upper part of the tibia, the matter was evacuated antiseptically. A piece of lint dipped in an oily solution of carbolic acid having been laid upon the part where the incision was to be made, its lower edge was raised to allow a knife smeared with the same solution to be plunged into the cavity of the abscess, when the curtain was at once dropped so that the pus might flow out beneath it. When all the matter had been pressed out, an external antiseptic dressing was applied, and this was afterwards changed daily. Four other abscesses afterwards made their appearance at intervals down the limb. Four were treated in the same way; and in every case when a probe, carefully guarded by being passed among folds of lint steeped in the antiseptic oil, was introduced into the incision, it came into contact with bare bone. This was of itself sufficient evidence that portions of the tibia, of greater or less thickness, were dead; for, had the periosteum been raised by suppuration from living bone, the osseous surface would have become covered with granulations during the process. But evidence which must satisfy the most incredulous is afforded by the fact that, between two and three weeks after the first abscess was opened, a probe introduced into the orifice still passed down to bare bone. Under such circumstances, what, it may be asked, could be the advantage of continuing the antiseptic dressing? If dead bone was present, whether in larger or smaller amount, must it not become detached from the living osseous tissue by a gradual process of exfoliation, which an antiseptic applied to the skin could neither promote nor hinder? Such may be a natural inquiry. But having seen a large mass of dead bone absorbed before my eyes by the granulations that enveloped it, in a case of compound fracture treated antiseptically; and having also had evidence from post mortem examination in a case of hip-joint disease where extensive necrosis existed in connection with caries, that bone killed by inflammation might, under antiseptic management, fail to induce suppuration; putting those facts together, I thought it not unlikely that, in the case we are considering, the dead portions of the tibia would be absorbed by the living tissues around them, if we perseveringly maintained an effectual external antiseptic guard. Such, then, was the practice we pursued, and the result was such as I had anticipated. The various incisions successively healed, till by the 6th of April, eleven weeks after the receipt of the injury which caused the attack, the abscess last opened was soundly closed and cicatrized, not a particle of dead bone having come away from any of the openings. At the same time, the swelling of the limb, instead of increasing, as is the case under ordinary treatment, from formation of new bone in the periosteum under the stimulating influence of exfoliations soaked with putrid liquids, had disappeared almost entirely from the upper part of the leg, which was that primarily affected, and was rapidly diminishing elsewhere. (On the 18th of May, the boy left the hospital with the full use of the limb. I had intended giving him a somewhat longer rest in bed as a measure of precaution. But I found that for a considerable time it had been impossible to keep him from getting up and running about the ward; and he was none the worse for his activity.) This certainly was very different from the tedious course of such cases under ordinary treatment.

With regard to the manner in which the dead bone has been disposed of, some who have not witnessed similar occurrences may doubt the possibility of its absorption, and believe that the necrosed pieces are still lying unchanged in the interior of that leg. But even those who take such a view must admit that we have here a most striking illustration of the important truth, that dead tissue, if protected from putrefaction, is of itself incapable of exerting any disturbing influence upon surrounding parts.

Carbolic Dressings.

I will now proceed to speak of the mode of dressing. Carbolic acid, as I have already remarked, is soluble in liquids of very different kinds, so different, for example, as water and one of the fixed oils; and each solution has its own special value. Water, having little affinity for the acid, dissolves but a small quantity, only one-twentieth part of the pure crystals, and holds that small quantity very loosely, so as to permit it to act with energy on any substance for which it has stronger attractions, and also to become soon dissipated on exposure. Hence, the watery solution is a pretty potent but transient application. Now this is exactly what we want when we apply carbolic acid to the interior of a wound for the purpose of destroying any germs which may have been introduced into it. We require something that will act with energy for the moment; but which, as soon as it has extinguished the vitality of the septic particles, may disappear from the wound, in order that the tissues may be left free from all unnecessary irritation. The fixed oils, on the other hand, have so strong an affinity for the acid that they will mix in any proportions with it, and hold it so firmly as not to permit it to act with much energy on the tissues, or to become soon dissipated into the atmosphere. Hence an oily solution is comparatively bland but permanent in its operation. These are just the properties which are desirable for an external application. We wish it to serve as a reservoir of the acid, retaining it for twenty-four hours at least, so that it may remain constantly exerting its antiseptic influence upon the discharges that flow out beneath it. At the same time it is most important that it should be mild in its action on the surface to which it is applied, in order to avoid irritation and excoriation. It appears clear, therefore, that a watery solution is best adapted for the treatment of the interior of a wound in the first instance, while an oily preparation is suited for an external dressing.

We have next to consider the best form for the oily application. I have used various forms; of which some have proved trustworthy, and others not so. One that has shown itself thoroughly reliable is a paste composed, like glazier's putty, of boiled linseed oil and whitening, but with the addition of about one part of carbolic acid to four of the oil. Even in the case of large abscesses, where there has been in the first instance a profuse discharge, the putty, if properly applied and retained securely in position, prevents with perfect certainty the spread of putrefaction into the interior. But the putty is a somewhat clumsy and inconvenient preparation, and I have been desirous, if possible, to get rid of it. Within the last few months I have given a full trial to cloths dipped in a solution of carbolic acid in olive oil, but I am sorry to say that this method, though attractive from its simplicity, is not reliable. It is true, indeed, that we have had some beautiful cases under this mode of management; as for example the following.

Case of Compound Fracture of the Right Leg and Severe Contused Wound in the Left Foot, in a Person of Advanced Age.—On the 31st of January last, a woman, aged seventy-four years, was admitted into the infirmary, having been run over by a heavily laden omnibus. The wheels had passed over both lower limbs, producing in the right leg compound fracture of both bones a little above the ankle, with a considerable wound on the outer side of the limb communicating with the broken fibula, and another on the opposite aspect, not directly connected with the seat of fracture. In the left limb the violence had been sustained by the foot, which presented at its inner aspect a large gaping contused wound, four inches long and two inches broad, while the skin was extensively detached, so that when a watery solution of carbolic acid had been introduced at the wound, pressure over the skin at the outer or opposite side caused some of the fluid to escape, showing that it had passed freely over the upper surface of the foot, beneath the undermined integument. She had also a wound on the forehead, two inches long, exposing the os frontis. From these various injuries she had lost a great deal of blood, and she was also suffering from contusions in other parts of the body. All the wounds were dressed with layers of lint soaked with a solution of carbolic acid in olive oil; the superficial layer, larger than the rest, being changed daily while the deeper layers were left undisturbed. Under this treatment the wound on the forehead healed without the formation of a drop of pus, and those in connection with the compound fracture were converted into superficial granulating sores, without any more disturbance, local or constitutional, than if the fracture had been a simple one; and the bones united in the usual period under the use of pasteboard splints. But the most remarkable circumstance in the case was the progress of the injury of the foot. Three days after the accident, my house surgeon, Mr. Appleton, observed that a considerable portion of the undermined skin on the dorsum of the foot had lost its vitality; and instead of adopting the usual course of applying wet lint or a poultice till the slough should separate, he extended the antiseptic dressings so that they overlapped the dead portion of tissue for a considerable extent in every direction; after which, the daily changing of the superficial layer was continued as before. The result, though in strict accordance with the principles which I am endeavouring to enforce, was strikingly opposed to ordinary experience. After the subsidence of the copious sanious effusion which took place immediately after the injury, the discharge became reduced to about one minim in twenty-four hours, without any distinct appearance of pus, while the foot remained free from the slightest uneasiness, so that she moved it as usual in the bed, and imagined it perfectly recovered. Such being the case, knowing, as I did, that to remove the deep dressings would be to induce, at the best, two large granulating sores which must, from that time foward, furnish a considerable amount of pus that would act as a drain upon the old lady's feeble system, I left the crust of lint and dried exudations untouched for seven weeks, at the end of which time it became spontaneously detached. On raising it, we found a narrow line of cicatrix along the inner side of the foot, complete healing by scabbing having occurred in, I suppose, the largest wound ever known to heal in that manner in the human subject. And on the dorsum of the foot, in place of the large slough, was a broad scar, a portion in the centre about as large as a fourpenny-piece alone remaining unhealed; the dead tissue having, apparently, been absorbed, as none of it was found on the dressing. The superficial layer of antiseptic lint, daily renewed, had answered the purpose of preventing putrefaction from spreading inwards, while the thickness of the permanent crust had kept the carbolic acid constantly supplied externally from penetrating to its deepest parts. Hence, the portion of the dressing in contact with the skin, having lost its original acid by diffusion into the circulation, before sufficient time had elapsed for granulation and suppuration to take place under the stimulating influence of the antiseptic, became a perfectly unirritating or neutral body, and the dead portion of tissue beneath it, being in like manner destitute of any stimulating properties, became amenable to absorption, like the bit of the external coat in the noose of the antiseptic ligature, or the dead bone in the case of necrosis, above related.

But, while I have mentioned this case as a good example of the behaviour of severe injuries under antiseptic management, I wish it to be distinctly understood that I do not recommend the mode of dressing adopted. For, as I have already stated, and as bitter experience in some other cases has but too clearly convinced me, it cannot be implicitly relied on. The reason why it is less trustworthy than the putty is sufficiently plain. The lint, being porous, absorbs the discharge, which, as it enters, displaces the antiseptic oil, and may thus, if profuse, establish a channel of putrescible materials from the external atmosphere to the wound. Again, when the discharge has passed through the dressing, even though it have been imbued with carbolic acid in its passage, it gives it off into the atmosphere on exposure, when it becomes again liable to putrefaction, and, having putrefied, may soak back into the porous dressing, and deprive it entirely of antiseptic virtue. For carbolic acid and the products of putrefaction exert a powerful chemical action upon each other; and, on this account, the former is a deodorant as well as an antiseptic, and, conversely, the latter, if in sufficient quantity, neutralize the acid and render it inert. In this way, I have known a dressing, consisting of several layers of the oiled lint, lose all odour of carbolic acid and acquire that of decomposition within twenty-four hours of its application. The putty, on the other hand, being impermeable to the discharge, retains the carbolic acid securely stored up, except in so far as it is exhaled from the surface, to maintain a constant antiseptic action upon the blood, serum, or pus that flows out beneath.

Impermeability to a watery fluid being thus evidently the essential cause of the superior efficacy of the putty, the chalk, which is its chief constituent, being of no other use than to give consistency to the mass, it naturally occurred to me that, if the oily vehicle of the carbolic acid were in a solid form, the chalk might be dispensed with, and the advantages of the putty might be obtained in a less bulky and more convenient form. I tried, in the first place, various kinds of *emplastra;* but these appeared objectionable on account of their adhesiveness, which is greatly increased by the admixture of carbolic acid, and which seemed likely to be mischievous by retaining the discharge. I next employed paraffin, mixed with a little wax to give it tenacity, and a little olive oil to confer the requisite softness. This certainly made, under ordinary circumstances, an effective as well as elegant substitute for the putty, being perfectly devoid of adhesiveness, while a comparatively thin layer proved securely antiseptic. But the paraffin cerate had this great disadvantage, that, in situations where it was subjected to much movement, such as the groin, it was apt to crumble down and become useless. Meanwhile I learned that Dr. Watson, of Edinburgh, was employing soap-plaster mixed with carbolic acid, and that, though adhesive, it appeared to work well; the discharge finding its way out beneath it. Thus I was again induced to try *emplastra;* and of late we have been using what seems to answer admirably, namely *emplastra plumbi* mixed with one-fourth part of beeswax to give it sufficient consistence, the carbolic acid being in the proportion of about one-tenth of the whole. This is used as a plaster spread on calico in a layer of about one-twentieth of an inch thick, and I can recommend it as thoroughly reliable. There is a case which I am dressing with it at the present time, which I may mention on account of its interest otherwise.

Case of Old Fracture at the Ankle with Fixed Displacement of the Foot, Rectified by Aid of the Antiseptic System.—A young man, aged twenty-nine, was engaged in mooring a vessel on the 11th of December, 1867, when one of the massive ropes, used for the purpose, slipped and struck him with violence at the outer and posterior aspect of the ankle, fracturing the fibula about two inches above the joint, and breaking off the internal malleolus at its base, driving the bones of the leg forwards and inwards with respect to the foot, or, in other words, producing displacement of the foot backwards and outwards. Four months after the receipt of this injury he came under my care in the infirmary, with the heel very prominent and the foot greatly everted, and firmly fixed in its abnormal position by osseous union of the fragments. In this condition the limb was absolutely useless, and the question arose whether anything could be done to restore it. It was clear that the foot could not be replaced without breaking through the 'callus' which could be plainly felt in both bones, and there seemed no prospect of being able to do this without cutting down and adopting means which, in the case of the tibia, would necessarily involve opening into the articulation, or producing artificially a compound fracture into the ankle-joint. This I certainly should not have dreamed of doing without the aid of the antiseptic system, being well aware of the disastrous course such injuries commonly run under ordinary management. If I had operated at all, I should have made a point of removing the end of the tibia, and even then I should have felt that I was subjecting the patient to some risk. But feeling confident that I had the means of converting a compound fracture into a simple one, I did not hesitate to adopt the following procedure. On the 11th inst. (April 1868), the man being under the influence of chloroform, I made a curved incision behind and below the prominent end of the tibia; and, a solution of carbolic acid in about four parts of olive oil being dropped into the wound during the progress of the operation, I detached the soft parts from the bone sufficiently to enable me to insinuate behind the callus one blade of a pair of cutting pliers, smeared with the same oil, and then having placed pieces of lint, soaked with the oil, around the blades of the pliers, so as to prevent the chance of septic air entering the joint when the bone should give way, divided the callus, and at once covered the wound with the antiseptic lint. I then made a longitudinal incision over the seat of fracture in the fibula, and divided it with similar precautions. Having thus overcome the obstacle presented by the bones, I proceeded to draw the foot towards its proper position by pulleys acting upon its outer and posterior part through the medium of a skein of worsted passed round it, while a padded belt supported the opposite aspect of the leg above the ankle: the wounds being kept carefully covered with the oiled lint. When a considerable amount of force had been used there was a sudden sensation of something giving way; and now, on removing the apparatus, the foot was found to have resumed its natural place. The wounds were then dressed with layers of lint soaked with a weak oily solution of carbolic acid, and covered with the antiseptic plaster; after which, a Dupuytren's splint was applied at the inner side of the limb to prevent eversion, and Mr. Syme's horseshoe splint anteriorly to obviate the tendency to displacement backwards. Fresh plaster has since been applied daily; and the result has been that, while the foot has retained its position satisfactorily, the patient has not suffered at all either locally or constitutionally, during the six days that have elapsed since the operation. His pulse has remained 68 or 70, he has not lost his sleep a single night, his tongue has been quite clean, and his appetite good. In fact, he has taken his food with better relish than before, because he has been freed from his previous gloomy prospect of hopeless lameness, while the operation has caused him no anxiety; as the assurance which I felt justified in giving him, that it was entirely free from danger, has been confirmed by the absence of pain or other annoyance. The discharge, which was sanious and copious in the first instance, has of late been only about three minims of clear serum in twenty-four hours; and judging from our previous experience with compound fractures, there is every reason to expect that in a few days more it will cease entirely.

(The subsequent progress of the case has been, on the whole, very satisfactory. But, for reasons to be soon referred to, healing by scabbing did not take place as was anticipated. The discharge, instead of drying up, showed rather a disposition to increase, and assumed a somewhat puriform character; and, although the renewal of the superficial plaster once in two or three days did not involve much disturbance of the limb, I thought it best to expose the wounds when sufficient time had passed to ensure the secure coalescence of their deeper parts. Accordingly, on the 1st of May I removed the lower portions of the dressings, disclosing two superficial granulating sores, with very prominent granulations, which explained the want of disposition to cicatrize. These, though treated with astringents, proved rather indolent, so that they were not completely healed till the 4th of June, though the bones were firmly united a fortnight before.

When he was allowed to walk, though he placed the sole fairly on the ground, he experienced inconvenience from a contracted state of the sural muscles, produced by the long-continued displacement of the foot backwards and consequent downward pointing of the toes, so that he could not bend the ankle beyond the right angle at which it had been maintained since the operation. I hoped that this inconvenience would be overcome by exercise; but in this I was disappointed; for though his power of walking improved it was by no means satisfactory. It also appeared that the abnormal position of the foot had led to an exaggeration of the curve of its arch, to such an extent as to make the foot half an inch shorter than the other, while the planter fascia was felt as a rigid band. I therefore divided that fascia and the tendo Achillis subcutaneously on the 26th of July, and this had the immediate effect of restoring the foot to its natural length, and permitting the ankle to be bent at an acute angle. Had I the case to treat over again I should perform the tenotomy at the same time as the main operation. But except the loss of time that has occurred, the result is nearly all that could be wished. Under the use of a Scarpa's shoe he has continued to improve steadily, and when I last saw him, in the early part of September, he could walk firmly and well, and complained only of some remaining stiffness of the ankle.

In compound fracture, as a general rule, healing by scabbing is that which should be aimed at. When this is attained, the treatment becomes greatly simplified; while the patient is saved any drain upon the system from purulent discharge, and any risks that may attend the presence of a granulating sore. With this object in view, it is necessary that the deeper layers of the dressing should be left to form the scab, and that, while the antiseptic is renewed from time to time externally, it should not penetrate to the surface of the wound permanently covered up? Is it not desir-the tissues to granulation and suppuration, though without putrefaction.

But, it may be asked, Is it not objectionable to keep the wound permenantly **covered up? Is it not** desirable to examine it from time to time, and ascertain what is going on in it? To this I would reply by another question. Does the surgeon think it needful, in a case of simple fracture, to make an incision and investigate the state of the broken bone, the torn muscles and fasciæ, and the other elements of the contused wound which, though the integument remains entire, exists as surely as in a compound fracture? No surgeon would think of such a course. And, on the same principles, provided no unfavorable symptoms are present, we may be well pleased to leave the deep portion of the dressing to serve as a temporary skin.

Yet it must be admitted, that to change the superficial layer of the dressing, without raising the deeper layers, is often a matter of great nicety, while the admission of septic air beneath the scab would be fatal to this mode of treatment. For, the dressing being purposely so arranged that the parts in immediate contact with the wound may be free from carbolic acid, receiving none from without to compensate for loss by absorption of that which they originally contained, the lower surface of the application becomes, in a day or two, devoid of all antiseptic properties, and the penetration of living germs beneath it would lead to putrefaction there, which would spread to any extravasated blood or dead tissue that might remain unabsorbed in the wound. Rather than run any serious risk of such an occurrence, it would be far better to change the whole dressing every day. For although this would necessitate granulation and suppuration, through the continued action of the acid upon the raw surface, yet the essential object of the antiseptic treatment would be attained; that object being not the avoidance of suppuration, but the prevention of putrefaction in the wound. It is of great importance to bear in mind this distinction, whch, from want of clear ideas regarding the conditions which determine suppuration, is very liable to be overlooked. A patient may die of poisoning and irritation in compound fracture, from putrefaction of the blood extravasated in the limb, before sufficient time has passed for any pus to be formed; and, on the contrary, suppuration may take place in connection with compound fracture, whether from the action of the stimulating antiseptic on the wound or from the occurrence of abscess in the contused limb independently of atmospheric influence, without the patient's life being at all endangered, provided always that antiseptic treatment is perseveringly continued.

Nevertheless, the advantages of healing by scabbing are so great that it is worth while to endeavour to attain them, and I have been long striving to improve the method of dressing, so as to get rid, if possible, of the attendant risk. A plan which has, in most cases, answered well when the putty has been used, is to make the permanent dressing of two or three layers of lint somewhat larger than the wound, wrung out of a pretty strong solution of carbolic acid in oil, say one of acid to four of oil, and covered with a piece of oiled calico or linen rag extending about an inch beyond the lint in every direction. Over this is appiled a stratum of antiseptic putty, which is changed daily, or once in two days, according to the amount of discharge. The blood from the wound soaking into the lint is acted on by the carbolic acid, and changed into a firm substance which consolidates the deep dressings into a crust or scab, and this crust, while sufficiently thick over the wound to prevent the carbolic acid of the putty from penetrating to the raw surface, is so thin at its margins formed by the rag as to be there kept antiseptic through and through. Then, in changing the putty, the first thing seen on lifting up its edge is the thin margin of the calico; and even if this be accidentally raised a little, its antiseptic property prevents any mischief from resulting. The putty is spread on calico, and the calico is applied next to the deep dressing, to prevent adhesion, while the external surface of the putty is covered either with thin block-tin or sheet-lead, or, what more recently we found to answer quite as well, gutta-percha tissue, which, though it permits carbolic acid to escape through it, is not objectionable on that account if the putty be sufficiently thick, while the gutta-percha, like the metallic plate, prevents the putty from becoming dry and hard. The putty is made to overlap the permanent dressing well on all sides, and I may remark that, whether the impermeable antiseptic guard be composed of putty or not, it is of the utmost importance that it should extend freely beyond the source of the discharge in every direction, so that the putrescible fluid may have to flow for some distance beneath it before it reaches the atmosphere or any dressing containing active putrefactive organisms. The degree of overlapping of the crust by the external dressing must vary according to the amount of discharge which may be anticipated. When this is large, it should be to the extent of three or four inches. Failures have undoubtedly often occurred for want of attention to this essential point.

But though this method will, with proper care, generally succeed, it would be very desirable, if possible, to get rid of the trouble involved in it. At one time I hoped this might be done by means of the plaster above mentioned, by employing a layer of it instead of the calico as the upper part of the permanent dressing, so that the adhesiveness of the emplastrum might keep the whole deep dressing securely applied to the skin, except at limited spots where the discharge might ooze out; another layer of plaster being used instead of the putty, with calico moistened with a watery solution of the acid interposed to prevent adhesion of the two layers of plaster. My anticipations, however, have not been verified in this respect. For the plaster, though it answers extremely well for an external antiseptic guard, whether in compound fracture, incised wounds, or abscesses, has proved unsuitable for the permanent dressing. The substance of the emplastrum becomes softened by the solution of carbolic acid used to moisten the calico, and permits it to enter beneath it and soak into the lint below, and stimulate the raw surface to granulate and suppurate, and this was what occurred in the case of displaced foot above mentioned. At the same time the lint is kept moist, instead of forming a dry crust, and hence it may gradually shift its place along with the plaster that covers it, involving the risk of leaving the wound insufficiently overlapped, if not exposed. I have experienced this inconvenience in two cases of compound fracture which have been treated in this way. One of these was an old lady, of seventy-five, in whom the os humeri was severely comminuted just above the elbow-joint, with a considerable wound from which six loose fragments were extracted; the other was a boy, twelve years old, whose right thigh was much contused as well as broken by machinery. These cases, indeed, have done well; osseous union having occurred as early as if the fractures had been simple ones. But in both of them the wounds healed by granulation instead of by scabbing.

With the view of getting over these difficulties I sought to obtain some kind of antiseptic cement, by which a portion of dressing might be glued down firmly upon the skin. Among other materials I tried shellac, and, in so doing, I accidentally hit upon a substance which appears preferable to the plaster for almost every purpose. I found that this resin could be mixed with carbolic acid in any amount by aid of heat, the result, when cooled, varying, according to the quantity of the acid, from brittleness to fluidity, the intermediate proportions giving a firm but flexible solid with a certain degree of elasticity, approaching to some extent the characters of caoutchouc. It further turned out that the lac thus associated with the carbolic acid retained it with great tenacity, so that a thin layer spread on calico may be used to store up a large quantity of the antiseptic, forming an application which retains its virtues for days at the temperature of the body, and, at the same time, fails to irritate the skin. It has also this great advantage over the lead plaster, that it cannot be softened by either a watery or an oily fluid. The only imperfection which it appeared to show, when used in practice as an external antiseptic guard, was that when long applied to the skin it adhered to the surface, whereas it is desirable that such a dressing should adhere very slightly if at all. This objection to it I attempted to obviate by spreading it upon gutta-percha, which, though insoluble in carbolic acid, allows it to travel through its substance. The lac when thus lined with gutta-percha proved none the less efficient as an antiseptic, and, being perfectly devoid of adhesiveness and of smooth surface, shed the discharge in a most perfect manner, greatly excelling, in this respect, the lead-plaster. But it had one fault, viz. that when subjected to much bending, as at the fold of a joint, the gutta-percha cracked and admitted the discharge, gradually insinuating itself, detached the gutta-percha more or less extensively, and introduced an element of risk through the interposition of a layer of liquid between the antiseptic lac and its lining. This fault has been got rid of by reducing the gutta-percha to a mere film, incapable of affording lodgement for fluid, by brushing over the antiseptic lac with a weak solution of gutta-percha in bisulphide of carbon, which, rapidly evaporating, leaves a coating of microscopic thinness, yet effectual for preventing adhesion. We have now given this lac dressing a sufficient trial in wounds and abscesses to entitle me to recommend it with confidence.

For an antiseptic dressing that is intended to be changed from time to time, perfect absence of adhesiveness is a most valuable property; not only because it permits all discharge to escape beneath it into the porous material placed outside to absorb it, but because it avoids traction upon any deeper dressing or upon the skin during the process of withdrawing it, with the concomitant risk of regurgitation of air or liquid charged with living putrefactve organisms.

But for the permanent dressing in compound fracture this complete want of adhesiveness is the converse of what we desire. Here, the material employed, being designed to form part of the scab, should stick to the skin or to anything else that lies beneath it. The lac prepared as above described may, however, be readily made suitable for this purpose, by rubbing off the film of gutta-percha by firm friction with a dry cloth, and then brushing the surface over with liquid carbolic acid. It then, at once, assumes a sufficient degree of adhesiveness.

In order to ensure healing without suppuration, it is requisite, as we have seen, not only to prevent the spreading of putrefaction into the wound, but also to protect the raw surface from perpetual stimulation by the carbolic acid. In the mode of dressing, above described, in which the putty was employed, the latter object was attained by means of layers of lint forming a crust too thick to be penetrated by the acid supplied externally; and the same plan would, no doubt, succeed as well with the lac. But to trust to the mere thickness of a penetrable crust is not altogether satisfactory. It would clearly be better, if possible, to protect the exposed tissues from the stimulating antiseptic in the lac by a layer of some substance chemically impermeable to carbolic acid. A metallic plate possesses this property; and in its more flexible forms, such as thin block-tin or sheet-lead, it seems likely, at least in ordinary cases, to answer well. I have, as yet, only had opportunity to try this method in two cases, but both of these have presented points of interest which make them deserving of mention.

Case of Contused Wound treated with Block-Tin and Antiseptic Lac.— The first was a contused wound, three inches long, over the lower part of the tibia, with some undermining of the skin, in a young man of twenty, occasioned by the limb being violently squeezed between a heavy iron pipe and a fixed piece of machinery. Happening to be at the infirmary soon after his admission, I dressed the case myself, washing and syringing out the wound with a saturated watery solution of carbolic acid, and covering it with a well-fitting piece of thin block-tin of rather larger size, washed with the watery solution, and then applying a piece of lac-plaster, deprived of its gutta-percha layer, overlapping the tin freely on all sides. A piece of calico was placed outside the lac-plaster, to prevent adhesion of its edges to a dry cloth, which was wrapped round the leg to absorb discharge, and was intended to be changed. Next day there was a good deal of sero-sanguineous effusion on the cloth, for which another was substituted, moistened with a solution of carbolic acid in four parts of olive oil. The same was afterwards done daily; the discharge diminishing rapidly, and the limb remaining free from swelling or pain, and the constitution from disturbance, till, on the fourth day, the patient, who was a silly youth, was seized with a desire to see the injured part, and tore off all the dressings. This foolish proceeding on his part gave us the opportunity of making an interesting observation. The wound was found perfectly level with the general surface of the skin, being filled with a clot of smooth surface corresponding to that of the tin which had covered it, while the edges of the skin were pale and natural in appearance. The dressing was re-applied as before, the wound being superficially washed with carbolic acid lotion in the process. Two days later the patient again, without any reason, laid bare the wound, which still presented the same characters, except that the surface of the smooth clot showed, here and there, some minute whitish specks, probably in consequence of the action of the watery solution of carbolic acid with which it was washed two days previously. A similar dressing was again employed, the use of carbolic lotion being again necessarily involved. After two more days, that is to say a week after the accident, the patient, though free from symptoms, having again removed the dressings, the wound was again examined. It was free from pus or odour of putrefaction, but its surface was mottled with red and yellow spots, and was not quite level. The dressing was continued one day longer, when it was abandoned, as the patient could not be induced to leave it alone, water dressing being used instead; and on the following day the wound presented the characters of a healing superficial granulating sore. Two days later, he was so unruly that he was discharged for misconduct.

In the following case we have had the opportunity of seeing the effects of this mode of dressing when left undisturbed.

Case of Compound Fracture of the Leg treated with Block-Tin and Antiseptic Lac.— On the 3rd of October, 1868, a porter, twenty-five years old, was unloading a wagon in a warehouse, when a box, weighing about four hundredweight, slipped, and, striking him upon the left leg, knocked him down over an opening in the floor, through which he would have fallen into the room below had not the heavy box, pressing upon the limb, pinned him down and kept him suspended. When rescued from this situation, he was taken to the infirmary, where my house surgeon, Mr. Malloch, found the leg much distended with extravasated blood, with a wound, three-eighths of an inch in length, on the inner side, about midway between the knee and ankle, bleeding freely and communicating with a transverse fracture of the tibia. A probe (smeared with an oily solution of carbolic acid to prevent the introduction of septic particles) could be introduced beneath the undermined fascia for about three inches in every direction except downwards, and also passed, for the same extent, directly outwards behind the tibia which was felt to be denuded of its periosteum. Having injected into the wound, with a syringe, several ounces of a saturated watery solution of the acid, and diffused it freely through the limb by pressure, to mix it with the extravasated blood, Mr. Malloch placed a piece of thin block-tin about an inch square over the orifice, and, after pressing out as much as possible of the blood and watery solution, applied a piece of lac-plaster deprived of its gutta-percha lining, overlapping the tin a couple of inches in every direction, and over this a folded cloth moistened with a solution of carbolic acid in four parts of olive oil. The limb was then put up in lateral pasteboard splints. This treatment relieved the severe pain which he was suffering; but it returned in the course of the next few hours, during which very free haemorrhagic effusion occurred. Next day the discharge became greatly diminished, and in the course of the following day it ceased entirely. The pain also left him about twelve hours after the accident and never returned. The after treatment consisted, for the first two days, in renewing the oily cloth once in the twenty-four hours; but from the third day onwards the cloth was left permanently upon the limb and merely brushed over with a mixture of equal parts of carbolic acid and oil, the inner splint being raised for the purpose without disturbing the limb, which lay upon its outer side with the knee bent. After the sixth day, the antiseptic oil was only applied once in forty-eight hours. On the third day, some wrinkling of the epidermis indicated subsidence of the swelling, which afterwards fell rapidly till, by the eleventh day, the calf was almost of natural size, having shrunk away considerably from the splint. His pulse never rose above 82, which was its number the day after the accident, and his general heatlh was from that time forward quite unaffected.

Ten days after the receipt of the injury, it was noticed that the oily cloth, which for a week past had indicated complete absence of discharge, exhibited an appearance of additional staining, corresponding to two or three drops of red serum which seemed to have pent up beneath the lac-plaster by inspissation of the blood and serum round its margins, till some accidental cause, such as the shrinking of the limb, cracked the dried exudation. Having been led to disturb the dressing to some extent in investigating the source of this discharge, I thought it best to remove it entirely, protecting the wound at the moment of its exposure with a bit of antiseptic lint. The under surface of the lac gave distinct indications of being impregnated with carbolic acid. The wound presented a very interesting appearance. It had shrunk considerably; but its margins resembled those of a perfectly recent wound; and its orifice was occupied by a projecting dark clot, which to the naked eye scarcely differed from a fresh coagulum. Hence there seemed reason still to hope for healing without suppuration, if the original mode of dressing were repeated. Accordingly, the tin smeared with carbolic acid was replaced, and overlapping it a fresh portion of lac-plaster, rendered adhesive by touching it with carbolic acid after removing the film of gutta-percha, except in a narrow space from the centre to one side. A dry cloth and the splint completed the dressing. Two days later, in order to maintain the lac-plaster in an antiseptic condition, two layers of calico, moistened with a solution of carbolic acid in four parts of olive oil, were substituted for the cloth; and afterwards, at intervals of from two to three days, the surface of the calico was lightly brushed over with a mixture of equal parts of the oil and acid. For six days, some yellowish serum, amounting at first to one or two minims in twenty-four hours, but gradually diminishing, exuded from below that part of margin of the lac-plaster where the gutta-percha film had been left, the amount being estimated by changing every day a little bit of antiseptic lint placed at the point of exudation. But, after the sixth day, the piece of lint was left unchanged, as the trifling discharge seemed to have ceased entirely. When eleven days more had passed without any change, I thought it well to ascertain again the state of the wound; and on the 30th of October, seventeen days after the second application of the deep dressing, and two days short of four weeks after the accident, I pulled off the lac-plaster with the tin adhering to it. The plaster was still sticking to the skin, and drew away the hairs along with it, except where the gutta-percha film remained. At this part, along the course of the track of exudation, the skin had an orange stain, from serum mixed with altered hæmatin, and was moist, except near the edge of the plaster. Beneath the tin, also, there was the same kind of orange moisture. The wound appeared at first unhealed, having an orange-red aspect; but, on wiping it with a piece of lint, a perfect cicatrix was disclosed, which had been covered with the remains of the little portion of clot seen projecting from the orifice on the former occasion of exposing it. A piece of dry lint was placed upon the scar; and the splints were readjusted, the fragments being in good position. The case was now reduced to one of simple fracture.

This case presents several features of great interest. In the first place, the appearances disclosed on the removal of the dressings on the tenth day after the accident afford as good an illustration as could be desired of the fact that the surface of a wound is not induced to suppurate, or indeed to undergo any appreciable change by the contact of a foreign body, destitute of chemically stimulating properties. The carbolic acid with which the surface of the tin was washed, like that injected into the wound, was absorbed into the circulation before it had time to bring those changes in the part which are the essential preliminary to suppuration. The tissues of a recent wound are incapable of forming pus, however much they may be stimulated, whether by nervous (i.e. inflammatory) excitement, or by chemical irritants, such as the products of putrefaction or pungent antiseptics. It is only when they have been gradually changed under the influence of prolonged abnormal stimulation into that rudimentary form of tissue which, when we see it on the surface of a sore, we term granulations, that they are liable to produce, when still further stimulated, the still more rudimentary pus corpuscle. It is upon this that the possibility of obtaining primary union on the antiseptic system depends. The antiseptic applied to the wound in the first instance is a powerful stimulant, but it is absorbed before it has time to bring about granulation in the tissues.

In the second place, it is very satisfactory to see, although theoretically it could hardly have been doubted, that, when a wound has been effectively protected from stimulation and consequent granulation, it may, even at a late period after its infliction, be again subjected to the temporary stimulus of an antiseptic application without being made to suppurate; for a knowledge of this fact will enable us to examine the wound when we think there is a fair prospect of healing being complete, confident that, should the reverse prove to be the case, we can again employ the original mode of dressing without interfering with the process of healing by scabbing.

Thirdly, I may remark that cicatrization without suppuration beneath a piece of tin is a novel mode of healing by scabbing. But the ordinary scab is in so far analogous to the metallic plate, that the exudations of which it is composed having dried before they had time to putrefy, the crust is, like the metal, a neutral or unstimulating solid. Further, there is putrescible moisture beneath the scab as beneath the tin; but the mode in which the putrefactive organisms are excluded is essentially different. The scab keeps them out mechanically, by adhering firmly to the surface of the integument; the metallic plate opposes no mechanical barrier to their entrance, but is guarded by a germ poison in the surrounding lac which no less imperatively forbids their access.

Altogether the case must be regarded as affording great encouragement for giving a further trial to this method, which seems to bring the treatment of compound fracture to something nearly approaching perfection. The lac, being impermeable to discharge, combines the properties of an external antiseptic guard with those of a permanent crust; and, as fresh carbolic acid can be supplied to it as often as may be desired without disturbing its position, the trouble and risk that attend the changing of the putty are entirely got rid of. At the same time the tin protects the raw surface from the acid with absolute certainty, while the tin and the lac constitute together so thin a layer as not to alter the contour of the limb, or interfere with the shape of splints such as would be used for simple fracture; a considerable advantage as compared with the mass constituted by a thick crust, covered with substantial putty. When the wound is large, I would advise the use of two layers of the lac-plaster for the sake of additional strength, the outer one overlapping the inner by an inch or two; and the outer, like the inner, rendered adhesive, as above described, so that the two may become incorporated into one mass. Also, I would recommend that, as was done in the second dressing of the last case, the film of gutta-percha should be left upon a track leading from the tin to what is to be the most dependent part of the edge of the plaster to afford free egress for sero-sanguineous discharge.

For treating the interior of the wound in compound fracture, I employed, till comparatively lately, the undiluted acid, and, as this afforded excellent results, I did not venture to change the practice without having some more substantial basis than hope to found upon. But rather more than a year ago, having observed that the injection of a saturated watery solution (one part of acid to twenty parts of water) among the fibrous tissues in a fetid suppurating wound of the palm, completely arrested the existing putrefaction, I concluded, that if the acid so diluted sufficed to destroy the abounding putrefactive organisms which must have been present among the textures in that case, it must surely be trustworthy for compound fracture. We have accordingly employed the saturated watery solution in all the numerous cases of compound fracture that have since come under my care, and in no instance has it failed. If it answers equally well, it is obviously superior to the strong acid, since it does not produce the slightest sloughing from caustic action, and, being a less powerful irritant, causes a less copious serous effusion. Besides, it may be injected and diffused among the tissues which are the seat of extravasation with a freedom which could not be used with the acid of full strength, and it is to this circumstance that I am disposed to attribute the fact that we have obtained success at a period after the infliction of the injury which I should formerly have thought quite hopeless, in one case, for example, as late as thirty-six hours after the accident. Lastly, we avoid a disagreeable symptom which we used to observe occasionally after applying the undiluted acid freely to large wounds, viz. obstinate vomiting for about twenty-four hours, occasioned, no doubt, by imbibition of a poisonous dose into the circulation.

Catgut, manufactured from the small intestine of the sheep, may be had at a very low price, from the thickness of a horsehair upwards. In the dry state, it is somewhat objectionable from its rigidity, and also from a tendency of the first half of the knot to slip before the second half is secured. Water renders it perfectly supple, and as little liable to slip as waxed silk. But if a watery solution of carbolic acid be used for the purpose of making it antiseptic, the protracted immersion requisite to ensure completeness of the effect makes the finer kinds too weak, and the stouter too clumsy so that it will not enter the eye of an ordinary aneurysm-needle. The method which I have found to answer best is to keep the catgut steeping in a solution of carbolic acid in five parts of olive oil, with a very small quantity of water diffused through it. A larger proportion of the acid would impair the tenacity of the thread. If a mere oily solution be employed, the gut remains rigid, the oil not entering at all into its substance. But a very small quantity of water, such as the acid enables the oil to dissolve, renders the gut supple, without making it materially weaker or thicker. And, curiously enough, the presence of this small amount of water in the oily solution gradually brings about a change in the gut, indicated by a deep brown colour, after which it may be placed in a watery solution for a long time, without swelling as a portion prepared in a simple oily solution does. This is a great convenience. For an oily solution is unpleasant to work with during an operation; and exposure to the air soon renders gut suppled with water rigid from drying. But, when it has been treated in the way above recommended, it may be transferred to a watery solution at the commencement of an operation, and so kept supple without having its strength or thickness altered.

For tying an arterial trunk in its continuity, catgut as thick when dry as ordinary purse-silk will be found best; but for ordinary wounds, where, if one ligature happen to break, another can be easily applied, much finer kinds may be employed, and are convenient from their smaller bulk. For everyday use, a small oil-tight capsule may be carried in the pocket-case; and this case can be replenished from a larger stock as may be necessary. I have had a small silver bottle with well-fitting screwed top adapted to my caustic case; and this contains two little rods of wood with gut of two sizes wound upon them, together with a few drops of the antiseptic oil; and now that torsion has almost entirely superseded the ligature in ordinary wounds, this small supply will probably last me for months.

OBSERVATIONS ON LIGATURE OF ARTERIES ON THE ANTISEPTIC SYSTEM

(*Lancet,* 1869, vol. i, p. 451. Corrected Febr. 1870.)

VARIOUS attempts have been made, both in the early part of the century and more recently, to improve the ligature, or to supersede it by other methods. Nevertheless, for obstructing the calibre of an arterial trunk in its continuity, no means hitherto devised have proved superior to a small silk thread tied in a secure knot, with the ends left projecting from the wound. Yet, as is implied by the numerous efforts at improvement, the ligature in this form is far from perfect. The internal and middle coats are ruptured by the constricting noose, while a portion of the tough external coat is pinched together and deprived of its vitality. The dead tissue, becoming contaminated by the putrefaction which occurs in the interstices of the silk fibres, acts, together with the septic ligature, as a cause of irritation to the neighbouring parts of the arterial wall, which consequently degenerate into an imperfect structure, inadequate to withstand the powerful cardiac impulse; and even before the slough separates by suppuration, the blood breaks through the feeble barrier, unless it be fortified by a firm plug of niternal coagulum. Hence, if a considerable branch takes origin close to the part tied, the formation of a clot being prevented by the current blood, secondary haemorrhage is the inevitable consequence; and thus the ligature is inapplicable in situations otherwise eligible for it, such as the femoral artery near Poupart's ligament, the origins and endings of the iliacs, and the innominate.

Even when the thread is distant from any considerable branch, the terrible risk of haemorrhage cannot be said to be altogether absent. The degenerate structure of the vessel near the ligature, unlike the arterial wall in its normal condition, is prone to ulceration, and the organizing coagulum is similarly circumstanced; so that an unhealthy state of the wound may open up the calibre of an artery tied in the most favourable situation.

Again, when the parts about the vessel communicate with loose cellular interspaces in important regions, as is the case with the iliac arteries or the subclavian, diffuse suppuration is frequently a cause of death. Finally, the cure is always rendered tedious by the time required for the separation of the ligature; while the presence of an external wound during the period thus protracted involves a risk, by no means inconsiderable in some localities, of hospital gangrene or erysipelas.

The Antiseptic System, however, places this branch of surgery, like most others, in a new light. One point which it has brought out in striking relief is, that a portion of dead tissue is not necessarily thrown off by suppuration, but, unless altered by putrefaction or artificially imbued with stimulating salts, serves as pabulum for the surrounding living parts, which remove it by a sure process of absorption. Hence, the death of a portion of the external coat included in the ligature does not of itself render it a cause of suppuration. And I conceived that if a silk thread, steeped in some liquid capable of destroying the septic organisms in its interstices, were tied round an artery, and left with short-cut ends in a wound dressed antiseptically, the foreign body, soon losing, by diffusion into the circulation, the stimulating salt with which it was saturated at the outset, and being in its own substance as unstimulating chemically as a pellet of lead from a fowling-piece, would either remain, like the latter, permanently encapsulated, or itself experience absorption together with the dead tissue in its grasp. In either case, being destitute of irritating properties, it should leave the primitive strength of the arterial coats unimpaired; when the objection to tying near a large branch would cease to exist.

The wound meanwhile would, under proper management, close rapidly, without any deep-seated suppuration, and would be efficiently protected against the evil influences of impure atmosphere. In short, the ligature of an arterial trunk in its continuity would be brought to a state of perfection.

I have subjected these theoretical views to the test of experience; and though the results have not turned out in all respects exactly as I had anticipated, yet those finally arrived at appearing satisfactory, I now present to the profession an account of all that I have done in the subject.

Case of Ligature of the External Iliac Artery on the Antiseptic System.— On the 29th of January, 1868, I was requested by Dr. Fergus to see a lady fifty-one years of age, who was suffering from an inguinal aneurysm which had existed for four years, but had of late been markedly on the increase, causing agonizing pain, which had confined her to bed for the last four weeks, and had considerably reduced her strength. The aneurysm was of the size of a large orange, affecting the uppermost part of the left femoral artery, and extending a little above Poupart's ligament. Any delay appearing undesirable, I tied the external iliac on the following day, in presence of Dr. Fergus, and assisted by Messrs. Hector Cameron, Appleton, and James Coats. There was nothing peculiar in the operation, except that the incision was made a little further outward than usual, in order to avoid the upper part of the aneurysm. The only bleeding vessel that required attention was twisted. The ligature employed had been previously steeped for two hours in strong fluid carbolic acid, prepared by adding a small proportion of water to the crystals. The tightly twisted thread requires a considerable period of immersion to ensure thorough soaking with the liquid; and the acid does not impair the tenacity of the fibre. At the time of the operation, the superfluous acid was removed by transferring the silk to a solution of carbolic acid in thirty parts of water; and the same lotion was used for the sponges, and also for washing the aneurysm-needle before it was passed round the vessel. The artery having been tied, and the ends of the ligature cut short, the wound was freely treated with the watery solution, some of which was poured in, to make sure that it penetrated to every part. The edges of the skin were then brought together with silver sutures, except in the middle, where I introduced a pledget of lint steeped in a solution of the acid in five parts of olive oil; passing it deeply, but leaving one end projecting externally, to serve as a drain for blood and serum. I then applied an external antiseptic dressing, the details of which I need not now describe. The pledget of lint was cautiously withdrawn on the following day, under cover of a pretty large piece of lint imbued with the antiseptic oil; and the external dressing was reapplied, and afterwards changed at intervals proportioned to the diminution of the serous discharge, which, at the end of a fortnight, was estimated at about three minims in three days. At this time, some portions of lint, which had been left till then undisturbed, were removed, when the wound was found quite free from pus, being perfectly cicatrized where the sutures were introduced; while the central part, where the pledget was placed after the operation, presented the appearance of a superficial sore, but not a granulating one; for the deep surface of the dressing, being devoid of stimulating properties, had failed to induce granulation in the tissues on which it lay. Meanwhile the patient had been relieved from the pain which she previously suffered, without experiencing febrile disturbance or any material inconvenience from the operation, except uneasiness in the wound the first two days, during retching occasioned by the chloroform. The tongue had been natural throughout; the pulse had only on one day been as high as 90, 72 to 84 being the usual rates; and her appetite, which had been absent during the four weeks of agony that preceded the operation, returned two days after it, as the derangement of the stomach from chloroform subsided. On the fourteenth day, as I was arranging her pillows, she sat upright without inconvenience. Four weeks after the operation, the wound being completely cicatrized, she was allowed to move about in her room; and, just six weeks from the date of the ligature of the artery, she descended three long flights of stairs, walked for some time in the streets, and reascended the steps to her lodgings; and, though fatigued by the effort, she left next day all the better for it. On the 31st of March, she called to see me, much improved in strength, though with still some tendency to swelling of the legs, especially the left, when in the erect posture. The aneurysmal swelling felt merely like a slight glandular thickening. On the 25th of July, 1868, I again visited her. She had derived much benefit from a stay at the seaside, and the tendency to oedema of the extremities was greatly diminished. There was still absence of pulsation in the external iliac artery, and the cicatrix remained quite sound twenty-five weeks after the operation.

She continued for about ten months in fair health and strength; but, in the latter part of November, she became affected with a peculiar spasmodic disorder of the respiration, and on the morning of the 30th month, while sitting up in bed, she suddenly exclaimed that something had given way within her, and that she was dying, and then immediately expired. Next day I made a post mortem examination, when the idea which she had expressed proved correct—an aneurysm of the descending part of the arch of the aorta having given way, and discharged an enormous quantity of blood into the mediastinal and subpleural cellular tissue. The parts concerned in the operation having been removed and dissected, the following appearances were disclosed. The aneurysm was not entirely obliterated; but remained about the size of a cherry or large filbert, of somewhat fusiform shape. The upper two-thirds were solid, being occupied by firm coagulum incorporated with the sac. The lower third, situated just at the bifurcation of the common femoral, had been kept free from coagulation by the regurgitant stream of blood from the profunda into the superficial trunk. This part of the sac appeared constituted by the wall of the vessel, very slightly distended. The external iliac artery was considerably shrunk throughout, and tapered from each end to near the middle, where it was only about a twentieth of an inch in diameter. In the greater part of its length the structure of the dwindled vessel could be distinctly recognised, with adherent coagula in the interior, decolourized and otherwise altered. But at the narrowest part the artery was reduced to mere fibrous tissue. constituting a dense white band five-eighths of an inch long, from the middle of which was seen projecting at one side a round, buff-coloured appendage about a line in diameter, somewhat obscured by a trifling amount of inflammatory condensation of texture in the immediate vicinity. On scratching this little body with the point of a knife, I found it to be a very thin-walled capsule, containing the knot of the ligature, with two tapering ends, which were shorter than the thread was cut at the operation, while the noose had vanished altogether. The surface of the knot also showed clear indications of having been subjected to an eroding agency, similar, no doubt, to that exerted by granulations upon dead bone absorbed by them. Besides the remnant of the ligature, the tiny capsule contained a minute quantity of yellowish, semi-fluid material, looking to the naked eye like very thick pus. Under the microscope, however, pus-corpuscles were seen to form but a small proportion of its constituents, which were principally rounded corpuscles of smaller size, and fibro-plastic corpuscles, together with some imperfect fibres and granular material. In addition to these elements were some which at first puzzled me; but which turned out to be fragments of silk fibre, of various lengths, and of jagged, tapering, or otherwise irregular forms, and many of them greatly reduced in thickness, contrasting strongly with the uniform bands of a fresh piece of silk from the same reel that had furnished the ligature.

Mingled with the puriform fluid were also some delicate filaments of silk, visible without the microscope; and these seemed to retain their natural elasticity. Nor was there anything about the more minute pieces into which the fibres had been so strangely chopped up, to indicate that they were undergoing a process of solution or softening by the fluid that soaked the thread. They had rather the appearance of having been superficially nibbled, so to speak; confirming the impression conveyed by the naked-eye characters of the knot, that the silk had been eroded by the absorbing action of the surrounding parts. Indeed, considering the organic origin of silk, the remarkable thing seems to be, not that it should be absorbed by the living tissues, but that it should resist their influence so long.

Why it was that the parts in immediate contact with the silk should have assumed so imperfect a structure is a difficult question, but one of great interest: because, although that structure could not be called pus, it was certainly a very near approach to it; and it is impossible to say that we had not here an incipient abscess. There can be no doubt that the presence of the thread was in some way or other the cause, and I think we can hardly be wrong in assuming that, in order to give rise to such degeneration of tissue, it must have operated as a persistent, if trifling, source of abnormal stimulation. Now, as putrefaction is here out of the question, and as the substance of silk is not chemically stimulating, we seem shut up to the conclusion that the thread must have occasioned disturbance of a mechanical nature. Further, the effect in question seems to be essentially connected with the disintegration of the silk. For in the horse's carotid the silk ligature, having remained unaltered during the six weeks that had passed after the operation, was found surrounded on all sides by compact tissue; and in the present case, so long a period as ten months having elapsed before the puriform condition was observed in an apparently incipient stage, it is probable that the thread had lain for a long time inert, producing irritation only when partially absorbed. If, then, we inquire how the disintegrating silk could prove a source of mechancal irritation, it seems not improbable that it may have been from the sharp and jagged fragments of the fibre perpetually fretting the elements of the living tissue around them. This view, if correct, would explain the curious fact observed by Lawrence and others, that when fine silk ligatures had been left with short-cut ends in a stump, though the wound might heal without their separation in the first instance, they were liable to make their appearance subsequently, sometimes at so late a period as seems to exclude the idea of putrefaction having occurred from organisms introduced into the threads. Indeed, such ligatures occasionally showed themselves encapsulated in little nodules in the cicatrix, without suppuration occurring at all. In other words, the apparently soft silk, instead of remaining, like a smooth leaden pellet, permanently embedded in the place where it was first introduced, made its way to the surface with or without suppuration, like a sharp spiculum of rigid glass; the silk being in its minute structure comparable to the pellet when in the primitive condition of smooth continuous fibres, and to glass spicula when in the form of jagged fragments as the result of partial absorption.

But whatever may be thought of this explanation,

it is clear that if there is any chance of silk, though used antiseptically, giving rise, even in exceptional cases, to abscess in the vicinity of an artery tied with it, this is a serious objection to its employment; and as the near approach to suppuration in the present instance was undoubtedly occasioned by the persistent presence of the thread, the case, while interesting as affording evidence that silk is susceptible of absorption, suggests the expediency of substituting for that material some other substance which can be more readily taken up by the tissues.

The use of 'animal ligatures', of catgut, leather, or tendon, was long since tried and abandoned as unsatisfactory; but after the experience which the antiseptic system has afforded of the disappearance, without suppuration, of large dead pieces of skin and other textures, there could be little doubt that threads of animal tissue, if applied antiseptically, would be similarly disposed of.

And even if chemical processes should have been used in preparing such threads, it did not seem likely that this would interfere with their absorption; for I knew that the free action of carbolic acid on blood and sloughs had no such deterring influence, and I have long been satisfied that the injection of a strong solution of perchloride of iron or tannic acid for the cure of naevi produces subcutaneous sloughs, which are imbued with the ingredients injected, and yet disappear, as a rule, without the formation of pus.

In order to put the antiseptic animal ligature fairly to the test, I made the following experiment:-

Ligature of the Carotid Artery in the Calf on the Antiseptic System, with Threads composed of Animal Tissue.—On the 31st of December, 1868, I tied the right carotid artery about the middle of the neck in a healthy calf a few days old, the animal being under chloroform. Ligatures of two different kinds were employed, at an interval of about an inch and a half, the sheath of the vessel being left undisturbed in the intervening part. The cardiac ligature was of home manufacture, composed of three strips of peritoneum from the small intestine of an ox, firmly twisted together into a three-fold cord. The distal thread was of fine catgut, called 'minikin gut' by the London makers. Both had been soaked for four hours in a saturated watery solution of carbolic acid, which swelled and softened them, so that the thread of my own making was too large to enter the eye of the aneurysm-needle except near the ends, where it was thinner than elsewhere. This substantial ligature bore the strain of tying well, but the fine catgut broke as I tightened the noose. I did not, however, remove it, but having a second piece at my disposal, passed it round at the same place, and with gentle traction completed the knot. There were thus two ligatures of the fine gut at the distal site. All were cut short, except one end of the catgut, which I purposely left about three-quarters of an inch long, to give a better opportunity of ascertaining what would become of the foreign material. The antiseptic arrangements were as follows: Before the operation the hair of the part was cut short, and a solution of carbolic acid in four parts of linseed oil (preferred for its cheapness) was rubbed well into the skin, to destroy any putrefactive organisms lying amongst the roots of the hairs; for any so situated might escape the action of the external antiseptic dressing, and communicate putrefaction to the discharges, and thence to the interior of the wound. The sponges used in the operation were wrung out of a watery solution of the acid, and all the instruments into the wound, together with the fingers of my left hand and the copper wire used for sutures, were treated with the same lotion, some of which was poured into the wound after the introduction of the last stitch, at one of the intervals left for the escape of discharge, to make sure against the chance of any fresh blood which had oozed out during the process of stitching having regurgitated and taken living germs in with it. The external dressing was a towel saturated with the oily solution, folded as broad as the length of the neck, round which it was wrapped so as to extend freely beyond the wound in all directions, prevented from slipping backward and forward by being stitched to a halter round the head, and to a girth behind the forelegs, while a bandage rolled round it kept it applied accurately to the surface. A sheet of gutta-percha tissue, to prevent contamination of the antiseptic towel from without, and another roller, completed the dressing; and a 'cradle' was placed upon the neck to check lateral movements which might disturb it. I have described these particulars because I am more and more convinced of the necessity for scrupulous attention to details such as the germ theory dictates, in order to attain anything like uniformity of successful results.

A few ounces of the oily solution were poured daily over the towel for the first week, after which the dressings were left untouched for three days, and then entirely removed. The wound was found quite dry and free from tenderness, and the cloth showed only a superficial bloody stain. The stitches being taken out, a drop of pus escaped from the track of the suture next the head; but this was the only appearance of suppuration in the case from first to last, and on the separation of the scab, a few days later, a sound cicatrix was disclosed. A month (thirty days) after the operation the animal, which had continued in perfect health, was killed, and the soft parts of the neck below the spine were removed for examination. On dissection I was struck with the entire absence of inflammatory thickening in the vicinity of the vessel, the cellular tissue being of perfectly normal softness and laxity. On exposing the artery itself, however, I was at first much disappointed to see the ligatures still there to all appearance as large as ever. But had I borne in mind what I had observed in some of my earlier cases of compound fracture treated antiseptically, I should have been prepared to find these threads present in appearance, though absent in reality. It may be well for me to quote from the account I have before given of one of these cases. It was a compound fracture of the leg, produced by direct violence, with a wound of considerable size, and a great deal of extravasation of blood into the limb. In accordance with the practice which I then followed, a piece of lint soaked with undiluted carbolic acid had been placed over the wound, and had formed with the blood a firm crust. 'Nearly three weeks after the accident I was detaching a portion of the adherent crust from the surface of the vascular structure into which the extravasated blood beneath had been converted by the process of organization, when I exposed a little spherical cavity about as big as a pea, containing brown serum, forming a sort of pocket in the living tissues, which, when scraped with the edge of a knife, bled even at the very margin of the cavity. This appearance showed that the deeper portions of the crust itself had been converted into living tissue. For cavities formed during the process of aggregation, like those with clear liquid contents in a Gruyere cheese, occur in the grumous mass which results from the action of carbolic acid upon blood; and that which I had exposed had evidently been one of these, though its walls were now alive and vascular.' Thus the dead, but nutritious mass, had served as a mould for the formation of new tissue, the growing elements of which had replaced the materials absorbed, so as to constitute a living solid of the same form.

Hence it might have been anticipated that the ligatures of peritoneum and catgut placed on the calf's carotid would, after the expiration of a month, be found transformed into bands of living tissue. Such was, in truth, the case, as was apparent on closer examination. They had, indeed, a deceptive resemblance to their former condition, from the persistence in their substance of the impurities of the original materials, the dark adventitious particles being of mineral nature incapable of absorption, so that they had remained as a sort of tattooing of the new structure. Nevertheless, a marked alteration in colour had taken place, especially in the distal ligature, where the dirty grey of the softened catgut had changed to a dirty pink tint. The two pieces of catgut which had been tied round the vessel at that part had become, as it were, fused together into a single fleshy band, inseparably blended with the external coat of the artery. The knots were nowhere discoverable, and the only indication of the end which had been left long at the time of the operation was the presence of a black-speck here and there upon a delicate thread of cellular tissue in connection with the vessel. The cardiac ligature was in like manner continuous in structure with the arterial wall. The short ends had disappeared; but the massive knot was represented by a soft smooth lump, which appeared at first entirely homogeneous, except that it was speckled with dark particles, as before referred to. On section, however, I discovered in the interior of the mass, and lying close to the wall of the artery, a small residual portion of the original knot, of comparatively firm consistence, and with the three-fold twisted character of the cord plainly visible. It was quite distinct from the living tissue that surrounded it, so that it could be readily picked out from its bed with a pair of needles. A slender and irregular remnant of the noose was also found lying in a sort of tubular cavity, extending about half round the vessel.

Thus the process of organization had not yet quite invaded the entire thickness of the foreign solid, and it was a happy circumstance that the thread had been so constructed that the distinction between the old structure and the new could be plainly recognised.

Ample as was the evidence afforded to the naked eye of the organization of these ligatures, it was satisfactory to find it confirmed in the clearest manner by the microscope. A bit of the residue of the peritoneal thread, having been teased out with needles in a drop of water, presented, like a fresh piece of peritoneum, the wavy bundles of parallel fibres characteristic of perfectly developed fibrous tissue. Adhering to the surface of the remnant of the ligature was some soft opaque material, readily washed off with water, consisting of corpuscles of different forms, most of them caudate or fibro-plastic, but some spherical, though not resembling those of pus; and here and there fragments of the original peritoneal tissue, affected more or less with interstitial cell-development. At a short distance from the remains of the old thread, the fleshy material which had been formed at its expense proved to be a most beautiful example of fibroplastic structure, the coarse fibres which mainly constituted it being composed of very large elongated cells, often containing several nuclei, and presenting in their course branchings and thickenings of various forms. Here and there were some fibres more perfectly formed, and also cells of a more rudimentary character. Again, the band which had resulted from the organization of the two fine threads of catgut, which, from the smallness of their bulk, had no doubt vanished early, having had longer time to perfect its structure, was a comparatively well-developed form of fibrous tissue, consisting of coarse fibres rather than of elongated cells, being thus intermediate between the merely fibro-plastic material of more recent growth and the completed texture of the original thread. For it is to be remarked that a piece of catgut exhibits under the microscope abundance of perfect fibrous tissue. A more favourable period for the investigation, with a view to establishing the nature of the change which ligatures of animal tissue experience under antiseptic management, could hardly have been selected.

Between the parts tied the calibre of the artery was occupied by adherent coagulum, which was for the most part decolourized, and exhibited under the microscope fibro-plastic cells of irregular forms. A similar clot was present between the distal ligature and a small branch that arose about a quarter of an inch beyond it. But between the proximal ligature and the heart the formation of a coagulum had been entirely prevented by a large vessel taking origin immediately above the part tied, which had thus borne for a month the full brunt of the cardiac impulse. Yet the vessel, so far from showing any sign of giving way, as it would inevitably have done had it been tied in such a situation without antiseptic precautions, appeared to have derived additional strength from the operation. The encircling ring of new tissue incorporated with the arterial wall must have had a corroborative effect; and within its grasp the inner coats, which seemed to have been but imperfectly ruptured by the soft and substantial ligature, were considerably thickened, and had coalesced so as to form a strong cul-de-sac, the irregularities of which had been smoothed over by a little fibrinous deposit, which had assumed the characters of a firm fibrous tissue, and presented a free surface undistinguishable from that of the lining membrane of the artery.

At the situation of the distal ligature the structure of the vessel seemed entirely unaffected. The middle coat was seen in longitudinal section as a pink streak between two white lines, representing the external and internal tunics, neither thicker nor thinner than in neighboring parts. The catgut threads had been tied too gently to produce rupture of the internal and middle layers, and their presence and the constriction which they occasioned, whatever may have been their effect in the first instance, had left no permanent marks of disturbance; while the fleshy band that had replaced them, though in time it would doubtless have dwindled down to an insignificant filament, was at least a temporary addition to the strength of the artery.

These appearances at the distal ligature are calculated to revive under a new aspect the old question whether it would not be better always to avoid rupture of the internal and middle coats, which could easily be done by using a pretty thick piece of catgut softened by steeping it in a watery solution of carbolic acid. In this way the wall of the vessel would be left from first to last entirely intact. This, however, is probably a matter of indifference. Indeed, judging from the condition of the artery at the cardiac ligature, the injury done to the vessel at the outset by tight tying seems to lead to changes which increase its power of resistance, which was certainly severely tested in the present instance.

It appears, then, that by applying a ligature of animal tissue antiseptically upon an artery, whether tightly or gently, we virtually surround it with a ring of living tissue, and strengthen the vessel where we obstruct it. The surgeon, therefore, may now tie an arterial trunk in its continuity close to a large branch, secure alike against secondary haemorrhage and deep-seated suppuration—provided always that he has so studied the principles of the antiseptic system, and so carefully considered the details of the mode of dressing best adapted to the particular case in hand, that he can feel certain of avoiding putrefaction in the wound. For my own part, I should now, without hesitation, undertake ligature of the innominate, believing that it would prove a very safe procedure.

Catgut, manufactured from the small intestine of the sheep, may be at a low price, from the thickness of a horsehair upwards. As sold in the shops, however, it is quite unfit for the purposes of the surgeon. For, when moistened with water or with the animal fluids, it becomes not only very soft and weak, but as slippery as a piece of recent intestine, so that a knot tied upon it yields to the slightest traction. But it is a happy circumstance that a simple process of preparation deprives it of these objectionable qualities. For this purpose, no method which I have yet tried answers better than that which I happened to use first of all for rendering the gut antiseptic—viz., suspending it in a mixture of five parts of some fixed oil (e.g., olive or linseed) with one part of carbolic acid liquefied by adding five per cent, of water to the crystals. Part of the water associated with the acid is disengaged by the oil, producing a very fine emulsion, which effects a remarkable physical change in the animal tissue. At first the gut is rendered swollen, soft, and opaque, though not to so great an extent as if placed in simple water; but in the course of a few days the opposite change begins to show itself, and the thread becomes gradually firmer and more transparent, till, after the lapse of a few weeks, it is quite free from opacity, and very strong, though supple. If drawn through the fingers, it is no longer slippery, but has a crisp feel like a thread of india-rubber, and a knot tied upon it holds more securely than one on waxed silk. Water, whether cold or at a temperature of 100 degrees Fahr., has now little effect upon the thread, and even putrid serum of blood acting upon it for days at the temperature of the body does not make the knots relax their hold. In this form the gut seems almost a perfect material for the ligature under any circumstances in which it is required.

'Prepared catgut' will, I hope, soon become a well-known article of commerce. But, for the sake of surgeons who may wish to prepare it for themselves, it is necessary to mention, in order to avoid disappointment, that the essence of the process is the action of an emulsion of water and oil upon the animal tissue. The same effect is produced upon the gut, though more slowly, by an emulsion formed by shaking up simple olive oil and water, as by one which contains carbolic acid. On the other hand, an oily solution of carbolic acid without water has no effect upon the gut beyond making it antiseptic, and if water be added only in the small proportion which the acid enables the oil to dissolve, though the gut is rendered supple, and acquires a dark tint from the colouring matter of the oil, it will be found, even after steeping for months in such a solution, that when transferred to water it swells up and becomes soft, opaque, and slippery, as if it had not been subjected to any preparation. How it is that an emulsion produces this remarkable change in the molecular constitution of the tissue I do not profess to understand. I was at first inclined to regard it as a closer aggregation of the particles, brought about by a kind of slow drying of the moistened gut in the oil, as the watery particles precipitate to the bottom of the vessel; but, not to mention other circumstances opposed to this view, the oil remains turbid for a very long time, the finer particles of water being extremely slow in precipitating, and if, after the lapse of weeks, a piece of dry unprepared gut is suspended in it, the thread is soon rendered soft and opaque by the very liquid in which gut has been longer immersed is growing constantly firmer and more transparent. It is necessary that the gut be kept suspended so as not to touch the bottom of the vessel, for any parts dipping into the layer of precipitated water would fail to undergo the change desired. The vessel containing the emulsion should be left undisturbed, for if the water is shaken up with the oil the process is retarded. An elevated temperature of about 100 degrees Fahr. seems for a while to promote the change, but ultimately leaves the gut in an unsatisfactory state compared with that obtained at an ordinary temperature. And conversely some portions of gut which I have prepared lately (February 1870) in a room without a fire, in cold weather, at a temperature of about 46 degrees, were in one week already in a trustworthy condition for surgical purposes. Hence the gut should be prepared in as cool a place as possible. The longer it is kept in the emulsion, the better the gut becomes. I once feared that it might in time grow too rigid for convenience, and possibly brittle also; but experience shows that this is not the case. When removed from the emulsion it soon dries in the air, but retains a considerable portion of its carbolic acid for several hours, so that no apprehension need be entertained of loss of its antiseptic property from exposure during the performance of an operation. In course of time it loses all the carbolic acid also, but retains permanently its altered molecular condition. If thus kept dry, as may prove the most convenient for the manufacturer on a large scale, it must be steeped thoroughly in some antiseptic lotion before it is used. And for the surgeon the most convenient way will probably be to keep it always in the antiseptic emulsion, so as to be ready for use whenever it is required.

For tying an arterial trunk in its continuity, catgut at least as thick as common purse-silk will be found best. But for ordinary wounds, where, if one ligature happens to break, another can be easily applied, much finer kinds may be employed, and are convenient from their smaller bulk. Several yards of fine gut may be carried in the pocket-case, on a winder contained in a little oil-tight silver capsule which I have had constructed for the purpose, as an appendage to a caustic-holder.

PREVENTION OF RABIES

A METHOD BY WHICH THE DEVELOPMENT OF RABIES AFTER A BITE MAY BE PREVENTED.

A real progress in the study of rabies was marked, without any doubt, by the papers in which I announced, in my own name and in the name of my fellow-workers, a prophylactic method; but the progress was scientific rather than practical. Accidents were liable to occur in its application. Of twenty dogs treated, I could not undertake to render more than fifteen or sixteen refractory to rabies.

Further, it was desirable, at the end of the treatment, to inoculate with a very virulent virus—a control virus—in order to confirm and reinforce the refractory condition. More than this, prudence demanded that the dogs should be kept under observation during a period longer than the period of incubation of the disease produced by the direct inoculation of this last virus. Therefore, in order to be quite sure that the refractory state had been produced, it was sometimes necessary to wait three or four months. The application of the method would have been very much limited by these troublesome conditions.

Finally, the method did not lend itself easily to the immediate treatment rendered necessary by the accidental and unforeseen way in which bites are inflicted by rabid animals.

It was necessary, therefore, to discover, if possible, a more rapid method, and yet one, I would venture to say, capable of affording perfect security to dogs.

Otherwise who would have the temerity, before this progress had been achieved, to make any experiment on man?

After making almost innumerable experiments, I have discovered a prophylactic method which is practical and prompt, and which has already in dogs afforded me results sufficiently numerous, certain, and successful, to warrant my having confidence in its general applicability to all animals, and even to man himself.

This method depends essentially on the following facts:-

The inoculation under the dura mater, after trephining, of the infective spinal cord of a dog suffering from ordinary rabies (*rage des rues*), always produces rabies in rabbits after a period of incubation having a mean duration of about fifteen days.

If, by the above method of inoculation, the virus of the first rabbit is passed into a second, and that of the second into a third, and so on, in series, a more and more striking tendency is soon manifested towards a diminution of the duration of the incubation period of rabies in the rabbits successively inoculated.

After passing twenty or twenty-five times from rabbit to rabbit, inoculation periods of eight days are met with, and continue for another interval, during which the virus is passed twenty or twenty-five times from rabbit to rabbit. Then an incubation period of seven days is reached, which is encountered with striking regularity throughout a new series extending as far as the ninetieth animal. This at least is the number which I have reached at the present time, and the most that can be said is that a slight tendency is manifested towards an incubation period of a little less than seven days.

Experiments of this class, begun in November, 1882, have now lasted for three years without any break in the continuity of the series, and without our ever being obliged to have recourse to any other virus than that of the rabbits successively dead of rabies. Consequently, nothing is easier than to have constantly at our disposal, over considerable intervals of time, a virus of rabies, quite pure, and always quite or very nearly identical. This is the central fact in the practical application of the method.

The virus of rabies at a constant degree of virulence is contained in the spinal cords of these rabbits throughout their whole extent.

If portions, a few centimetres long, are removed from these spinal cords with every possible precaution to preserve their purity, and are then suspended in dry air, the virulence slowly disappears, until at last it entirely vanishes. The time within which this extinction of virulence is brought about varies a little with the thickness of the morsels of spinal cord, but chiefly with the external temperature. The lower the temperature the longer is the virulence preserved. These results form the central scientific point in the method.

These facts being established, a dog may be rendered refractory to rabies in a relatively short time in the following way:-

Every day morsels of fresh infective spinal cord from a rabbit which has died of rabies developed after an incubation period of seven days, are suspended in a series of flasks, the air in which is kept dry by placing fragments of potash at the bottom of the flask. Every day also a dog is inoculated under the skin with a Pravaz' syringe full of sterilized broth, in which a small fragment of one of the spinal cords has been broken up, commencing with a spinal cord far enough removed in order of time from the day of the operation to render it certain that the cord was not at all virulent. (This date had been ascertained by previous experiments.) On the following days the same operation is performed with more recent cords, separated from each other by an interval of two days, until at last a very virulent cord, which has only been in the flask for two days, is used.

The dog has now been rendered refractory to rabies. It may be inoculated with the virus of rabies under the skin, or even after trephining, on the surface of the brain, without any subsequent development of rabies.

Never having once failed when using this method, I had in my possession fifty dogs, of all ages and of every race, refractory to rabies, when three individuals from Alsace unexpectedly presented themselves at my laboratory, on Monday the 6th of last July.

Théodore Vone, grocer, of Meissengott, near Schlestadt, bitten in the arm, July 4th, by his own dog, which had gone mad.

Joseph Meister, aged 9 years, also bitten on July 4th, at eight o'clock in the morning, by the same dog. This child had been knocked over by the dog and presented numerous bites, on the hands, legs, and thighs, some of them so deep as to render walking difficult. The principal bites had been cauterized at eight o'clock in the evening of July 4th, only twelve hours after the accident, with phenic acid, by Dr. Weber, of Villé.

The third person, who had not been bitten, was the mother of little Joseph Meister.

At the examination of the dog, afer its death by the hand of its master, the stomach was found full of hay, straw, and scraps of wood. The dog was certainly rabid. Joseph Meister had been pulled out from under him covered with foam and blood.

M. Vone had some severe contusions on the arm, but he assured me that his shirt had not been pierced by the dog's fangs. As he had nothing to fear, I told him that he could return to Alsace the same day, which he did. But I kept young Meister and his mother with me.

The weekly meeting of the Académie des Sciences took place on July 6th. At it I met our colleague Dr. Vulpian, to whom I related what had just happened. M. Vulpian, and Dr. Grancher, Professor in the Faculté de Medicine, had the goodness to come and see little Joseph Meister at once, and to take note of the condition and the number of his wounds. There were no less than fourteen.

The opinion of our learned colleague, and of Dr. Grancher, was that, owing to the severity and the number of the bites, Joseph Meister was almost certain to take rabies. I then communicated to M. Vulpian and to M. Grancher the new results which I had obtained from the study of rabies since the address which I had given at Copenhagen a year earlier.

The death of this child appearing to be inevitable, I decided, not without lively and sore anxiety, as may well be believed, to try upon Joseph Meister the method which I had found constantly successful with dogs.

My fifty dogs, it is true, had not been bitten before I brought them into the condition of being refractory to rabies; but I knew that that circumstance might be left out of my calculations, because I had previously rendered a large number of dogs refractory to rabies after they had been bitten. I have this year given the members of the Commission de la Rage evidence of this new and important advance.

Consequently, on July 6th, at 8 o'clock in the evening, sixty hours after the bites on July 4th, and in the presence of Drs. Vulpian and Grancher, young Meister was inoculated under a fold of skin raised in the right hypochondrium, with half a Pravaz' syringeful of the spinal cord of a rabbit, which had died of rabies on June 21st. It had been preserved since then, that is to say, fifteen days, in a flask of dry air.

On the following days fresh inoculations were made. I thus made thirteen inoculations, and prolonged the treatment to ten days. I shall say later on that a smaller number of inoculations would have been sufficient. But it will be understood how, in the first attempt, I would act with a very special circumspection.

In order to follow the condition as to virulence of the spinal cords, two fresh rabbits were inoculated, by trephining, with the various spinal cords employed.

Observation of these rabbits enabled us to ascertain that the spinal cords of July 6th, 7th, 8th, 9th, 10th, were not virulent, for they did not render the rabbits rabid; the spinal cords of July 11th, 12th, 14th, 15th, 16th, were all virulent, and the virulent material was present in larger and larger proportion. Rabies appeared after an incubation of seven days in the rabbits of July 15th and 16th; after eight days in those of the 12th and 14th; after fifteen days in those of July 11th.

On the last days, therefore, I had inoculated Joseph Meister with the most virulent virus of rabies, that, namely, of the dog, reinforced by passing a great number of times from rabbit to rabbit, a virus which produced rabies after seven days incubation in these animals, after eight or ten days in dogs.

When the condition of immunity has been attained, the most virulent virus can be inoculated, in considerable quantity, without ill effects. It has always seemed to me that the only possible effect of this must be to make immunity more assured.

Joseph Meister, therefore, has escaped, not only the rabies which would have been caused by the bites he received, but also the rabies with which I have inoculated him in order to test the immunity produced by the treatment, a rabies more virulent than ordinary canine rabies.

The final inoculation with very virulent virus has this further advantage, that it puts a period to the apprehensions which arise as to the consequences of the bites. If rabies could occur it would declare itself more quickly after a more virulent virus than after the virus of the bites. Since the middle of August I have looked forward with confidence to the future good health of Joseph Meister. At the present time, three months and three weeks having elapsed since the accident, his state of health leaves nothing to be desired.

What interpretation is to be given of this new method which I have just made known, of preventing rabies after bites? I have not at the present moment any intention of treating this question in a complete manner. I wish to confine myself to certain preliminary details essential to the comprehension of the significance of the experiments, which I am continuing, in order to adopt eventually the best of the various possible interpretations.

Bearing in mind the methods of progressively attenuating various lethal virus, and the prophylaxis in that way attained, and admitting also the influence of the air in bringing about this attenuation the first explanation to accounting for the effects of this method which suggests itself is, that while the morsels of spinal cord are left in contact with the dry air, the intensity of their virulence is progressively dimininshed, until it is entirely abolished.

This reflection would lead us to believe that the prophylactic method now described depended upon the employment at first of a virus without any appreciable activity, then of feeble intensity, and then of more and more virulence.

I will show that facts do not lend support to this view. I will prove that the increase in the length of the period of incubation of the rabies, each day, communicated to the rabbits, as I have just described, in order to test the virulence of the spinal-cords dried in contact with air, is an effect of a diminution of the quantity of the virus of rabies contained in the spinal cords, and not an effect of a diminution of its virulence.

Can it be admitted that the inoculation of a virus, always of identical virulence, could be capable of producing a refractory state, when it is used in very small but daily increasing quantities? I am studying experimentally this interpretation of the facts.

Another interpretation may be given of the new method, an interpretation certainly at first sight very strange, but which deserves every consideration, because it is in harmony with certain facts already known with regard to the vital phenomena of certain low organisms, and notably of certain pathogenic microbes.

Many microbes appear to give origin in their cultivations to matters which are injurious to their own development.

Since the year 1880, I have carried on researches in order to ascertain whether the microbe of fowl-cholera produced a kind of poison for itself (see *Comptes Rendus,* T. xc., 1880). I have not been able to establish the presence of such a material; but I think that this study ought now to be resumed—and so far as concerns myself I shall not be wanting—by working in an atmosphere of pure carbonic acid gas.

The microbe of swine-plague (*rouget*) can be grown in various broths, but the weight of it which is grown is so small and so soon arrested at that proportion, that sometimes the cultivation can only be detected as slight silky waves in the nutritive material. It would be said that a product which arrests the development of this microbe comes into existence whether the cultivations be made in contact with air or in vacuo.

M. Raulin, a former assistant of mine, now Professor in the Faculty at Lyons, has proved in the remarkable thesis which he sustained at Paris on March 22, 1870, that the vegetation of *Aspergillus niger* develops a substance which in some measure checks the growth of that mould, when the nutritive material does not contain iron salts.

Can it be that that which constitutes the virus of rabies is formed of two distinct substances, and that side by side with that one which is living and capable of growing in the nervous system there is another, not living, which, when it is in suitable proportion, has the power of arresting the development of the first? In a later communication I will experimentally examine, with all the care which it deserves, this third interpretation of the method of prophylaxis of rabies.

In conclusion I need not say that perhaps the most important of the problems to be solved at the present time is that of the inerval which may be allowed between the occurrence of the bites and the commencement of the treatment. In the case of Joseph Meister this interval was two days and a half. But it must be expected to be often much longer.

On Tuesday last, October 20th, with the kind assistance of MM. Vulpian and Grancher, I commenced to treat a youth of 15 years, bitten six full days before, on both hands, under exceptionally grave circumstances. I will promptly make known to the Academy the result of this new trial.